Play, Learning and the
Early Childhood Curriculum

(2nd edition)

Elizabeth Wood is Reader in Early Childhood Education at the University of Exeter. She teaches on a range of post-graduate programmes and runs in-service courses for teachers and other early years practitioners. Elizabeth has co-directed two ESRC funded research projects with Neville Bennett: Reception Teachers' Theories of Play (1995–97) and Progression and Continuity in the Early Years (1999–2000). She was involved in the JUDE project on literacy and underachievement, which spans Key Stages 1 to 4. She has authored books and articles based on her research interests in play, young children's learning, early childhood pedagogy, and underachievement.

Jane Attfield is an experienced early years teacher who has taught in nursery and infant classes in New Guinea, England and Australia. She was the coordinator of a Local Authority funded Play Project at a school in Dorset. Jane completed her Master of Education degree at Exeter University, and her research into the Play Project is used substantially in the book.

Play, Learning and the Early Childhood Curriculum

(2nd edition)

Elizabeth Wood and
Jane Attfield

P·C·P
Paul Chapman
Publishing

First published in 1996
Second Edition published in 2005

Paul Chapman Publishing
A SAGE Publications Company
1 Oliver's Yard
55 City Road
London EC1Y 1SP

SAGE Publications Inc
2455 Teller Road
Thousand Oaks
California 91320

SAGE Publications India Pvt Ltd
B-42, Panchsheel Enclave
Post Box 4109
New Delhi 110 017

Library of Congress Control Number: 2004117260

British Library Cataloguing in Publication Data

Wood, Elizabeth
  Play, learning and the early childhood curriculum
  1. Early childhood education 2. Play
  I. Title II. Attfield, Jane
  372.2'1

ISBN 0-7619-4173-8 (cased)
    0-7619-4174-6 (paperback)

Typeset by TW Typesetting, Plymouth, Devon
Printed in Great Britain by Athenaeum Press Ltd, Gateshead

Contents

Preface   *vii*

1   The Problems with Play   1

2   Ideologies, Ideals and Theories   28

3   Understanding Children's Learning: Multi-theoretical
    Perspectives   59

4   Contemporary Socio-cultural Theories   90

5   Developing Play in the Curriculum   118

6   Developing a Pedagogy of Play   158

7   Assessing Children's Learning in Play   184

8   Improving the Quality of Play   217

Bibliography   *238*

Author Index   *245*

Subject Index   *246*

For Liz and David, two master players

Preface

We were delighted when we were asked to write the second edition of this book. Much has happened since the first edition in the arenas of policy development, research and practice. Early childhood education is at the heart of policy-making agendas in England and many other developed and developing countries. Concerns with the quality of provision have sparked a massive international research endeavour, which is seeking to identify effective provision and practice in different cultures, and in different early childhood settings. There is also a thriving international play scholarship which ranges broadly across many different themes that are central to high-quality provision and effective teaching and learning. Contemporary research studies in the field of play are exciting in their foci, innovative in their methods and contentious in the eclecticism of their theoretical frameworks. The field remains open to debate, discussion and argument regarding the role and value of play in learning and development. Nevertheless, there have been many practical outcomes that are of direct relevance to practitioners as they strive towards improving the quality of play.

This second edition reflects these trends, and draws substantially on academic and practitioner research. Guided by feedback from readers of the first edition, we have aimed to integrate theory and practice throughout the book. The first four chapters focus mainly on theoretical frameworks, which explain different aspects of learning, the benefits of different forms of play, and a rationale for a play-based curriculum and pedagogy. The second half of the book develops the theme of creating unity between playing, learning and teaching. We have highlighted ongoing issues, questions and dilemmas that practitioners encounter, and have provided many practical examples to show how these have been addressed.

The first edition was based substantially on Jane's research for her Master of Education degree. Her observations and documentation of children's play-based activities remain just as relevant. In addition, we are privileged to present the practice-based evidence from the work of early childhood practitioners who have been involved in in-service and modular degree programmes at Exeter University. Our thanks are due to all these dedicated and enthusiastic practitioners, and especially to Joanna Cook, Amanda Kersey, Charlotte Rowland, Sheena Wright, Diann Cudmore and Jaqui Bamford for their observations and analyses of children and adults at play. The practitioners that Elizabeth has worked with have provided inspiration in their ongoing commitment to valuing, defending and improving play in their settings. They form a resilient core of enthusiastic proponents for play, and active resisters of policy directives that are not in tune with how young children learn.

We hope that this second edition will inform and inspire practitioners, provoke debate, encourage reflection and raise awareness of the importance of lifelong playing and learning.

Elizabeth Wood and Jane Attfield

CHAPTER ONE

The Problems with Play

Early childhood education is underpinned by a strong tradition which regards play as essential to learning and development. This is based substantially on the work of pioneer educators such as Jean-Jacques Rousseau, John Dewey, Maria Montessori, Friedrich Froebel, Margaret MacMillan and Rudolf Steiner. More recently, this tradition has been related to contemporary contexts, receiving further validation and critical examination from researchers, policy-makers and practitioners. However, in spite of continuing enthusiastic endorsements for play, its place in the curriculum remains problematic, particularly beyond the early years of school. The role, purposes and value of play in the early years curriculum continue to be debated. What counts as play is contested, and there are ongoing debates about the relationship between playing, learning and teaching. These issues have been particularly relevant for early years practitioners since the implementation of the Education Reform Act in 1988, and the subsequent flow of educational policies which have see-sawed between an anti- and pro-play ethos. These debates have had a positive outcome because they have kept play high on educational agendas in policy, research and practice. Play continues to be taken seriously in the academic community, as evidenced by extensive research that is providing new theoretical frameworks and guidance for practice. Play is also being taken much more seriously by policy-makers, as evidenced by the endorsement for a pedagogy of play in the British Government's framework Birth to Three Matters, and the Foundation Stage for three- to five-year-old children. These trends can also be seen in many other countries, in a thriving international play scholarship, and ongoing debates about the role and value of play and its contribution to effective teaching and learning. Play also continues to fascinate and challenge practitioners who are concerned with improving the quality of their provision, understanding the meaning and value of play, and providing evidence of learning through play.

However, play remains problematic both in theory and in practice. The purpose of this introductory chapter is to explore some of these problems in relation to four key areas: defining play, exploring the status of play, the play/work divide, and lifelong playing and learning. Some of the paradoxes of play are explored: is it orderly or rule-bound, spontaneous or chaotic, highly significant or little more than messing about? The final section examines play in the context of National Curriculum policies, and highlights current trends towards developing a more coherent pedagogy of play within and beyond early childhood.

WHAT IS PLAY?

Two key questions continue to challenge the research and practitioner communities: what is play, and what does play do for the child? Chazan (2002: 198) takes a broad and positive view of the functions of play:

> Playing and growing are synonymous with life itself. Playfulness bespeaks creativity and action, change and possibility of transformation. Play activity thus reflects the very existence of the self, that part of the organism that exists both independently and interdependently, that can reflect upon itself and be aware of its own existence. In being playful the child attains a degree of autonomy sustained by representations of his inner and outer worlds.

Play activities involve a wide range of behaviours and can be situated in different contexts, which may have multiple meanings for children and adults. Play can be regarded as deeply serious and purposeful, or trivial and purposeless. It can be characterized by high levels of motivation, creativity and learning, or relegated to little more than aimless messing about. Ambiguities surrounding the definition of play have done little to substantiate claims that children learn through play or that a play-based curriculum is the best or only approach to supporting early learning. Hutt *et al* (1989) argue that play is a jumbo category that encompasses a multiplicity of activities, some of which are conducive to learning, but many of which are not. On transition to school, children will be expected to play in certain ways, and at certain times, so that play in school can encompass different experiences from play at home and in the community. For example, many children dislike outdoor playtime because it provides opportunities for conflict, aggression, bullying and other anti-social behaviours. The following observation was recorded by a newly qualified teacher, and shows how, for the youngest children, playtime can be a traumatic experience:

> It appeared to me that for many of the children playtime was a total mystery. They did not know what was going to happen to them and were very apprehensive. I headed for the staff room and soon became aware that I was being followed by Luke (aged four). I explained that it was time to go out to the playground. 'I'm not doing it, I'll come with you', he said. I realised that he was afraid to lose sight of the adults into whose care his mother had entrusted him. He did not know which (if any) adult would be in the playground. Probably his entire life up to that moment had been spent in the sight of his trusted carer, and suddenly he felt he would be abandoned.

Paradoxically, playtime was not a welcome interlude but an apparent threat to this young child. In school contexts, playfulness can also be seen as naughtiness when it disrupts work. Neill and Jamel (both aged five) did not settle immediately to a maths activity. Instead they began play-fighting, using their pencils as swords. Their play was not aggressive or malicious, but as it became more energetic and noisy they fell off their chairs, were reprimanded by the teacher and separated for the rest of the session. Young children soon learn what is accepted, ignored or banned in their school-based play lives.

In contrast, deep and serious play can be respected and encouraged by teachers. In a nursery, some boys were playing with Duplo⊛ and made a large layout on the floor. As the complexity of their play developed, they used other resources to create a town, including Playmobil⊛ figures that were used to act out various scenarios. The teacher realized the need to 'go with the flow' of their ideas and asked other children not to cut across their space or take away their equipment. The children were not made to join in with mid-session circle time as their play continued to evolve over two hours. At review time they proudly explained their layout to the whole class, and dismantled it only after it had been shown to parents and caregivers.

Considering these contrasting observations, there is little wonder that clear definitions of play have proved elusive. Garvey (1991) suggests that not everything that young children do together can be classified as play. There is a continuous moving back and forth among different activities with different modes of action, interaction and communication. Garvey regards play as an attitude or orientation that can manifest itself in numerous kinds of behaviour. There are endless possibilities for what children play with, what they can play at, and the imaginary worlds and scenarios they create. These possibilities expand as new areas of experience are encountered, and as children's skills as players develop through childhood and into adulthood. Thus what play is, and what it does for the player, cannot be constrained by theoretical or temporal definitions.

Meckley (2002) has drawn on Garvey's definition of play characteristics, in order to make links between what play is, what it does for the child, and how children make links between their inner and outer worlds (see Figure 1.1).

---

1. Play is child-chosen
Before children play, they have ideas about what they want to do and who they want to play with. As children start to play, they choose materials, activities and other players. Although children are in control of their own play, they must cooperate and negotiate with others to play together. Because children choose their play and playmates, they are usually successful. They feel satisfied and proud of their accomplishments. Within a child's own play, no one but the child is determining what is the right way or the wrong way because the child makes the rules for her play within the framework of what is acceptable at home or in school. If adults choose children's activities or assign children to play areas, children tell us this is work and not play. Children learn the most from play if it belongs to them.

2. Play is child-invented
Play is not only chosen by children but also invented by them. Children are always creating something new when they play whether it is a new construction, or a new idea, or group of ideas. Even though it may seem to an adult as if the construction is not new because it may look just like another child's construction, to the child it is new because they tried and completed something that *they* never did before. In play, children are the inventors and experimenters: they take risks to try something they have never tried before or think an idea they have never thought before. Through play they are developing creativity and thinking skills.

3. Play is pretend but done as if the activity were real
Children learn a great deal in pretending with activities and ideas that are like real events but are not real. They develop understanding of cognitive, social and emotional concepts by playing with these concepts. They develop perspective about people, events, relationships and rules through playing about them. Children use play to make sense of their world.

4. Play focuses on the doing (process not product)
Play is a basic activity of childhood. The process or activity of play is where the learning occurs. Communication is essential to play. For example, there is a relationship between language and play. In play children use more complex language than in conversations with adults. Children frequently make their first attempts at reading and writing when they are playing, by acting as if they are competent readers and writers.

5. Play is done by the players (children) not the adults (teachers or parents)
Play is something children not only choose to do but also prefer to do. Because children learn through the process of playing, they need plenty of time, materials and other players. Adults cannot plan children's play, but can help to

---

plan for the children's play, and to support children's own plans. Adults provide the proper environment, the support, the rules, the safety, so that children can obtain the maximum learning from playing.

6. Play requires active involvement
Children's bodies and minds are active in play. Research tells us that the maximum learning occurs when children interact and co-operate with the environment, materials and with others (peers and adults). Play is where the activity of childhood is occurring.

7. Play is fun
Play is fun and enjoyable because children choose their activities and playmates, and draw on their own motivation and ideas.

FIGURE 1.1 THE CHARACTERISTICS OF PLAY

Meckley's framework captures some of the complexities, diversity and unpredictability of play, and provides 'ideal' conceptions of what play is and what it does for the child. The purposes and goals of play often shift as children manipulate play and non-play situations because they understand implicitly that different types of behaviour are permitted, whereas others, such as mock aggression and play-fighting, are often banned. Play does not take place in a vacuum: everything that children play at, or play with, is influenced by wider social, historical and cultural factors, so that understanding what play is and learning how to play are culturally situated processes.

Play cannot easily be defined or categorized because it is always context dependent, and the contexts are varied. There are many different forms of play including: role play, imaginative play, socio-dramatic play, heuristic play, constructive play, fantasy play, free-flow play, structured play, rough-and-tumble play, all of which involve a wide range of activities and behaviours, and result in varied learning and developmental outcomes. For example, fantasy play involving characters and events is considered to be a higher form of play as it encourages representational thinking and symbolic actions (making one thing stand for something else). Constructive play tends to involve opportunities for mathematical and technological learning, while sand and water play may provide opportunities for scientific learning (Worthington and Carruthers, 2003). Socio-dramatic play can encourage children to become competent users of literacy where practitioners encourage literacy-rich environments and events (Hall, 2000). Given that play is varied and complex, can definitions help us to solve the problem of what play is, and what it does for the child?

- Play is personally motivated by the satisfaction embedded in the activity and is not governed either by basic needs and drives or by social demands.
- Players are concerned with activities more than with goals. Goals are self-imposed, and the behaviour of the players is spontaneous.
- Play occurs with familiar objects, or following the exploration of unfamiliar objects. Children supply their own meanings to play activities and control the activities themselves.
- Play activities can be non-literal.
- Play is free from rules imposed from the outside, and the rules that do exist can be modified by the players.
- Play requires the active engagement of the players.

FIGURE 1.2 DISPOSITIONS IN PLAY

Pellegrini (1991) and Saracho (1991) define play in terms of dispositions that players bring to events and activities (Figure 1.2).

Fromberg's (1987: 36) broad definition states that play is:

> *Symbolic*, in that it represents reality with 'as if' or 'what if' attitude;
> *Meaningful*, in that it connects or relates experiences;
> *Pleasurable*, even when children engage seriously in an activity;
> *Voluntary and intrinsically motivated*, whether the motives are curiosity, mastery, affiliation or others;
> *Rule-governed*, whether implicitly or explicitly expressed;
> *Episodic*, characterized by emerging and shifting goals that children develop spontaneously.

These criteria can be used differentially to categorize children's behaviour in play situations:

> As a result, play can be categorized as 'more or less play', not dichotomously as 'play or not play'. Behaviours meeting all criteria might be categorized as 'pure play', whereas behaviours with fewer components are 'less purely play'. Simply put, acts should not be categorized as 'play' or 'not play': they should be related along a continuum from 'pure play' to 'non-play'. (Pellegrini, 1991: 215)

The pure play–non-play continuum is a useful concept for early childhood practitioners for several reasons. First, children step in and out of play in order to provide a framework for their activity, and to maintain the flow and direction of the play. Second, practitioners often adopt playful orientations to teaching and learning, for example by animating stories, providing imaginary scenarios for mathematics or technological problems, or encouraging historical imagination through authentic activities such as museum visits, investigating artefacts and dramatizing factual events (Wood and Holden, 1995). They can also model humour and playfulness, both of which can be seen as important elements of effective practice, by encouraging engagement, involvement, interest and enjoyment.

THE PARADOXICAL NATURE OF PLAY Definitions of play should take into account different contexts as well as the needs, interests, affective states and preferences of children at different ages: what counts as play will vary according to who is playing and the choice of play activity. As these different definitions indicate, play is infinitely varied and complex. Play is also paradoxical because children play to detach themselves from reality but, at the same time, they get closer to reality. Play represents cognitive, cultural, historical, social and physical interconnections, involving dialogue between:

■ reality and fantasy

■ real and not real

■ real worlds and play worlds

■ past, present and future

■ the logical and the absurd

■ the known and unknown

■ the actual and the possible

■ safety and risk

■ chaos and order.

In aiming to define and categorize play, we may be in danger of overlooking the fact that children have their own definitions of play. In order to establish mutual awareness of play and non-play situations, they create roles, use symbols, redefine objects, transform ideas and determine the action through negotiation and shared meanings. Their enactments of play themes and stories, or their creation of play scripts, reveal far more subtleties than academic definitions can capture. Moreover, play is not just about fantasy. Children continuously weave in and out of play, transferring 'real world' knowledge, skills and understanding from other areas of their lives. Play is also rich with meanings that children create for themselves. These meanings may not be understood if little time is devoted to observing and interpreting children's play and the transformational processes involved.

It is debatable whether academic definitions can accurately capture the spirit and essence of play, which can happen at any time, and in any place. The following vignettes exemplify 'instant play' – the 'in the moment' playfulness of the human mind.

> Nicky (age four years five months) spent over an hour sorting buttons, using different criteria. She talked about sorting buttons into pairs and invited the adult to make pairs of buttons. Nicky joked about pairs of buttons and pears that you eat. At the end of the session, she extended this word play further with the researcher who had been observing her throughout the morning:
>
> *Researcher*: I remember you telling me something about pairs – you said there were pairs of buttons. Can you remember telling me that?
> *Nicky*: Ya.
> *Researcher*: What did you tell me? What's a pair?
> *Nicky*: It's not an apple!

Nicky's joke involved communicating her understanding of the homonyms 'pairs'/'pears', while at the same time playing with pairs/pears as 'not apples'. Nicky was playing at not knowing, but let the researcher know that she did know the difference (quite a feat of inter-subjectivity and mind-reading on her part). Her knowledge was sufficiently secure that it could be played with, and she may have been playfully resisting adult questioning by not giving the expected or correct answer (Wood, 2004). The next example also reveals sophisticated mind and word play:

> The science theme in a Year 2 class was life processes and living things. The children had investigated eggs, learning the difference between the albumen and yolk. They had also incubated eggs, and were waiting for them to hatch. Paul (age six years seven months) was fascinated by this topic. One day he brought in an egg to show his teacher. Unknown to him, Paul's father (a keen ornithologist) had 'blown' the content of the egg, leaving a hollow shell. Paul showed the egg to his teacher, carefully concealing the holes:
>
> *Paul*: Can you guess what's inside this egg?
> *Teacher*: I guess there's some transparent albumen, and a yellow egg yolk.

> Paul: No, you're wrong (crushes the egg in his hand). This is an egg joke!

The teacher was being 'teacherly' by taking the opportunity to reinforce factual knowledge, which perhaps makes Paul's punch-line all the more amusing. He successfully manipulated the play/not play situation by setting up the serious question, and, like Nicky, he understood the ritual and structure of playing a practical joke. Given its enormous diversity, there is little wonder that play defies precise definitions. As the next section shows, despite its complexity and potential, the status of play is also problematic.

THE STATUS OF PLAY

Play has an idealized status in early childhood, but there are competing discourses inside education, and more widely in society, which challenge this viewpoint. As Anning (1997) argues, play has been defined as trivial by a male-dominated society which emphasizes the power of rational thought. Work is the serious, rational business of life, while play is for leisure and fun. Assumptions about the centrality of play to children's learning and development and its place in the curriculum have been taken for granted by some, and challenged by others. For example, Meadows and Cashdan (1988: 47) argue that play has been portrayed as spontaneous, absorbing, refreshing, enjoyable, creative and the ideal way of learning:

> If children aren't enabled to play as they choose, it has been claimed, their development will be impaired. Enthusiasts for play suggest that human beings have evolved so that they need to play in order to learn, to work off their surplus energy, to practise skills they will need in later life. While each of these claims has some truth in it, none of them is an entirely watertight reason for elevating them into *the* way of learning.

Perspectives from practice reveal tensions between the rhetoric and reality of play. The commonly held view that early years teachers encourage learning through play is more myth than reality. A study of the quality of provision in Reception classes (age 4–5) revealed a mismatch between teachers' aims and practice (Bennett and Kell, 1989). Although teachers mentioned play in their aims, only 6 per cent of the observations were classified as play activities, and these were regarded as:

> ... very limited and very limiting. The teachers appeared to have low expectations of it, often acting as a time filler, and far too frequently

> there was no clear purpose or challenge, a lack of pupil involvement,
> very little monitoring or attempt at extension. In other words, play
> tended not to provide learning experiences of an acceptable quality.
> (Bennett and Kell, 1989: 79)

On the basis of these observations, the authors conclude that: 'The view
that the education of young children is founded on play has attained the
status of a commandment, but it is a commandment far more observed
in the telling than in the doing' (1989: 78). Within the current policy
framework, the status of play is seen in relation to learning outcomes,
rather than the more complex processes discussed earlier in this chapter.
Even in the pre-school phase, play can be seen as preparatory to 'real'
learning in 'big school' and may not be taken seriously by parents or
colleagues in school. Work is often disguised as play as early childhood
teachers strive to engage children in activities with defined teaching
objectives. While policy discourses emphasize the need for 'more challenging work', there is no acknowledgement of children's needs (and their
rights) for more challenging play.

■ RHETORIC AND REALITY

The gap between rhetoric and reality can be seen as one of the main
weaknesses of play in schools. This long-standing problem provided the
impetus for a study of the relationship between teachers' thinking and
classroom practice (Bennett *et al*, 1997). Nine Reception class teachers
were studied for one year, with a focus on their beliefs and theories about
the role and value of play, how they planned for play in the curriculum,
and what factors enabled or constrained play in their classrooms. The
teachers selected episodes of play to be videotaped, and subsequently
analyzed these in order to discover whether their intentions were realized
in practice. The evidence challenged the teachers' theories and practice,
and revealed some of the reasons for the rhetoric–reality divide. While all
the teachers defined play as child-initiated, play was structured by time,
resources, the learning environment, the planned or anticipated learning
outcomes and downward pressures from the National Curriculum. Free
play sometimes became noisy and disruptive, with children following
their own, rather than the teacher's, agenda. Although all the teachers
valued play as a medium for learning, other curriculum priorities meant
that they did not involve themselves as co-players, and they spent little
time assessing or understanding learning through play. Downward
pressures from colleagues, parents and the National Curriculum meant
that the teachers needed evidence of children's learning to show pro-

gression and achievement, and play did not readily provide such evidence. The teachers found it difficult to understand patterns of learning and activity in play because they did not have time to observe, discuss and reflect, and feed their understanding into subsequent planning. One teacher described the complexities of managing play in a Reception class as 'spinning plates'. Other factors such as classroom layout, lack of resources, class size and the lack of adult support also intervened between teachers' theories and practice so that their idealized notions about play could not always be put into practice.

In spite of these constraints, the teachers provided some interesting models of how they integrated play into the curriculum. The study provided clear evidence that achieving good quality play is resource-intensive, and requires high levels of pedagogical skill and organization, as well as time and expertise to observe, assess and interpret the meaning of children's play behaviours and activities. Many of the activities the teachers planned could not be classified as 'pure play', but nevertheless enabled children to engage with curriculum content in playful ways. The study highlighted the need for a more secure theoretical and pedagogical underpinning for play to address some of these dilemmas and improve the status of play.

■ PLAY AND POPULAR CULTURE

The status of play can also be seen as related to the status of children. Giving children a voice and allowing them to make choices and decisions can be threatening to adults' control and may not accord with their choices or fit comfortably with their values. Adults often make value judgements about what is 'good' and 'bad' play in relation to potential learning outcomes. Play can have a life of its own because it belongs to the private worlds of children and is often invested with a mystique that is integral to childhood. Play can be chaotic, anarchic, subversive and unpredictable. Perhaps because of this adults have sought to control and manipulate play both inside and outside the home. In educational settings, practitioners have become increasingly focused on ensuring that play is purposeful, educationally worthwhile and results in defined learning outcomes, all of which are recurring themes in the contemporary policy framework. Children's natural tendencies to play provide a lucrative market in popular culture, which in turn influences children's choices and activities. They are exposed to many different media influen-ces, and readily use 'pester power' to demand the latest must-have collectable toys, games, comics and other spin-off products that are often tied in to films and television programmes, which are themselves little more than 'product placement' advertisements. There are different view-points about these trends: educators and parents may resent this commer-cial and economic exploitation, and may question the educational value and quality of these products. Marsh and Millard (2000) note that possibly the single most overriding adult objection to popular cultural texts is the prevalence of violence, especially in superhero sagas, cartoons, action-adventure films and programmes, comics, magazines and video games. In contrast, Cohen (1993) argues that toys and characters from television programmes and films can provide rich 'springboards for fantasy'. In their detailed exploration of literacy and popular culture, Marsh and Millard (2000) lead us to question who is really providing the springboards and controlling the fantasies – adults or children? They argue that children are not passive recipients of shifting and often transient trends in popular culture: they both accept and reject the products offered, and create their own cultural practices based on their experiences in the home, community and friendship groups. Marsh and Millard also argue that practitioners should use rather than ignore children's popular cultural forms as a means of building on children's interests and experiences, and enabling them to experiment with different forms for representing the world.

■ PROBLEMS WITH PLAY

There are other influences in society that question the status of play and reflect some of the paradoxes of postmodern life. More formal approaches to schooling in early childhood are based on the assumption that 'earlier is better'. In their leisure time, children may be channelled into clubs and activities that some parents see as having higher status and lower risk than more traditional forms of play. Fears for children's safety have reportedly reduced opportunities for outdoor play, thereby imposing restrictions on different forms of play. New technologies such as computers, the Internet and interactive video games provide mostly sedentary opportunities for play and leisure, which can be used outside the controlling gaze of adults. Decreasing levels of physical activity have given rise to concerns about increasing levels of obesity in childhood, so that there are almost as many 'dangers' in the home play environment as out of it. Physical play may be seen more as part of a health and fitness regime (again under adults' control) rather than as a freely chosen activity for adventure and fun.

The status of play beyond early childhood is undermined because there is relatively little research to inform practitioners how children's play progresses as they get older, and how the school curriculum can support progression through play. There is an assumption that play becomes less relevant to children beyond the age of five, although it may be allowed in 'choosing time' in Key Stage 1. By Key Stage 2, play in school tends to become a distant memory except as organized games and outdoor playtime. This is ironic given that toy and games manufacturers have perceived the inherent need for play to change and progress from childhood into adulthood. For example, Lego™ provides a carefully sequenced range from Duplo™ for pre-school children, to the more complex LegoTechnik™ and computer programs for older children. Beyond childhood, the status of play is enhanced when it contributes to productivity and effective working practices. As the next section shows, confining play to the realms of childhood may be underestimating its importance to lifelong learning.

LIFELONG PLAYING AND LEARNING

If playing and growing are synonymous with life itself, then lifelong playing can be seen as an important aspect of lifelong learning. In adulthood we are encouraged to use our leisure time productively in playing games to maintain health and fitness. Role play techniques are often used in training programmes in business as a way of enabling people to deal with difficult situations, rehearse strategies and cope with feelings. Firefighters, police officers, paramedics and the armed forces use invented scenarios and replica environments to learn techniques and strategies, and to act out their feelings and responses in difficult situations. Play is often used as an incentive and reward for successful performance in business: there are companies that specialize in organizing 'executive play' breaks, including white-water rafting, health and beauty weekends, rally driving, sky diving and bungee jumping. A stroll around a toyshop reveals a wide range of board games for adults and increasingly sophisticated electronic games that can be played at home or on the move. Many virtual-reality computer/video games are based on role play scenarios where players take on a character and work out strategies and actions in response to problems. We are encouraged to adopt a 'use it or lose it' approach to our brains and bodies as we age: studies have shown that doing crosswords, playing games such as bridge and bingo, and remaining physically and socially active can maintain mental, emotional and physical health. Far from being an exclusive occupation of childhood,

Playful contests (such as beauty pageants and drinking games)
Carnivals, circuses and parades
Festivals and feasts
Playgrounds and theme parks
Community and national celebrations
Games and sports, including national and international contests and
    championships (for example the Olympics)
Extreme sports that involve high levels of challenge and risk (bungee jumping,
    white-water rafting, sky diving)
Theatrical performances (music, dance, drama, comedy acts, pantomime, films)
Clubs and leisure activities
Travel, exploration and adventure activities
Mind play (dreams, fantasies, word games, puzzles, mind games).

FIGURE 1.3 DIFFERENT FORMS OF PLAY

play is an inherent need throughout our lives, whether organized or spontaneous, sedate or chaotic.

In a scholarly review of play research, Sutton-Smith (1997) notes the disagreement among Western philosophers as to whether play is basically orderly and rule-governed, or a chaotic, violent and indeterminate interaction of forces. He describes many different forms of play and play contexts that span childhood and adulthood, including those that represent expert levels of skill (such as in sport) and bring high rewards and social status (Figure 1.3).

Playing and playfulness are deeply embedded across the lifespan as cultural activities which have a wide variety of meanings and significance. Different forms of play serve many different purposes, from the individual mind at play in a game of chess, to whole communities at play in carnivals and festivals.

▓ LINKING PLAY IN CHILDHOOD AND ADULTHOOD

There are lifelong links between children's play worlds and subsequent adult roles, identities and occupations. Imaginary worlds constructed in childhood can last through adolescence and into adulthood, and become more elaborate and structured (Cohen and MacKeith, 1991). For example, the architect Frank Lloyd Wright played with Froebelian building blocks, and acknowledged the influence these had on his later career. The musicians Jacqueline and Hilary du Pré grew up in a playful musical world, with a mother who was an inspiring co-player:

> From as early as I can remember, Mum entertained us with music. She
> was always singing, playing the piano, clapping and stepping rhythms,
> making shapes in the air according to the phrase shapes. We curled
> into the tiniest forms when the music was soft, and burst out jumping
> in the air when it was loud. We tiptoed and crouched for creepy music
> and skipped to dotted rhythms. We had to convey ferocity or tragedy
> and all as a spontaneous reaction to her playing. (du Pré and du Pré,
> 1997: 29)

Their mother also wrote tunes especially for Jacqueline because there was
nothing suitable for a young budding cellist. The tunes were illustrated
with drawings and stories and drew on everyday events such as a visit to
the zoo, as well as fantastical tales about witches and elves. In contrast,
the formative years of the writers Charlotte and Emily Brontë could not
have been more different. Their mother was often ill; their father was
stern, aloof and absorbed in his work. The children found escape from a
gloomy and rather lonely childhood through inventing and acting out
plays which often drew on their knowledge of famous characters in
history. Their brother Branwell's box of toy soldiers provided the props
for the stories. By the age of 13, Charlotte Brontë was an avid writer of
tales, dramas, romances and poems, which were written out in minute
handwriting in their 'little magazines'. Perhaps not surprisingly, there was
a strong element of escapism in their tales of adventure, shipwreck and
creating new societies in far-off islands. These examples show how
children's play worlds can influence their subsequent pathways into
adulthood. It is always interesting to ask students and teachers how they
played and what they played with as children. Almost invariably there is
a lot of 'school play' involving toys, peers and sometimes adults.

Playfulness, imagination and creativity are inextricably linked in our
playing and working lives. Increasingly in adulthood we engage in
different forms of play; for example playing with ideas, roles, words,
media, meanings, and with relationships between events, people, concepts, materials and systems. Young people have one foot in childhood
and the other in adulthood. They gradually play their way into the next
stage of their lives by projecting images and adopting roles that are often
influenced by the media and popular culture. The dressing-up box of
childhood becomes the wardrobe of adulthood, whether it is a suit for
work, the latest fashions for going out clubbing, a hi-tech outfit for the
gym or sports activity, or a fancy-dress outfit for a party. For many adults,
play is still a deeply enjoyable experience, and maintains the possibilities
for change and transformation that Chazan (2002) identified. Observations of families at the seaside consistently reveal the playfulness of adults,

with or without children. For example, a group of girls and boys played energetically for two hours on a beach, digging holes and burying each other, building sand castles and sand sculptures, and creating a miniature Neolithic stone circle which closely resembled Stonehenge. Their playfulness flowed between rough and tumble, construction, teasing and joking. Between the playful banter these young people (who were 17–18 years old) discussed their forthcoming exam results, their preparations for going to university, and their hopes and fears for the future. Play is riddled with paradoxes: children and adults often work quite hard at their play in terms of effort, motivation, concentration and outcomes. Children play at being adults, while adults want to play in the sand. Play in childhood is seen as trivial: play in adulthood can have high status and bring rich rewards, for example through being a skilled player in a sport. However, being a skilled player in adulthood may also involve the drudgery of practice, the discipline of training and endless competitions to maintain status. As the next section shows, creating a continuum between lifelong playing and learning is perhaps even more critical in the 21st century as economic success becomes dependent on people who are creative, flexible, innovative, imaginative and playful in the workplace.

PLAY AND WORK

As we have seen, society has a general mistrust of play in educational contexts and the lack of a precise operational definition of play ensures that it is viewed as the opposite of work. Research evidence shows consistently that while play may be encouraged in early childhood, the boundaries between work and play become increasingly evident in the primary school, often from Reception class onwards. In the study by Bennett *et al* (1997), teachers considered that play activities were more motivating and engaging than work for young children, and provided a 'natural way to learn'. At the same time, play was sometimes used as a way of teaching children skills such as independence and concentration, which were necessary for work. The play/work divide has evolved because of conflicting perspectives about the relationship between playing and learning. With more status being given to formal education and defined learning outcomes, teachers are faced with increasing demands for evidence of achievement from parents who typically undervalue play as a learning process. For example, a small rural primary school successfully integrated play across the curriculum. However articulate the teachers' justifications to parents, the use of the word 'play' was objected to because of its trivial, anti-work connotations and a concern that the children would not be 'doing' the National Curriculum. The teachers decided to call play-based sessions 'workshops'. This compromise was a pragmatic response to a difficult problem, but might also be seen as a betrayal of the ideals of play.

Children also have their own distinctions between work and play: they often associate work with teacher-directed activity rather than choice, and with sitting down rather than being active. The following comments from children aged six to seven reflect a range of views: they were recorded after a morning of play activities organized by students on an Early Years teacher training course:

- 'No, we haven't been working this morning because we could choose.'

- 'Play is what you do when you choose, like Lego and things, but work is what the teacher tells you to do like reading and writing things down.'

- 'I think we've been playing and working. It was hard work making that go-kart because it kept falling to bits.'

Debates about play tend to go round in ever-decreasing circles: just as rigid definitions are unhelpful to practitioners, so too are narrow demarcations between work and play. One further point is important here: it has been suggested that we need to distinguish between play 'as such' and play in schools (Guha, 1988). Play 'as such' has been studied intensively from many different perspectives with the intention of understanding why children play, what they play and what effects it has on their learning and development. Play in school is structured (and sometimes constrained) by contextual influences, and the need to provide evidence of learning in relation to measurable outcomes (Bennett *et al*, 1997). Practitioners therefore have to justify play as a vehicle for learning and demonstrate the ways in which a play-based curriculum and pedagogy can contribute to effective teaching and learning. However, as we will show in subsequent chapters, there are different constructs of 'effectiveness' in early childhood education. In summary, early childhood specialists need to value play through creating appropriate contexts and conditions for learning, which promote a continuum between play and work, and incorporate playful approaches to teaching and learning. The following section provides an overview of policy developments, and considers whether the problems with play are being solved or exacerbated.

PLAY AND NATIONAL CURRICULUM POLICIES

Since the first edition of this book was published in 1996, the education community has continued to be deluged by waves of policy changes and initiatives, to the extent of innovation overload. One of the key changes has been the expansion of pre-school provision and the extension of government policies to this phase. This has been a mixed blessing in the sense that substantially increased funding has been allocated to this phase, along with policy interventions that have sought to improve the quality of provision, promote accountability and provide continuity with Key Stage 1. Play has remained a political issue, with the early childhood community defending a play-based curriculum, and successive governments pushing towards defining teaching intentions, learning outcomes and goals. In the first edition, we argued strongly for articulating a play-based pedagogy, alongside a play-based curriculum. So what progress has been made in the intervening period, and is there a stronger validation for play?

Policy changes have kept play high on the educational agenda for different reasons. Following the introduction of the National Curriculum, there were widespread concerns that play would be squeezed out of the curriculum, and that pre-school education would be subject to 'top-down' influences. At the same time, play advocates in the academic and practitioner communities continued to lobby for play as an integral part of a broad, balanced and responsive early childhood curriculum. The Education Reform Act (1988) was based predominantly on a party political agenda of the Conservative New Right, and introduced an unprecedented degree of control that was widely regarded as threatening to teachers' traditional autonomy in determining what should be taught, when and how. In early childhood, traditional autonomy was synonymous with insularity, lack of clarity in aims, idiosyncratic approaches and low accountability. The ideologies of the New Right orchestrated a discourse of derision that exposed these perceived weaknesses and introduced more centralized control of curriculum and assessment practices and, subsequently, pedagogy. The extent and pace of change were daunting: there was a clash of ideology and counter-ideology as politicians attacked the hallowed principles of play, and the early childhood community maintained a staunch defence. The reforms aimed to change the culture of early childhood and primary education, and concretized the downward influence of the National Curriculum on Reception and nursery classes.

Opinions were divided about the impact of the National Curriculum. Anning (1997) stated that Key Stage 1 teachers knuckled down to making the best compromises they could between their preferred ways of designing the curriculum, implementing new policies and taking a proactive role in contributing to change processes. More pessimistic views were also expressed. According to Hurst (1994), play was seen increasingly as the enemy of education and was relegated to the margins of school experience. Furthermore, the top-down pressures of the National Curriculum on pre-school education became a 'malign influence' (Hurst, 1994: 58). Blenkin and Kelly (1994: 1) gave further support to these views:

> It is plain to anyone who has had direct experience of early years education in the UK that the advent of the National Curriculum has had the effect of turning it on its head. The direction of its development has been reversed; the advances it has made towards establishing a new and sophisticated form of curriculum have been discounted and arrested; and those teachers in the sector who continue to adhere to the values and ideals implicit in the approaches which have been displaced are struggling against all odds to maintain those values and ideals in a context which is not only incompatible but hostile to them.

These forthright critiques reflect some of the pain, struggle and frustrations that practitioners have faced as a result of policy changes. However, it became increasingly evident that the early childhood community needed to clarify what they were hanging on to and defending: the ideology which underpinned this phase was made to appear outdated and irrelevant, and politicians were not convinced about the significance of play for learning and development. Research evidence showed that the status of play was already tenuous, particularly beyond the pre-school phase. The lack of clear principles and a secure theoretical base created discrepancies between the rhetoric and reality of play, and between aims and practice. There were disagreements about the role of the adult in children's play, and the efficacy of free versus structured play. The dichotomy between work and play meant that play lacked status and credibility, particularly in relation to obtaining evidence of progression in children's learning. Play was increasingly exposed in the context of a political agenda that emphasized accountability, performance, competition and league tables and demanded evidence of effectiveness and outcomes, as was seen in numerous Ofsted inspection reports. The vulnerability of play was not caused by the National Curriculum but was undoubtedly exacerbated by it. The need to retain play within the curriculum was upheld by many advocates, but with the proviso that more attention should be paid to planning, assessment, evaluation, progression and continuity (as we also argued in the first edition of this book).

There were attempts to legitimize play within the developing policy framework. A report by Her Majesty's Inspectorate examined the implications of the National Curriculum for children under five and accorded central status to play, with particular emphasis on planning, structuring the learning environment and developing skilled interactions between adults and children:

> Purposeful play features strongly in good pre-school education. It is not a free or wholly unstructured activity. Through the selection of materials and equipment . . . teachers ensure that, in their play, children encounter the learning experiences that they intend . . . Play that is well planned and pleasurable helps children to think, to increase their understanding and to improve their language competence. It allows children to be creative, to explore and investigate materials, to experiment and to draw and test their conclusions . . . Such experience is important in catching and sustaining children's interests and motivating their learning as individuals in co-operation with others. (DES, 1989: 8)

The endorsement for planned, structured, purposeful play was reinforced by the influential report of the Rumbold Committee (DES, 1990) as a key aspect of ensuring quality provision for the under-fives, including children in Reception classes. Play and talk were identified as key approaches to learning, alongside other conditions for learning:

- sensitive, knowledgeable and informed adult involvement and intervention

- careful planning and organization of play settings in order to provide for and extend learning

- enough time for children to develop their play

- careful observation of children's activities to facilitate assessment and planning for progression and continuity.

The impetus for change was being externally driven; however, practitioners needed to reconceptualize their practice in their own terms, and create new ways of thinking about a play-based pedagogy and curriculum. To this end, they were assisted by wider trends in education and society, which eventually led to a clearer policy framework for children aged three to five, and subsequently children up to the age of three, across all pre-school settings. The distinction between play 'as such' and play 'in schools' become more crystallized in policy terms, as reflected in the government's first attempt to define a curriculum framework for four- to five-year-old children. The Desirable Outcomes for Children's Learning (SCAA, 1996) included six areas of learning (personal and social development, language and literacy, mathematics, knowledge and understanding of the world, physical development and creative development). Outcomes were defined in each area, and were related to Level 1 descriptions in the subject areas of the National Curriculum. Play and talk were identified as common features of good practice; however, the explicit political agenda was to provide Reception children with a head start into Key Stage 1. Teachers were required to carry out Baseline Assessment of Reception children in the term of entry, with the resulting data being used to measure 'value added' between Reception and Standard Attainment Tests (SATs) in Year 2 (age seven). This framework was problematic from its inception: Anning (1995) warned of the dangers of misinterpreting these outcomes and communicating false ideas of what are reasonable expectations for young children. These dangers were identified as whole-class teaching, overemphasis on formal, sedentary activities, and worksheets or rote learning in literacy and numeracy activities.

In a subsequent review by QCA (1999), the Desirable Outcomes were considered to be helpful for:

■ providing a common language and foundation

■ establishing national expectations

■ encouraging a broad curriculum

■ encouraging educators to review and make changes to their provision

■ strengthening links between pre-school and Reception classes

■ promoting whole-school issues.

The following areas were considered to be problematic, and echoed the concerns expressed by many early childhood specialists:

■ the outcomes were difficult to manage and understand

■ they focused on subjects not children, and on outcomes rather than processes

■ play was not mentioned, leading to formal approaches too early, and children being put under pressure to learn in ways that are not appropriate

- the outcomes did not acknowledge children's prior experience and failed to take account of children with special
  educational needs and those for whom English is an
  additional language

- personal and social development were not given sufficient
  priority

- oracy was insufficiently emphasized

- the outcomes confused knowledge, skills and dispositions,
  and were poorly written. (QCA, 1999)

The Desirable Outcomes worked against the principle of using play and
talk as media for learning because of 'over-formalisation of the curriculum and the proliferation of worksheets' in some settings (QCA, 1999).
Not surprisingly, this framework proved to have a short life, and the
persistence of the early childhood lobby paid dividends in the design of
a new framework. The Foundation Stage for three- to five-year-old
children was introduced in England (QCA/DfEE, 2000) (with similar
frameworks in Wales and Scotland), and provided a clear endorsement for
a play-based curriculum and pedagogy.

DEVELOPING A PEDAGOGY OF PLAY

PLAY IN THE FOUNDATION STAGE

The *Curriculum Guidance for the Foundation Stage* (CGFS) (QCA/DfEE,
2000) articulates sound principles for making connections between
playing, learning and teaching, and sets out a pedagogy of play. This is
broadly defined as the ways in which early childhood educators make
provision for playful and play-based activities, how they design play-
learning environments, and all the pedagogical techniques and strategies
they use to support or enhance teaching and learning through play
(Wood, 2004). The CGFS validates adult-directed and child-initiated play
and, in theory at least, provides guiding principles that address some of
the problems with play:

- Well-planned play, both indoors and outdoors, is a key
  way in which children learn with enjoyment and challenge.

- Children do not make a distinction between 'play' and
  'work' and neither should practitioners. Children need

time to become engrossed, work in depth, and complete activities.

■ Creative and imaginative play activities promote the development and use of language.

■ Practitioners should make good use of opportunities to talk 'mathematically' as children play or take part in daily activities.

■ Practitioners should encourage children's mathematical development by intervening in their play.

■ Creative development includes art, music, dance, role play and imaginative play.

The role of the practitioner is crucial to:

■ planning and resourcing a challenging learning environment

■ supporting children's learning through planned play activity

■ extending and supporting children's spontaneous play

■ extending and developing children's language and communication in their play

■ assessment and evaluation

■ ensuring continuity and progression.

The use of the terms 'well-planned' and 'structured' play can have different meanings, depending on how they are interpreted in practice. For example, structure can imply a tight (and possibly restrictive) pedagogical framework that focuses attention on defined learning outcomes. Alternatively, structure can imply a more open framework which ensures that play activities include processes that support learning and potentially lead to a variety of outcomes. The CGFS incorporates both approaches across a variety of different contexts; therefore practitioners need to look carefully at their own meanings of these terms, and how they are interpreted in practice. The following teaching–learning processes are central to good practice, and help to foster positive learning dispositions:

Creativity, imagination, challenge, investigation, curiosity, concentration, confidence, control, perseverance, engagement, participation, planning and reflecting, building on what they already know, being challenged, taking risks, building self-esteem and self-efficacy, developing positive attitudes and learning dispositions, exploration, experimentation, making choices and decisions, planning their own tasks and activities, sensory exploration, making connections, using language for different purposes, playing/working alone or in collaboration with others (peers and adults), creating and solving problems.

Pedagogical approaches include:

Using language that is rich and using correct grammar, developing linguistic structures for thinking, providing rich and simulating experiences, responding to spontaneous learning, planning real-life situations, involving children in planning and initiating their own activities, direct teaching, responding to different needs and learning styles, planning a high-quality learning environment, informed understanding of how children learn, knowledge of SEN, EAL and equal opportunities, modelling positive behaviour, ensuring breadth and balance across the six areas of learning.

Practitioners should use their professional knowledge to decide how to interpret this guidance, in order to create unity between playing, learning and teaching. The CGFS provides guidance for developing the curriculum, and should not be interpreted as prescribing a curriculum. The stepping stones exemplify a range of learning outcomes, but are not exhaustive in defining all the possible and actual learning outcomes that will be embedded in a high-quality curriculum. These frameworks provide a considerable challenge, especially for Reception and Key Stage 1 teachers, because they also have to follow the national frameworks for teaching as described in the National Literacy and Numeracy Strategies (DfEE, 1998, 1999), which are not consistent with the more flexible pedagogy embodied in the CGFS. Some of the National Literacy and Numeracy Strategies teaching objectives are linked to play and playful approaches.

▨ PLAY IN THE LITERACY AND NUMERACY STRATEGIES

LITERACY STRATEGY: FRAMEWORK FOR TEACHING OBJECTIVES

- To use knowledge and familiar texts to re-enact or re-tell to others, recounting the main points in correct sequence.

- To experiment with writing in a variety of play, exploratory play and role play situations.

- To use writing to communicate in a variety of ways, incorporating it into play and everyday classroom life.

- To draw on grammatical awareness, to read with appropriate expression and intonation, e.g. in reading to others, or to dolls, puppets.

- To recite stories and rhymes, inventing patterns and playing with rhyme.

- To write and draw simple instructions and labels for everyday classroom use, e.g. in the role play area.

- To identify and discuss characters . . . and to compare characters from different stories or plays.

- To become aware of character and dialogue, e.g. by role-playing parts when reading aloud stories or playing with others.

NUMERACY STRATEGY: FRAMEWORK FOR TEACHING OBJECTIVES

- Teachers should provide structured learning 'opportunities' indoors and outdoors, e.g. sand and water, stories, physical movement, singing and acting number stories and rhymes, cooking and shopping, two- and three-dimensional creative work, observing numbers and patterns in the environment and daily routines.

- Small groups can be scheduled to play freely in the 'opportunity' area, but [practitioners] need to intervene in the play to question the children and develop their understanding in ways that you have planned in advance.

- Children should have experience of real-life and imagined situations, and learn how to use mathematics in authentic contexts, e.g. cooking, measuring, shopping.

- Teachers should plan interesting, linked activities and talking points with chosen objectives in mind. In this way, teaching is focused on the mathematics and is not left to chance.

- Teachers should build on children's everyday 'real world' mathematical knowledge and personal experience of numbers, such as door and bus numbers, ages of people in the family, TV programme times, bed times, family lottery numbers, telephone numbers.

These teaching objectives fail to capture the spirit of playful teaching and the complexity of play as a medium for learning. Not surprisingly, there remain concerns about the appropriateness of the Literacy and Numeracy Frameworks for Teaching Reception children, and transition from Foundation Stage to Key Stage 1 (Ofsted, 2004). A report commissioned by the Association for Teachers and Lecturers (Adams *et al*, 2004) notes the continued ambiguous position of the Reception year, in which children below statutory school age receive full-time education within a school setting. They recommend that practice should become less like the Key Stage 1 model (dominated by lessons, subjects, timetables, tightly defined learning objectives and assessments) and more like best nursery practice:

> where learning is seen in a holistic, non-compartmentalized way, where play, first-hand experiences and talk are the principal means of learning, where children's capacity to explore and imagine for themselves is nourished by open-ended invitations to engage with the world, and where observation of individual children is the key to developing both curriculum and pedagogy. (Adams *et al*, 2004: 81)

Many early childhood specialists argue that the Foundation Stage should be extended upwards into Key Stage 1, to make it less like the Key Stage 2 model and improve progression and continuity from birth to seven years. This aspiration is embedded in the policy framework in Wales with the development of a Foundation Stage for children aged three to seven. Some of the problematic issues associated with the implementation of the CGFS and the Literacy and Numeracy Strategies will be addressed in subsequent chapters, along with an exploration of how contemporary theory and research can inform shared understanding of effective practice in the early years.

To summarize, policy developments in early childhood have proved to be a mixed blessing. Play has remained high on the agenda, but with greater emphasis on what constitutes good-quality play. Greater attention is being paid to developing a pedagogy of play, which validates the role of adults in planning, supporting and extending children's learning through many different approaches, as well as recognizing the educationally powerful content of children's self-initiated activities. The early childhood community has been influential in articulating the needs and characteristics of young learners, and how these should influence provision. More attention is being paid to the additional or special play needs of children as the government's policy for special educational needs promotes access and inclusion. As subsequent chapters will show, research and practice-based evidence support the role and value of play in different areas of learning.

Despite the problems with play, a key message of this book is that early childhood educators will find it difficult, if not impossible, to provide a high-quality curriculum without providing high-quality play. However, a cautionary note must be sounded here: the policy agenda validates play as an approach to learning which pays into the outcomes that are defined in the CGFS, the Literacy and Numeracy Strategies, and Key Stage 1 of the National Curriculum. Practitioners should not be constrained by following this agenda slavishly; while these frameworks constitute an official (and politically driven) version of desirable skills, knowledge and understanding, there are other versions and other visions which can inform provision. A key challenge for practitioners is to develop their abilities to tune into other potential outcomes, including the outcomes that children construct for themselves, and co-construct with others in their play and work. The implications of the new policy initiatives are that all practitioners need a powerful understanding of young children's learning, and diverse funds of pedagogical knowledge and expertise to plan a curriculum that is fit for children in the 21st century. In the next chapter, we will look in more detail at past and present perspectives from ideology and theory that provide a justification for play.

FURTHER READING

The following texts provide good accounts of the rhetoric and reality of play, and the everyday problems and constraints that practitioners face.

Adams, S., Alexander, E., Drummond, M.J. and Moyles, J. (2004) *Inside the Foundation Stage: Recreating the Reception Year*, London, Association of Teachers and Lecturers.

Anning, A. (1997) *The First Years at School*, Buckingham, Open University Press.

Anning, A. and Edwards, A. (1999) *Promoting Children's Learning from Birth to Five*, Buckingham, Open University Press.

Anning, J. Cullen, J. and Fleer, M. (eds) (2004) *Early Childhood Education: Society and Culture*, London, Sage.

Bennett, N., Wood, E. and Rogers, S. (1997) *Teaching Through Play: Teachers' Thinking and Classroom Practice*, Buckingham, Open University Press.

CHAPTER TWO

Ideologies, Ideals and Theories

The validation of child- and adult-initiated play has been broadly welcomed by early childhood specialists, but at the same time it creates some interesting challenges. Practitioners on continuing professional development courses frequently ask for input on the latest research, theories and ideas that underpin play, as well as opportunities to identify their own theories and beliefs. This chapter focuses on these areas. Because of its enduring influence, we revisit the ideological tradition to show some of the continuities and developments with contemporary theory and practice. This is followed by a detailed exploration of what theory and research can tell us about why children play, and the role and value of different forms of play. The research evidence on learning through play is not always conclusive, but is nevertheless persuasive. The evidence on teaching through play is more problematic, and tends to highlight the tensions between the rhetoric and reality of play.

THE IDEOLOGICAL TRADITION

The ideological tradition has provided a foundation for how early childhood education has been conceptualized and has validated the role and value of play in early learning. This tradition is by no means uniform, because it emanates from a variety of philosophers, educators and developmental psychologists from different ages and cultures. The heady mix of ideas ranges from the rhapsodic to the pragmatic, regarding the nature of childhood, the purposes of education, the rights of the child, the responsibilities of adults and the role of play. Central to this tradition is the work of Johann Pestalozzi, Freidrich Froebel, Rudolf Steiner, John Dewey, Maria Montessori, Margaret and Rachel McMillan, Susan Isaacs and Anna Freud as well as the literary and philosophical writing of social and political reformers such as Jean Jacques Rousseau, William Wordsworth and Charles Dickens. Their ideas were innovative and transformational, and exerted a profound impact on how childhood was conceptualized, and how children should be treated in society. Until the 19th century, childhood was seen as an immature form of adulthood and children from all social classes had little status in society. Children were frequently abused and exploited and had few legal rights or protection. For many, childhood was cut short by the need to work in the home or in factories, often for long hours and in dangerous conditions. The concept of original sin meant that children were regarded as naturally evil: there was an enduring belief that children needed to have moral rectitude instilled in them by whatever means adults thought acceptable, whether in the home, school or workplace. The child's mind was seen as an empty vessel, or a blank slate, which could be filled with the knowledge, skills and behaviour deemed valuable by society. Froebel and Rousseau took the opposite view: children are naturally good, and their goodness could be harnessed through nurture, care and appropriate education. Along with other social reformers, the early pioneers created new visions of childhood, changed entrenched attitudes towards children and developed appropriate provision for their development, care and education, where freedom to learn could be combined with appropriate nurturing and guidance. Intrinsically bound with this movement were wider ideals about social justice and, ultimately, a more egalitarian society.

◼ FRIEDRICH FROEBEL (1782–1852)

Froebel is regarded as one of the most significant pioneers of early childhood education because of his continued international influence on practitioners. Froebel saw the child as an individual and as part of the family and community. He proposed that learning is a holistic process involving the child, other adults and the wider environment. He believed that children's natural goodness needed to be encouraged and nurtured through sound educational practices that would develop unity between the outer and inner life of the child. He saw childhood as a stage in its own right, not just a preparation for adult life, and emphasized development and transformation through play, first-hand experiences, self-chosen activities and intrinsic motivation. Play for Froebel was a spiritual activity which reflected deep inner processes and transformations. His 'kindergarten' represented metaphors of growth, freedom and an idyllic balance between nature, nurture and spirituality. The developmental tradition was firmly established with Froebel's belief that the role of the adult was to begin where the learner is, and to intervene sensitively in the child's activities, including play. The curricula devised by the early pioneers were not just innovative but revolutionary, which did not always sit easily with the dominant social and political order. Froebel's new system of education was perceived as a political threat and, by the mid-19th century, he was regarded as a subversive by the authorities in Germany. He was accused of being an atheist and a socialist and all of his nurseries were closed down (Cohen, 1993). However, his ideas not only endured but spread beyond Germany with the establishment of training colleges and kindergartens.

▧ RUDOLF STEINER (1861–1925)

Steiner continued Froebelian principles in focusing on holistic development, through a curriculum based on learning through social interaction, drama, imagination, play, music, poetry and movement. He emphasized the facilitative, heuristic role of the teacher in enabling the development of the individual child, and the fulfilment of individual potential.

▧ JOHN DEWEY (1859–1952)

In the USA, the work of John Dewey became increasingly influential in the 20th century, and echoed many of these developmental principles. Dewey also emphasized the ways in which children act as co-constructors of their learning; he saw them as active agents and active participants in shaping their learning environments and experiences.

▧ MARIA MONTESSORI (1869–1952)

Montessori also came to enjoy an enduring international influence as her theories and beliefs were translated into practice through training colleges and schools. Montessori's approaches were based on Séguin's work with cognitively impaired children, and her own research with deprived children. Montessori's model of child development was based on the accretion of skills in a simple to complex approach, based on the use of didactic materials. Montessori believed in a planned environment and devised a sequence of learning activities to support sense training, through which children progressed with the support of a trained 'directress'. Although she regarded fantasy play as trivial and patronizing to the child, Montessori provided a child-sized environment in which children could learn and practice real-life skills without the presence or intervention of an adult. She was more pragmatic in her prescribed curriculum and pedagogy, and placed less emphasis than Froebel, Steiner and Dewey on the child's natural tendencies for free play, exploration and fantasy, and representations of thought and action through different media.

MARGARET MACMILLAN (1860–1931)

Pragmatism was also the focus of MacMillan's work. Along with her sister Rachel, she established an enduring relationship between care, health and education at community level (Bradburn, 1976; Steedman, 1990). Margaret MacMillan originally set up clinics to address the severe health problems found among children in urban slum areas, and extended this provision to include education. The curriculum in the open-air nurseries focused on sensory training and speech training, with an emphasis on discovery methods of learning in a structured environment (indoors and outdoors), which was planned to support the child's needs and interests. Provision was made for discipline-based learning, for example in science, maths and literacy, through integrated experiences that fostered children's motivation and readiness to learn. MacMillan was a humanitarian, a Christian socialist and a social reformer who agitated for increasing state provision based on her new form of education, not as a luxury but as a necessity. She saw her nursery schools as part of a new social movement, which would lead to community development and regeneration, and would gradually create a more informed electorate (Bradburn, 1976). Her ideas established a blueprint for nursery education, the legacy of which can be discerned in contemporary policy and practice, with the development of community-based services (for example Sure Start and Early Excellence Centres) that combine health, education and welfare for children and their families.

SUSAN ISAACS (1885–1948)

Isaacs carried out pioneering research of a more theoretical nature, which bridged philosophy, psychology and psychoanalysis. Along with her assistants, Isaacs carried out systematic observations of children aged two to nine years in the naturalistic setting of the experimental Malting House School. Isaacs saw the child as an active learner:

> Errors and surprises are the main impetus to the further development of knowledge, based on the distinction of differences. Each new assimilation of experiences gives rise in its turn to a new expectation. The art of perception is thus always active and living. It is a process, not a passive experience (1936: 28).

She also emphasized the value of spontaneous, imaginative and manipulative play as a means of satisfying frustrated desires and working out inner conflicts, and of gaining understanding of the external world of objects and their relations. Isaacs was interested in the child's construction of knowledge, which she advanced through her scientific analyses of young children's social, intellectual and emotional development. She made direct links between her theories of learning and early childhood curriculum and pedagogy, advocating systematic observations and record keeping to inform planning and provision. Play was central to the curriculum, and provided children with opportunities for problem-solving and developing skills in reading, writing and number. Children's self-education was prioritized, with the minimum of interference from adults. The role of the teacher was essentially to observe and identify the child's needs and interests, and to design the curriculum accordingly, thus reinforcing the developmental orientation established by Froebel.

▓ 'MISS BOYCE'

A detailed account of Isaacs' theories in practice was given by Boyce (1946) at the experimental Raleigh School in the East End of London, which catered for children age four to seven and a half years, all from economically disadvantaged families. They experienced poor health, speech and language problems and many physical disabilities that were associated with poverty, inadequate sanitation and poor health care. The accounts by 'Miss Boyce' of the children's learning and development revealed a seamless progression towards a more structured timetable, with child-initiated activities gradually leading towards more teacher-directed inputs based on fostering and responding to children's needs and interests, and identifying their readiness for new learning. The older children continued to have sustained periods of time for 'free activities' and play, with play themes often developing over a period of weeks, alongside a more structured timetable for teacher-directed sessions. Boyce stated that planning the curriculum around individual needs and interests is a complex and demanding pedagogical endeavour, a point with which practitioners today would readily agree. She disagreed with Isaacs' standpoint on minimal interference from adults, and considered that they could actively nurture children's interests, by offering different stimuli, resources and activities to promote new learning. In this respect, Boyce anticipated more contemporary theories about a proactive, but not overly intrusive, role for the practitioner.

These ideologies and theories melded with those of the Progressive movement in early childhood and primary education, which emerged in the early 20th century from the work of John Dewey, Nathan Isaacs and their followers. Progressivism rejected the formality and instrumentalism of established approaches, and heralded new approaches based on child-centred methods of teaching and greater autonomy for the child. Progressivism made fundamental assumptions about the nature of childhood, the child as learner, the nature of knowledge, and the developmental processes of knowledge acquisition. Education was conceptualized not as something that is done to the child, but as a complex process within which the child is an active participant. This orientation was theoretically seductive, because it reflected powerful notions of childhood innocence and freedom, and empowerment through education, both of which were central tenets of the social and educational reform movements. These assumptions were a direct challenge to behaviourist/instrumental discourses which positioned the child as a blank slate or empty vessel.

FROM PAST TO PRESENT

The work of the pioneers reflected several enduring themes that have influenced culture and practices in early childhood education nationally and internationally (Saracho and Spodek, 2002; Slentz and Krogh, 2001). Within a broadly developmental theoretical orientation, curriculum provision and pedagogic approaches are essentially child-centred, and are informed by children's ongoing needs and interests and their readiness for new learning. Readiness can be determined by close observation of the child, which then informs the next sequences or steps in learning and curriculum provision. The curriculum is conceptualized as integrated experiences rather than discrete subjects, with a wide range of activities leading potentially towards multiple outcomes, which may not always be predetermined. The distinction between play and work is not clearly drawn: rather the quality of activities and experiences determines effective teaching and learning. There is consistent agreement that children learn best in enriched environments, with a variety of resources and activities to support freedom of choice, active learning and problem-solving. In such environments, practitioners make learning inevitable through fostering the child's interest, engagement and motivation to learn. There are differing emphases on the role of adult intervention and interaction, particularly in free play and child-initiated activities. The predominant pedagogical orientations are enabling and facilitating children's learning, alongside opportunities for direct instruction and support where necessary and appropriate. While many of these principles have been ideologically seductive, they are nevertheless open to debate. There is consistent agreement that a contemporary framework for early childhood education needs to be grounded in reliable evidence, useful theories and sound principles (Anning *et al*, 2004).

The pioneer educators aimed to establish the uniqueness and importance of childhood as a stage in its own right, and to respect children's natural affinity for play. However, they did not demonstrate consistent agreement in their principles or practices. Although play was valued differently by each of the pioneers, they were concerned to harness its educational potential in different ways. The Romantic, child-centred ideology emphasized the importance of allowing children to indulge their naturalness and playfulness. Montessori did not believe that children needed to play and did not value play as a creative force in itself. In designing special child-sized environments, she was not directly stimulating imaginative role play, but encouraging practical independence and autonomy. She had an instrumental view of play as a means to further cognitive, social, moral and emotional development. The pioneers recognized that play allows children to express their inner needs, emotions, desires and conflicts but, in terms of their curriculum models, it was not the dominant activity. The models devised by Froebel and Montessori were based substantially on special materials to be used in particular sequences and in carefully structured environments. The curricula designed by the pioneers also included more pragmatic adult-directed elements such as sense-training, language and speech training, self-discipline, orderliness, cleanliness and the formation of good habits and dispositions.

These curricula were socially, culturally and temporally situated: they were designed with reference to particular values and purposes within rapidly changing societies. For example, the Progressive movement, which developed in the USA at the turn of the 20th century, criticized the programmes of Froebel and Montessori as being highly structured, formal and ritualized. Montessori's emphasis on sensory training, individualism and academic learning was considered to be at odds with notions of freedom, creativity, play, fantasy and self-expression. We might also question whether Romantic notions of childhood freedom and innocence remain relevant in contemporary society: a Reception class teacher questioned why she was bothering to teach her children nursery rhymes (as recommended in the National Literacy Strategy) when they knew all the words, actions and dance routines to the latest songs from popular girl bands, and pop idols such as Britney Spears and Kylie Minogue.

In spite of these different emphases, there are remarkable continuities in some of the fundamental principles that underpin good quality provision for children, which are exemplified in the work of Miss Boyce in the experimental Raleigh School. The staff developed an integrated (child-initiated and teacher-directed) curriculum that echoes many of the recommendations in contemporary curriculum frameworks, both nationally and internationally. The staff aimed to create a 'child-centred school' that prioritized the development of the individual:

> We looked forward to their development socially, but determined to allow this to grow spontaneously in an atmosphere we should provide. Organization of large groups with set purposes was to be avoided. We hoped also, that reading and writing, and number, with other knowledge of the world around them, would arise as interests from problems encountered during play, and from the practical necessities of self-chosen pursuits . . .

> The principle of activity as a means of learning guided the efforts of the staff to foster the development of each child. Whatever they could undertake without too heavy a responsibility was given into their care . . . Nature study was entirely a matter of doing; number knowledge was the result of daily experiences in and out of school. Reading and writing interests were levered from the post-office play and picture books. Knowledge of the world was gained through first-hand observation supplemented by the teachers' questions. Experiment was encouraged and led to further discussion and investigation. Most of the information needed was given at moments when some incident had aroused the curiosity of the group. (Boyce, 1946: 4–5)

Miss Boyce describes a range of 'mixed methods' that we are familiar with today. Creative activity and play were encouraged, and children were allowed to plan their own activities and develop their interests over a period of time, with support and enrichment from the staff. Teachers also planned 'formal instruction' in reading, writing and number as well as stories, verse readings and group teaching. They aimed to build on children's everyday experiences, for example their home and street experiences of mathematics. Miss Boyce records that 'All these activities were considered real school-life; there was no antithesis between work and play. In fact, no one quite understood which was which' (1946: 6). She describes many different activities with the oldest children (age six to seven and a half) which were stimulated by visits in the local environment, for example to the park, the blacksmiths, the County Hall, the gas works, to watch boats on the River Thames, and explore Covent Garden market. She also describes in detail how these 'excursions' led to energetic and imaginative role-play themes which were led by the children, but constantly enriched by the staff: answering children's questions, responding to their ideas, and providing resources, books and photographs. In the adult-initiated activities, Miss Boyce talks about the children becoming infected with the enthusiasm of the teachers, and outlines how the teachers both responded to and stimulated children's interests. Thus there are some significant continuities between the work of the early pioneers and contemporary policy and practice. These principles remain fundamental to contemporary provision both nationally and internationally.

As conceptions of childhood changed and investment in schooling expanded, education was seen as playing a vital role in the social and economic welfare of the nation. However, there were radically different views of what form mass education should take and the Romantic and Progressive movements, both in the UK and USA, sat uneasily with the continuing influence of the utilitarian model. Control of the curriculum became a political and economic issue and, as public investment in education increased, so too did the need to raise standards of achievement, to provide evidence of effectiveness and accountability and demonstrate value for money. Curricula based on more traditional approaches – drill, rote-learning, sequenced exercises and prioritizing 'the three Rs' – seemed more likely to produce a literate, numerate workforce in the drive towards global economic competitiveness. These wider trends resulted in two distinct theoretical and pedagogical frameworks which have informed contemporary policy and practice: the naturalist, developmental tradition derived from the pioneers, and the instrumental, utilitarian elementary tradition derived variously from the public schools and the Protestant work ethic (Anning, 1997).

The tensions and ambiguities at the level of ideology, policy and practice, which are rooted in the past, have a familiar resonance in the present. What constitutes an appropriate curriculum in the early years has been the subject of intense debate and, increasingly, of political intervention. The eclectic principles of the ideological tradition have contributed to the vulnerability of play and some of the weaknesses inherent in early childhood education. The developmental, child-centred tradition lacked a clear, unified theoretical, psychological and pedagogical base, and systematic guidance for practice. Although play was central to this ideology, there was little clear specification of how play leads to learning, what purposes it serves at different ages in a child's life, and what forms of play are appropriate at different ages. The powerful rhetoric of play was inconsistent with play in practice in contemporary settings. The early childhood community has been articulate at making claims about the importance of play, but less competent at demonstrating the relationship between playing and learning. So what can theory and research tell us about this relationship, and how useful is this evidence in informing practice?

THEORETICAL PERSPECTIVES ON PLAYING AND LEARNING

In providing sound justifications for play, we can draw on a thriving national and international community of play research and scholarship, and a wide range of studies, utilizing diverse research designs, methods and theoretical orientations. Inevitably the outcomes of play scholarship are varied, but there have been some significant advances in theory and practice. Because the field of play is so broad, many play scholars have chosen to focus on types of play (such as role play) or areas of learning (such as literacy), or groups of children, for example those with additional or special educational needs. Early childhood education has been reliant on psychological theory and research, with a particular emphasis on child development. However, more recent studies draw on socio-cultural theories (Chapters 3 and 4) and provide a broader picture of play in theory and practice. This section provides an overview of the main trends in play theory and research, and describes some of the key findings, along with their implications for developing a play-based curriculum and pedagogy, and practical examples. Four key themes are addressed:

- Why do children play?

- What are the main forms of play in early childhood?

- What do children play with, and what do they play at?

- What does play do for the child?

WHY DO CHILDREN PLAY?

Theories of play have changed over time, and there are different emphases according to the disciplinary focus of play research (psychological, biological, sociological, educational). Figure 2.1 summarizes classic theories (Hughes, 1991) and contemporary theories about why children play.

As these multiple theories indicate, play can serve different purposes across children's learning careers: different forms of play appear to be valuable in the here and now and for future learning. There has been a distinct change in emphasis from theories that describe play as a biologically predetermined activity (a natural, instinctive way of

Play allows children to express ideas, emotions and feelings. Play can be seen as emotionally and psychologically cathartic, and provides a safe outlet for tensions and anxieties. Children consciously express, and may exaggerate emotions (for example fear, anger, aggression) in order to learn how to handle these more rationally.

Play provides opportunities for relaxation and recreation, allowing children to regenerate energy expended during work-based activities.

Play enables children to use surplus energy.

Play enables children to practice for the next stage of development, including adulthood, for example through role reversal (child becomes parent, pupil becomes teacher).

Play enables children to engage in a wide range of problem-solving activities (cognitive, manipulative, social), and contributes to intellectual growth.

Play facilitates learning across the three domains of development – cognitive, socio-affective, psycho-motor.

Play facilitates learning relevant processes such as rehearsing, practising, repeating, imitating, exploring, discovering, revising, extending, combining, transforming, testing.

Play contributes to the development of learning dispositions such as intrinsic motivation, engagement, perseverance, positive social interactions, self-esteem, self-confidence and 'can-do' orientations. Play thus contributes to mastery of learning.

FIGURE 2.1   THEORETICAL PERSPECTIVES ON WHY CHILDREN PLAY

promoting optimal development) to those that focus on the role of play in the social, emotional and cultural adaptation of children in different societies. More recently, play scholars have provided evidence of links between play and the subject disciplines such as literacy and numeracy, and the different contexts in which play occurs. As we argued in Chapter 1, there is also an important distinction between play 'as such' and play in educational settings, a view that has been endorsed by policy developments, both nationally and internationally. Thus how we conceptualize play in educational settings depends on understanding the relationship between playing, learning and teaching.

■ WHAT ARE THE MAIN FORMS OF PLAY IN EARLY CHILDHOOD?

Many researchers have distinguished between different forms of play and have sought to define their characteristics or qualities. Because the theories

- *Practice play* – sensori-motor and exploratory play based on physical activities (six months to two years).
- *Symbolic play* – pretend, fantasy and socio-dramatic play, involving the use of mental representations. When play becomes representational, it is regarded as intellectual activity (two to six years).
- *Games with rules* – from six or seven years upwards.

FIGURE 2.2   PIAGET'S CATEGORIES AND STAGES OF PLAY

of Jean Piaget have been so influential on research and practice in early childhood, the following section gives a brief summary of his key theories about play and learning. Piaget (1962) defined three categories and stages of play (Figure 2.2).

These categories have been challenged, refined and extended. Smilansky (1990) added a fourth category of *constructive play* because of the dominance of such play in early childhood. Constructive play is characterized by the manipulation of objects to build or create something, and can be based on blocks and other constructional equipment, as well as playdough or collage materials which may involve symbolic, spatial and multi-dimensional constructions and representational forms.

PIAGETIAN PERSPECTIVES ON EARLY LEARNING Piaget was interested mainly in the origins of logical, mathematical and scientific thinking and aimed to establish the relationship between biological and cognitive development. While he acknowledged the importance of language, social interaction and communication, these were not the main focus of his research. Piaget's theory of cognitive development placed action and self-directed problem-solving at the heart of learning and development: by acting on the world the learner comes to discover how to control it and how to understand the consequences of action. Piaget saw the child as a scientist working actively on materials, objects, events and the environment to construct knowledge and understanding through experience. The emphasis on internal construction of mental schemas is the basis for constructivist theories of learning. Piaget conceptualized learning as a series of transitions through age-related stages, and from immature to mature forms of thinking, which progress from simple to complex, and from concrete to abstract. These stages are linked to the concept of *readiness* – critical periods when a child is ready to learn and to progress to a new level of understanding. Interventionist teaching which ran ahead of these stages could not facilitate development or learning and, in Piaget's view, could actively prevent children from learning something for themselves. Many Piagetian ideas have been challenged and refined by subsequent research. For example, Meadows (1993: 349) challenges notions about 'ages and stages', and argues that the development of performance is age-related, but being stagelike in the sense of being clearly discontinuous, cohesive, synchronous or even across tasks requires stronger evidence than is available in most areas.

Piaget proposed that three processes are important in learning – assimilation, accommodation and equilibration. *Accommodation* is the child's ability to adapt to the environment, whereas *assimilation* is the child's ability to change the environment to suit the imagination. Assimilation involves transforming experiences within the mind, whereas accommodation involves adjusting the mind to new experiences, thus building, modifying or extending schemas. When children encounter new experiences, concepts or knowledge, their existing internal schema have to adjust, causing a state of disequilibrium or cognitive conflict. Disequilibrium motivates learning until a state of equilibrium is reached.

Piaget argued that children's play promoted assimilation rather than accommodation, thereby consolidating newly learned behaviours. Therefore playing was not the same as learning but could facilitate learning by exposing the child to new experiences and new possibilities for acting in and on the world. Thus play was not seen as a leading source of learning and development, but could actively contribute to these processes. Piaget's theories melded easily with the work of the early pioneers, and the ideologies of the Progressive movement, because of his emphasis on discovery and exploration, and child-centred views of learning. His theories were interpreted to imply that educators should create environments in which children could be active learners, free to explore, experiment, combine different materials, and create and solve problems through their self-chosen and self-directed initiatives. The educator is an enabler and facilitator who responds to children's initiatives and values their thinking processes and ongoing cognitive concerns, but does not impart knowledge which children ideally should construct for themselves.

Piaget's three stages and categories of play implied a developmental progression. However, play does not seem to fall consistently into such categories, and children combine different forms of play. Sensori-motor and exploratory play may be the dominant forms of play in infancy, but continue throughout childhood. Infants and toddlers also engage in symbolic and imaginative play. Smilansky (1990) questioned Piaget's categories of play on the basis that both dramatic and socio-dramatic play develop in parallel to other forms of play, beginning at around two and continuing well beyond the age of ten. For example, Elizabeth had a collection of cotton reels which, from around eighteen months, were variously transformed into food, goods to load on a train wagon, people, items of shopping and naughty children in school. She transformed the meaning of the cotton reels 'inside her head', and communicated new meanings in the context of play, combining symbolic and dramatic play forms. As children develop, they build up a repertoire of play skills and knowledge so that they may need less time in epistemic or practice play (what does this object do?) and more time in ludic or creative play (what can I do with this object?) (Hutt *et al*, 1989). Piaget also had a limited view of progression to games with rules. As the next section shows, research studies of children's dramatic and socio-dramatic play reveal how they construct their own internal rules, and reflect the rules embedded in their social and cultural worlds.

DRAMATIC AND SOCIO-DRAMATIC PLAY Much research has focused on the significance of dramatic and socio-dramatic play as a means for learning, particularly in the socio-affective domain. Smilansky distinguishes between these two types of play (Figure 2.3).

Both types of play involve imitation, make believe, imagination and creativity, and involve symbolic activity. Both make complex, and often high cognitive and socio-affective demands on children:

> Children derive satisfaction not only from the ability to imitate but also to form make-believe play, which provides unlimited access to the exciting world of adults ... Make-believe in dramatic and socio-dramatic play, as opposed to other circumstances where it serves as a means of escape from the real world, extends the scope of the imitative activity and provides a comprehensive and comprehensible context that increases the realism of the behaviour. (Smilansky, 1990: 20)

There are six elements of dramatic and socio-dramatic play:

- *Dramatic play* involves pretending to be someone else, role taking, imitating a person's speech actions and patterns, using real and imagined props, using first and second hand experience and knowledge of characters and situations.
- *Socio-dramatic play* involves cooperation between at least two children: the play develops on the basis of interaction between players acting out their roles, both verbally and in terms of the acts performed.

FIGURE 2.3   FORMS OF SOCIAL PLAY ACTIVITY

1 role play by imitation

2 make-believe with objects

3 make-believe with actions and situations

4 persistence in the role play

5 interaction

6 verbal communication.

Each element incorporates play skills and play knowledge. The richness of the play depends on the extent to which these various elements are used and developed. For example, verbalizations in children's socio-dramatic play can be complex, highly developed, and reflect the patterns and content of adult verbal interactions. Children:

- set the scene for speaking

- make behaviour understandable

- provide proper interpretation and direction for the activity

- provide the means of management and problem-solving reflecting child-reality and child-interaction (Smilansky, 1990: 20).

Dramatic and socio-dramatic play involve complex cognitive, social and emotional processes such as imitation, make-believe, symbolic transform-ations, communication and meta-communication, interpreting social and cultural rules, taking on and acting in role, sustaining the theme and sequence of a play episode, motivation, involvement and emotional engagement. Children use metacommunicative and metacognitive skills and processes as they step in and out of the play frame to comment on past and present conversations, and to clarify, maintain, negotiate and direct social and pretend play (Sawyer, 2003). The richness and quality of play can be evaluated in relation to how the various elements are used and developed.

Contemporary studies challenge deficit notions of children's thinking; rather than progressing in stages from concrete to abstract modes of thinking, children move along a continuum. Between the ages of three and four, children develop a 'theory of mind': they begin to show awareness of others' mental states and feelings, and can adapt their behaviour accordingly. These 'mind-reading' skills are evident when they construct and share pretend worlds, thereby engaging in quite sophisticated activities, such as stepping into a role, acting in role, imagining different feeling states, and developing empathy (seeing things from another's perspective). Children do not just play with objects and materials: they also play with meanings, ideas, roles, rules and relationships, and can make significant cognitive leaps and transformations. The ability to think in quite sophisticated, abstract ways is an undervalued aspect of children's play. Imitation, make-believe and symbolic activity are complex cognitive and social processes which are not always understood by practitioners in terms of their relationship to learning. As Kelly-Byrne (1989: 212) argues, these complex forms of play may be a neglected resource:

> it is the excitement and compulsion of a personal agenda that motivates much self-initiated and self-directed play in the lives of children . . . In the privacy of a space of their choosing and among friends, the dramatic play of children is an alluring and incredibly complex kind of behaviour that is likely to encompass most, if not all, of a child's resources and integrate them into a whole. The value of tapping its momentum and power, in the child's own terms, should be obvious to those of us concerned with facilitating children's communication and their sense of their own power.

For younger children, action tends to arise more from things: therefore they tend to be more absorbed in assigning roles and arranging props. In solitary dramatic play, children may use self-speech or out-loud thinking to communicate the pretence (often in different voices), and provide a commentary on the action as they play in role. Themes that are rehearsed in this way may be transferred to socio-dramatic contexts as children gain confidence in their skills as players and progress to more complex forms of social/cooperative play. Although it may appear chaotic, children's dramatic and socio-dramatic play reveals patterns and consistencies (Meckley 1994a,b). In an ethnographic study of play, Meckley's observations show that each play event had distinct, consistent and predictable patterns of actions, objects and players: there was always a set sequence of actions for each play event which identified this specific event to the children enacting the event, and to those engaged in other activities in the room. Sustained and systematic observation allowed Meckley (1994b: 47) to interpret the meaning of play in the children's own terms as they communicated and interpreted their individual and collective social realities:

> Shared knowledge of the subjective and collective realities of child participants in this social culture can also be known by the adult participants through attention to metacommunicative signals which

regularly occur during the play period. These signals include but are not limited to gaze or watching, body orientation or movement, specific actions with objects, specific sequences of action, imitation, language, and voice change. In fact, adults should note any attention-causing behaviour from play participants. Such behaviour reveals information concerning the play events and players' understandings about these events.

When children organize socio-dramatic play, they may recall what has been previously played in terms of characters, plot and sequence of activities. These actions define the 'play frame' (Broström, 1999) and often include certain rituals that begin the play. Children thus create a play frame and a psychological frame. Negotiating a play frame provides some direction and internal consistency to the actions and interactions. This is sustained by the play script, which reveals their knowledge of plot, characterization and sequence of events, and depends on a wide repertoire of cognitive, social and emotional dispositions in order to sustain the flow. Players can make transformations and reversals, and create real/not-real paradoxes so that a wide variety of imaginary situations can be played into the action. Imagination and creativity are essential as children invest objects and actions with new meanings and intentions that have to be accepted and understood by the players. As the play develops they may revise, repeat or extend previous themes, combine and recombine ideas, negotiate rules, and perhaps accommodate new players with different perspectives and contributions. Children step in and out of the frame to reformulate or elaborate plans, renegotiate rules, reconstruct the plot, reason about cause and effect, direct actions and behaviour, rehearse dialogue and roles. Such transformations involve sophisticated levels of thinking and action as children communicate multiple meanings through language, gestures, symbolic and iconic representations.

With age and experience, action arises more from ideas than from things. Children become increasingly adept at negotiating the play frame and determining the actions and interactions. As experienced players, older children can more readily formulate goals, which they realize through cooperation and reciprocity (Broadhead, 2004). (Evidence of these skills can be seen in the episodes of play described in Chapters 5, 6 and 7). Children become more skilled at exercising and controlling their will, in order to engage in successful, sustained play. Such control is dependent on the skills, dispositions and mood states of the group of players. The benefits of successful play are inclusion, enjoyment, shared control, peer-group identity and self-efficacy. Gradually they learn to understand and integrate the perspectives of others: in taking on or assigning roles, they interpret how other people behave and coordinate each other's interpretations. They build their play skills and their play knowledge (what is involved in being a successful player).

Creativity and imagination are both important cognitive processes that serve to direct, influence and generate complexity. The roles that children create involve actions and speech, and generate feeling states that link both affective and cognitive processes. Children use stories as a powerful means of making sense of the world, and play with a wide range of human emotions: love, hate, fear, anger, jealousy. These are often played out as opposing forces – good and evil, cruelty and kindness, strength and weakness, protection and abandonment, friendship and enmity. Such powerful moral and affective themes are often drawn from children's popular culture, as well as their everyday experiences (Marsh and Millard, 2000; Anning and Ring, 2004). The driving forces for play are intrinsic motivation, the pleasure afforded by play and the ability to take control and exercise power in an adult-dominated world.

Broadhead (2004) provides further evidence to support the educational significance of different forms of play. In a collaborative study with early years teachers, Broadhead focused on children's language, sociability and cooperation, and developed the Social Play Continuum (SPC), which identified four domains of play (see Figure 2.4).

- associative
- social
- highly social
- cooperative

FIGURE 2.4   BROADHEAD'S FOUR DOMAINS OF PLAY

The SPC challenges Piagetian notions about forms of play in relation to ages and stages, because it tracks increasing complexity in language, action and behaviour, thereby identifying continuity and progression in play. The SPC is based on sustained observations of play, with children from three to six years, and has enabled practitioners to enhance their understanding of the meanings that children construct and communicate in their play, and how these can be interpreted within and beyond defined curriculum frameworks. The report of the study (Broadhead, 2004) is detailed and informative, and provides guidance for practitioners using the SPC as a tool for understanding and assessing play. Broadhead uses socio-cultural theories for interpreting children's meanings and actions within social contexts, thus shifting the emphasis away from the Piagetian view of the individual child as learner to the child as a social actor and co-constructor of learning.

Play is not an entirely spontaneous activity: children learn how to play in different contexts, with the support of skilled peers and adults. Research shows that from birth, children are naturally active, curious and sociable, dispositions that typically provoke a synergistic response from knowledgeable others. Parents and carers are the child's first co-players, and invest a great deal of time in being playful, teaching children how to play, and teaching children through play (Gopnik *et al*, 1999). Practitioners have an important role in enriching and extending children's play (see Chapter 6). More structured approaches to play tutoring may be particularly significant for children with special educational needs, with English as an additional language, and with diverse cultural backgrounds, because they are likely to have special play needs.

▓ CONTEMPORARY PERSPECTIVES ON THE ADULT'S ROLE IN PLAY

The implications of these studies are that play activities stimulate a wide range of social, emotional and cognitive processes that are important for learning in a variety of contexts. There is consistent agreement that the kinds of interactions used by adults should simultaneously:

- ■ support and respond to children's needs and potential
- ■ support children's skills as players and learners
- ■ enrich the content of their play
- ■ support their own ideas and provide additional ideas and stimuli
- ■ enable children to elaborate and develop their own themes
- ■ be responsive to the level of play development
- ■ remain sensitive to the ideas that children are trying to express.

Dramatic and socio-dramatic play create dynamic, unifying activities that integrate many areas of learning across the curriculum, which will be explored in greater detail in Chapters 5–7 (see Figure 2.5).

CONSTRUCTIVE PLAY Constructive play involves the manipulation of objects and materials to build or create something, using natural and

- language and communication
- planning and organization
- developing social and cooperative skills
- acquiring social knowledge
- acquiring discipline-based knowledge
- relating to peers and adults
- understanding self and others
- developing empathy and mind-reading skills
- creativity and imagination
- representation and symbolization
- creating plots, themes, stories, routines
- developing and using play knowledge.

FIGURE 2.5   INTEGRATING LEARNING ACROSS THE CURRICULUM

manufactured materials such as blocks and other constructional kits, as well as playdough, junk and collage materials, sand and water. Constructive play involves exploration and discovery, tactile stimulation, problem-solving, social interaction, engagement and concentration, and attention to processes and outcomes. It may be combined with socio-dramatic and dramatic play because children often enjoy making props to support their play, and playing with what they have created. Constructive play enables children to represent their ideas, knowledge and interests through different forms such as layouts, buildings, plans, sculptures and collages. These processes and outcomes can give practitioners a window into patterns of children's thinking and learning, as described by Gura's (1992) report of the Froebel Block Play research study. The focus of the study was on processes (what the children did with the blocks), and content (what they learned). Much of the children's learning was identified as scientific, mathematical and technological, and linguistic, and was situated in creative, flexible contexts that enabled them to explore the materials and their ideas and represent their thinking. By encouraging the children to record their constructions and layouts, they made transformations between two-dimensional and three-dimensional symbolic representations. These were rich in meanings as the children used conventional and invented signs and symbols to represent the blocks. They also needed knowledge about the blocks (names and properties), in order to have mastery of them, and use them for different functions. For example, knowledge about size, shape, tessellations and configurations was needed to solve practical and conceptual problems. The adults acted as play partners, providing appropriate support for learning, providing challenge or helping the children to succeed in self-created problems and challenges. The children became master block-players and master builders as they used their knowledge in increasingly complex ways. This study extends Smilansky's standpoint, by demonstrating that adult interventions in play need to be content-, skill- and ideas-oriented in order to support children's learning and development. The project demonstrated the following conditions for learning through play:

- the importance of adult involvement, particularly enabling the children to share the initiative about what is to be learned, and how

- creating contexts for learning which encourage exploration and investigation

- enabling children to be creative, take risks and be playful in their ideas

- organizing the physical setting to maximize the potential for learning

- developing continuity and progression through observation and record keeping

Gura emphasizes the importance of providing block play beyond the pre-school phase, so that children have opportunities to build on their expertise, as exemplified in these observations:

> Robert (age six, Year 1) played alone, making a large castle from the blocks. During the early stages he was involved in selecting materials for the task, designing, and making decisions about where to place each block for strength and stability. He was representing his inner thought processes and at the same time, talked to the adult observer about a holiday visit to castles in Wales.

> In the second stage, he combined Playmobil(TM) figures with his castle, and introduced fantasy elements, thus flowing into dramatic play. Robert allowed other children to join in and explained the different parts of the castle, and what the game would be (a siege between the English and Welsh). In the final stage, they decided as a group to build a tall look-out tower in the centre of the castle, and played co-operatively, using problem-solving skills to combine height with strength and stability. Finally the tower collapsed and the castle was broken up. This was an energizing, satisfying episode of play in which the children used a repertoire of social and manipulative skills. Their dialogue revealed a great deal of real-world knowledge about castles and structures, and enabled the observing teacher to make some informed assessments of their skills, knowledge and understanding.

> Martin (age four, Nursery) built a racing car with hollow blocks and, for a while, was content to sit behind the steering wheel by himself making engine noises. Other friends joined the activity and negotiated with Martin to extend the size of the car and include extra seats. They went for a long drive, visiting different places on the way, stopping for petrol and oil. At some point Martin felt that he was losing control of his original intentions because he told the others to leave: the car was really a Grand Prix racing car and could only take one person. He removed the extra seats, returned to his solitary play and put a blanket over his head to signify a helmet and/or the cockpit, as well as to exclude other children. This sequence incorporated constructive, manipulative, symbolic and socio-dramatic play. It was also rule bound: the children negotiated the rules and maintained them in order to sustain the pretence. They displayed their real world knowledge and understanding of social conventions. They also deferred to Martin's ownership and control, partly because he had made the car. This was a common pattern in the collaborative play of this group of four year old boys. Martin was popular, articulate, inventive and capable of directing imaginative play sequences. His friends usually accepted his dominance because he was a skilled player and they enjoyed inclusion in his games.

Both these episodes involved boys with constructive play, an area that is often chosen by boys rather than girls. Gender is an important and often contentious issue in play (MacNaughton, 2000), particularly in rough-and-tumble and superhero play.

ROUGH-AND-TUMBLE, AND SUPERHERO PLAY Rough-and-tumble, and superhero play often provoke energetic debates among practitioners as they strive to reconcile their personal values about what forms of play can be allowed, tolerated or banned. They often have clear ideas about what is 'appropriate play' (taking into account safety factors), but at the same time struggle with their commitment to nurturing children's interests and play themes when these include play-fighting and aggression. Real conflicts occur in many forms of play (not only superhero and rough and tumble), especially where children lack the skills of cooperation, sharing, negotiation and turn-taking. Practitioners report that play-fighting can develop into real fighting as children either do not understand or go beyond the real–not real boundaries of rough-and-tumble play. It follows that not all play is good play: some children use play times and play spaces to engage in bullying and social aggression, showing 'the dark side of play' (Sutton-Smith, 1997). As a consequence, rough-and-tumble and superhero play are often banned (but still occur in spaces away from the gaze of adults). Inevitably gender issues come to the forefront, because these forms of play are typically, but not exclusively, dominated by boys and involve a lot of physical activity such as chasing, running, jumping, wrestling, rolling, crawling, as well as dramatic gestures and actions. So what can research tell us about the benefits and problems in superhero and rough-and-tumble play?

As we noted in Chapter 1, these forms of play are often related to children's popular culture, and are accessed through many different media – television, computers, videos, films, games, comics, books, toys and tailor-made dressing-up clothes. Superheroes are not a recent social and cultural phenomena: there is a long tradition of myths, legends, folk tales and stories that portray struggles between heroes and villains, good and evil, right and wrong. Sports personalities and adventurers are portrayed as heroic and often take on the same iconic, almost mythic status of legendary gods and warriors. Children's literature portrays children, not just adults, as heroes and villains: for example in J.K. Rowling's Harry Potter books, the children have magic powers which enable them to fight the forces of evil, as well as bullying from their own peer group.

Superhero play is often combined with rough-and-tumble play as children engage in play-fighting, using weapons and displaying mock aggression. There are ongoing debates about whether these forms of play enable children to work through difficult emotions and behaviours and control difficult feelings such as fear, anxiety, aggression, anger and powerlessness. Children may feel a sense of agency, control and excitement as they, rather than the adults, call the shots. They may also use these forms of play to deal with the real and often disturbing images they see of war, conflict and violence in the media (and possibly in their own families and communities). Alternatively, they may use role models from popular culture to learn how to be aggressive, and use violence to solve problems or establish dominance and control over others. The central theme of superhero programmes is that the 'good guys' (they are almost always male) triumph over the 'bad guys', usually through conflict and might rather than through dialogue and moral reasoning. This arguably offers children limited role models, and few choices about how they resolve conflict in their own lives. Taking into account the real concerns about violence and aggression, are practitioners always right to ban these forms of play? Marsh and Millard (2000) take a positive view of the potential benefits of superhero play (see Figure 2.6).

On the basis of their research, practitioners need to adopt a critical stance to their own values and develop informed insights as to the potential meaning and value of superhero play. Pellegrini and Blatchford (2000) also identify many benefits of rough-and-tumble play (Figure 2.7).

- Children are attracted by the discourses of power, which serve as a counterpoint to the dominant rules and regulations imposed by adults.
- Children can explore complex realities and role models (good/evil, male/female, right/wrong) rather than accepting these as bipolar concepts.
- Children are attracted to the dressing up clothes and props that characterize the different superheroes.
- Girls as well as boys engage in superhero play, and may challenge its masculinist nature.
- Superhero play can have powerful effects on children's motivation to engage in literacy practices where practitioners consciously incorporate this into their role play areas and themes.
- Superhero play is a potential site for language development, and is particularly strong for bilingual children. Because English is most often the language in which superhero narratives are experienced, children may use key words and phrases in their play.
- Practitioners can use these forms of play to build critical discourses with older children, in which they learn to challenge the images and messages that they convey. (Marsh and Millard, 2000: 51–52)

FIGURE 2.6   THE BENEFITS OF SUPERHERO PLAY

- Reciprocal role-taking helps to sustain play as children alternate between hero and villain, chaser and chased, aggressor and victim.
- Bouts of rough-and-tumble play often lead to other forms of social play, such as cooperative games. This is more typical for popular children, but for rejected children often leads to further real (rather than mock) aggression.
- Rough-and-tumble play develops from around age three to four, peaks at around age seven, and declines by around age eleven, so it has its own particular place in children's development.
- More boys than girls engage in rough-and-tumble play, and their play tends to be more vigorous, particularly after long periods of sedentary work.
- Children engage in social problem-solving and experiment with different social roles (but again this is more typical of popular rather than rejected children).
- Children learn to encode and decode emotions, which contributes to their social competence.

FIGURE 2.7   THE BENEFITS OF ROUGH-AND-TUMBLE PLAY

It appears that rough-and-tumble play may have positive benefits for some children, but not for others. Where children engage in pro-social rough-and-tumble, their play scripts and themes can develop over time, becoming increasingly organized and coordinated. These play bouts share the positive features of dramatic and socio-dramatic play: they provide opportunities for developing language, creating stories and events, developing play themes and patterns, and engaging the players socially and emotionally. Children can also remain sensitive to the comfort and safety of other players while playing vigorously (Broadhead, 2004), and can reason about their perspectives and experiences. Given ongoing national and international concerns about the performance of boys (especially in literacy), it may be that banning rough-and-tumble and superhero play denies them the opportunities to engage in activities that are intrinsically valuable. We will return to this theme in the second half of the book, and consider how these forms of play can be facilitated, but managed in pro-social ways.

■ WHAT DO CHILDREN PLAY WITH, AND WHAT DO THEY PLAY AT?

The work of Vivian Gussin Paley and Dianne Kelly-Byrne provides fascinating insights into children's play lives, which exemplify what they play with, and what they play at. In *Wally's Stories*, Paley (1981) followed a group of five-year-olds through their kindergarten year. A wide variety of thinking emerged from the children's conversations, stories and play acting, as concepts of morality, science and society shared the stage with fantasy. The children were encouraged to tell their own stories and create play themes and scripts; these included monsters, superheroes, good guys and bad guys, and concepts of danger, threat, strength, bravery, triumph and fear.

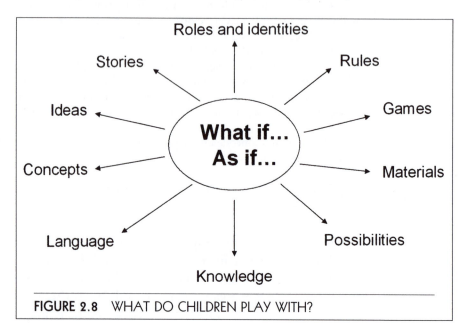

FIGURE 2.8   WHAT DO CHILDREN PLAY WITH?

Inevitably, themes derived from well-known stories, fairy tales and television programmes influenced the children's play worlds. They often made sense of events and concerns in their own lives in ways that went beyond emotional catharsis, such as rules, power, conflict, control, coercion, jealousy, anger, punishment, justice and self-determination. They demonstrated emerging knowledge of physics, mathematics, space and time, and made connections between actions and events in their real-worlds and play worlds. They were involved in complex actions and interactions which entailed communicating their intentions to others, negotiating, taking into account the needs and perspectives of others, adjusting the script and, in the midst of wild and wonderful fantasies, using logic, reasoning and real-world knowledge to sustain the fantasy. The following conversation took place after reading the story of 'The Three Pigs'. Earlier, Wally had been on the 'time-out' chair, and he invented a 'time-out' chimney in the script:

> Andy: There's a boy Jeffrey on the other block from me. I went to his house once and he wouldn't let me in.
> Lisa: Why?
> Andy: Someone else was there.
> Wally: You should have gone down the chimney.
> Lisa: You shouldn't sneak into someone's house.
> Eddie: He should shape his hair in a different way and then come back and Jeffrey'll say 'Come in' and tell the other boy to go home.
> Fred: If he went down the chimney he might get boiled.
> Wally: He could come down with a gun.
> Eddie: Just to scare him. If he puts a boiling pot there, just jump over it.
> Lisa: Not a gun.
> Eddie: Here's a great idea. Get bullets and put it in a gun and aim it at Jeffrey.
> Teacher: That's a great idea?
> Eddie: No, I mean it's a bad idea.
> Lisa: Well, let him come down the chimney but not with a gun.
> Wally: Let's all go to Jeffrey's house and climb down his chimney and make him let Andy come in.
> Andy: I'll find out if he has a chimney.
> Wally: I'll get a time out chimney and he has to stay in there until he lets you come in. (Paley, 1981: 19–20)

Similar perspectives are revealed by Kelly-Byrne's study of the play life of six-year-old Helen, which was a 'mass of diffuse yet intricately patterned symbols, structures and rhetoric' (1989: 209). Helen's home was the naturalistic setting for the fieldwork and included both solitary and peer group play. Kelly-Byrne involved herself in Helen's play, at her request and under her direction. Helen's preferred mode of play was make-

- The child's origin and identity.
- The battle between good and evil.
- The testing of her powers and weaknesses.
- Her relationships with parents, peers, males and females.
- Strong women rescuing men who were weak and abandoned.
- The upgrading of her own supposedly inferior status as a girl by performing super feats.
- Understanding the polarities of smartness versus dumbness.
- Sorting out differences between good and bad mothering.
- Making sense of her own sexuality.
- Exploring the power of language to posit worlds and transform situations. (Kelly-Byrne, 1989: 211)

FIGURE 2.9   THEMES IN HELEN'S PLAY LIFE

believe, with themes derived from myths and legends, television characters (including Wonderwoman) and her everyday life at home and school. These themes were interwoven with immense complexity, and were further elaborated and transformed by Helen's creativity and imagination. The predominant play themes included are listed in Figure 2.9.

This study demonstrates contemporary theories regarding the role of play in the transmission of culture through social interaction and communication. These processes contribute to children's social cognition – their understanding of roles, rules, relationships, values, beliefs, how society is organized, how it functions, and their own place in the world. Helen's preoccupation with powerfulness and powerlessness was explored in her Wonderwoman play, reflecting her position as a child, and her interpretation of gender socialization processes, especially those relating to images of women portrayed in the media. Kelly-Byrne was struck by Helen's deep involvement, abundant energy levels and intense excitement during play sequences, and argues that this evidence challenges the 'wishy-washy' and idealized views adults often hold about children's play:

> Helen learned that play is a special kind of medium for packaging life's contradictions, for ordering confusion, and for destroying and transforming patterns and realities that are disliked; and, moreover, for doing so with a spirit of involvement, happy abandon, madness and festival. The materials she used in shaping her imaginary worlds were provided by the culture and motivated by her inner conflicts and agenda. She also had a sense of the spirit of play, one that was in keeping with the negative cultural state that play holds in our society. Therefore her play was often irrational, exuberant, combative, unbridled, and grotesque in its moments of intense passion. (Kelly-Byrne, 1989: 216)

'DISAPPEARING PEGS IN THE ROAD' Meckley (1994a,b, 1996) demonstrates how young children communicate shared knowledge through their social play and argues that it is essential to gather data on children's play over an extended period of time to fully understand its social organization. She reveals the immense complexity in children's play with repeating themes that were enacted through *play frames* (play sequences or actions), and enabled them to communicate and interpret their individual and collective social realities. The play frame creates a shared context that makes behaviour comprehensible and prescribes appropriate responses. Meckley argues that children are extremely competent in their construction of play frames and present themselves with tasks, problems and situations that demand complex interactions and a variety of social and communicative skills. Far from being chaotic, the play maintained stability, order, interconnectedness and consistency through an inherent rule system that was socially constructed by the players. Within the play events children used metacommunicative cues and techniques for sharing knowledge among all the players, and maintaining the play (1994b). In the 'Disappearing Pegs in Road' play, they regularly constructed a road layout with blocks, then poured a can of pegs into the spaces between the blocks. The actions were communicated verbally and non-verbally:

- Signalling of others to join in this play is done by getting the peg can and taking it to the block area.

- Handing the peg can to a child immediately confers leadership on the peg can holder for the ensuing play.

- Changing voice by Jason, the disappearing peg play events' inventor and director, always signals a change in the play, usually that Jason is about to wreck the blocks. When other children in the area hear this voice change, they usually move away from Jason and/or exit the block area. Jason uses a specific singsong voice that always signals that destruction will follow.

- Searching for players often occurs during these play events. Disappearing Pegs in Road, once started, is a continual play event that may span thirty minutes or more. During this time, other happenings in the room attract the players away and only one may remain. When this player realizes he is alone, he searches for the others to come back to the play or he may briefly join them in their new activity.

There is substantial evidence of children learning through these peer group interactions: Meckley identified social and communicative competence, social affiliation and social knowledge. As in Broadhead's study (2004), the children were using symbolic, abstract forms of thinking and communicating these to each other in quite sophisticated ways, including signs, symbols, gestures, facial expressions and body language.

Other studies have investigated social and cognitive processes in children's play (and work) that reveal patterns of activity, learning, thinking and understanding (Athey, 1990; Nutbrown, 1999; Broadhead, 2004; Worthington and Carruthers, 2004). These provide further evidence of the complexity of play and demonstrate how children reveal persistent cognitive concerns across a range of activities, which give educators a window on learning and development. Worthington and Carruthers (2004) provide detailed exploration, grounded in their own practice, of children's mathematical learning, and the playful ways in which emerging mathematical knowledge is communicated and represented through many different activities. Broadhead's research into children's social and cooperative play demonstrates that we need to attend to the content of children's play, particularly their language and behaviour, in order to understand the nature and quality of their thinking and learning. Figure 2.10 describes an episode of sand play involving three girls and a boy (all in a Reception class). It captures the flow of play, and the connections between the observable behaviours, and the implicit meanings.

In terms of what play does for the child, the studies reviewed here show that play offers many benefits to all areas of learning and development, acting as a potential motivating force which integrates different processes and activities.

However, we must also remember that the same or similar benefits are not necessarily available to all children, and the forms of play described above are not equally accessible to all. For example, children with autistic spectrum disorders may find dramatic and socio-dramatic play incomprehensible and potentially threatening. Children with physical disabilities may have difficulties with rough-and-tumble play. Because play is valued differently in many cultures, some children have different home-based play themes and patterns that may not transfer readily into pre-school and school settings, without awareness and sensitivity from practitioners (Brooker, 2002). Later chapters of this book, which focus on play in practice, will provide more detail regarding play for children with special or additional educational needs.

Two of the girls begin turning the sand wheel very quickly by putting the sand through the top of the sand wheel. They make this difficult by piling several pebbles and shells in the opening to the sand wheel. The third girl instructs them: 'You keep it going and I'll get more things', and turns to select pebbles and shells from the tray. The two girls keep dropping the sand through the restricted opening of the wheel. The boy gives instructions to the girl about which pebbles to select. They seem urgent and focused: 'Keep it going, don't let it stop', referring to the turning of the wheel. The play is quite noisy, with all four voices raised at some point . . .

One girl draws a heart on the floor of the sand tray and calls to the others to look. This leads to a shout: 'The monster's here' with lively discussion on this theme. One girl crawls under the sand tray and begins banging on the bottom of it. The two above remain anxious to ensure the sand keeps flowing: 'put a finger in': 'hurry, it's running out'. The boy is putting sand in with some urgency. The girl bangs again on the underside of the tray, laughing . . . She then explains to the others, almost in narrative style, that the monster is coming (we now realize that this is the banging on the bottom of the sand tray). It also becomes apparent that the sand through the wheel is designed to 'invoke' the genie to come and save them. (Broadhead, 2004: 67–68)

FIGURE 2.10   ACTIVITY AND MEANING IN PLAY

CONTEMPORARY DIRECTIONS IN THEORY AND RESEARCH

This chapter has identified three significant trends. First, contemporary research has moved play beyond the seductive principles of the early pioneers, towards a more secure evidence base, which specifies the processes that link playing and learning. Second, studies of play have moved out of the experimental frameworks of developmental psychology and into more naturalistic settings such as the home, community and school. Understanding the child as player/learner and the child in playing/learning contexts is valuable in terms of understanding the role and value of play, and providing recommendations for practice that reflect the realities of play in school. Third, there has been a shift away from broad-scale theories towards more detailed descriptions of the characteristics, patterns and processes of early learning and development (which will be outlined in more detail in Chapters 3 and 4). Practitioners do not have to limit the way they conceptualize play to how it is defined and categorized by academics, researchers and policy-makers. The theory and research base in early childhood can inform our understanding about the relationship between play and learning but, ultimately, practitioners create their own knowledge about what works, taking into account the complex contextual variables in their settings. Practitioners are unlikely to use abstract theoretical language. However, they do need to raise their own theories, values and beliefs to a conscious level of awareness in terms of how these influence their practice and what aspects of their thinking and practice need to be changed, as exemplified in studies by Bennett *et al* (1997), Anning and Edwards (1999), MacNaughton (2000) and Broadhead (2004). There is no single definition of play, and no single theory which can explain the role of play in children's learning and development. The next chapter focuses on research studies that have examined the relationship between different forms of play and different areas of learning. Having examined what play is, and what it does for the child, we will addresses the thorny issue of what play leads to, within and beyond curriculum frameworks.

FURTHER READING

The following authors provide a range of perspectives on play and learning across early childhood and primary education, making clear links between theory and practice.

Bishop, J.C. and Curtis, M. (2001) *Play Today in the Primary School Playground*, Buckingham, Open University Press.

Broadhead, P. (2004) *Early Years Play and Learning, Developing Social Skills and Co-operation*, London, RoutledgeFalmer.

Brooker, L. (2002) *Starting School – Young Children Learning Cultures*, Buckingham, Open University Press.

Lytle, D.E. (ed.) (2003) *Play and Educational Theory and Practice*, Westport, Conn., Praeger.

MacNaughton, G. (2000) *Rethinking Gender in Early Childhood Education*, Buckingham, Open University Press.

Pellegrini, A. and Blatchford, P. (2000) *The Child at School: Interactions with Peers and Teachers*, London, Arnold.

CHAPTER THREE

Understanding Children's Learning: Multi-theoretical Perspectives

Learning and development in humans are so complex that no single theory can adequately account for all the interrelated processes involved. Knowledge about these areas is constantly expanding, particularly as new technologies allow researchers to delve into the complexities of how the human brain develops and functions. Some theories are broad scale and focus on what happens in the child's mind (a predominantly cognitive orientation), or what happens in the social and cultural contexts in which learning is situated (a predominantly social orientation). Both these orientations will be explored in Chapters 3 and 4, with further specification of their practical implications in Chapters 5 to 8. Some theories provide more detailed explanations of how children learn in specific subject areas such as literacy, numeracy, the creative arts and technology, as well as in the interpersonal, social and emotional domains. Recent studies have also been concerned with examining the contexts and conditions that appear to best support children's learning, and the ways in which practitioners can enhance the potential of play. Most theories inevitably imply ideal transitions through ideal processes and into ideal states. However, as all practitioners know, the contexts in which they work are often far from ideal, and children are individuals who learn and develop in different ways and at different rates across their learning careers.

The purpose of this chapter is to explore a range of theories about playing, learning and teaching. Research into play has been dominated by developmental and cognitive psychology, with its traditions of scientific modes of enquiry. Contemporary studies have adopted a more naturalistic, interpretive stance and aim to understand play from the perspectives of children as social actors, as well as their multiple patterns of meaning, knowing, representing and understanding. We have illustrated many of these theoretical ideas with examples from practice-based research studies in order to demonstrate the complexities of play, adults and children's roles in play, and playful orientations to teaching and learning.

The chapter begins with a brief overview of recent advances in cognitive neuro-science, including what research has revealed about how the brain develops, and whether we can make connections with how children learn. The second section describes 'meta' skills and processes in cognition, memory, language and communication, and how these can be identified in play. This leads on to the third section on schema theory, and the implications for understanding how children construct and represent meaning. The two final sections look at social cognition and emotional literacy, and creativity.

HOW DOES THE HUMAN BRAIN DEVELOP AND FUNCTION?

Advances in technology, such as magnetic resonance imaging (MRI), have facilitated new approaches to conducting research on how the brain develops and functions, which could have implications for understanding how humans learn. Researchers in this field remain cautious about the implications for educational policy and practice, but their findings are filtering into these domains. We begin by looking at the neurophysiological development of the human brain because learning and development are dependent on how cognitive structures are formed, connected and coordinated (Meadows, 1993).

The brain is a highly complex organ and its range of functions is not fully understood. Looking at the architecture of the brain, different parts have different functions: the left hemisphere dominates in speech and language comprehension, while large areas at the front and back deal with thinking, storing and processing information. Both hemispheres and all areas of the brain are interconnected via neurons, synapses, axons and dendrites. There are around 100 billion *neurons* (brain cells) in the human brain, most of which are present at birth. *Axons* and *dendrites* (the brain's electrical wiring system) carry the messages that are sent and received from external stimuli ('There's a new climbing frame in the playground') and internal stimuli ('I want to have a go on that'). The *synapses* are the connectors or junctions that pass on messages between the neurons, helping to process and store information.

The brain is not just a mechanical device for coordinating actions, storing and processing information. Different areas of the brain are responsible for coordinating and controlling highly complex functions, from breathing, swallowing and body temperature, to playing a piano concerto. Emotion and cognition are not separate brain functions, but work together in a continuous dialogue which we recognize as thought processes or inner speech and physical sensations. Many brain functions are so seamlessly coordinated that we are not conscious of all aspects of their orchestration in our everyday lives. For example, being interested in the new climbing frame may motivate the child to have a go, and could lead to further emotional as well as physical challenge, such as negotiating a new or unfamiliar layout, climbing to a higher level, overcoming fear and expressing pleasure in a new achievement. Therefore it is difficult to separate out the development and functions of the brain from the development of the individual mind and the concept of self.

In normal patterns of development the architecture of the brain develops in response to stimulation which is actively sought and used. The wiring between the neurons changes significantly as infrequently used connections are pruned and new ones grow. In the early years children's brains undergo substantial and rapid growth in *synaptogenesis* (connections between the neurons), which appears to make this a particularly sensitive period for learning. This process of synaptic development has been studied using MRI, and helps to explain why adults in certain occupations (such as a taxi driver or concert pianist) have areas of greater development and complexity in specific areas of their brains. However, the brain remains flexible throughout childhood and into adolescence, and the notion that there are 'critical periods' for learning is not as fixed as was once considered. For example, a number of studies have been carried out on children from Romanian orphanages, many of whom endured severe and sustained levels of deprivation and, interestingly, were not able to engage in spontaneous play. However, many of the children (depending on the duration and severity of deprivation) showed remarkable resilience, progress and achievements with appropriate support, care and stimulation (Blakemore, 2002).

The brain is not a blank slate, nor is the child's mind an empty vessel. The architecture of the brain is incredibly complex: activity stimulates development. Learning and development involve complex interrelating factors such as our biological make-up, genes, everything around us in the environment, and our experiences, actions and interactions within that environment. From birth onwards the child is an active participant in these processes, seeking out and co-constructing experiences and interactions. Life experiences determine how neural networks develop. The human brain has been compared to a computer, but its range of processes, and its plasticity make it infinitely more superior:

> The electronic computers we have now don't work until they are built. They are assembled using chips and circuits according to a very specific diagram. When all the connections are soldered together, we turn on the computer for the first time and it begins to work (or at least we hope). The hardware of the computer doesn't change as we use it any more than the wiring on a Christmas tree changes when we flip the switch and the lights go on.

> But the human brain works very differently. The brain keeps rewiring itself even after it is turned on. And the circuits that are laid down depend deeply on experience. Experience is changing the brain from the very beginning. Everything a baby sees, hears, tastes, touches, and smells influences the way the brain gets hooked up. (Gopnik *et al*, 1999: 180–181)

These experiences assist in the processes of editing, sorting and pruning connections, strengthening some and discarding others. The brain selects what is stored in short-term and long-term memory; not everything can be stored so the brain actively prunes out redundant information and becomes more skilled at retrieving information, and using it for specific purposes (Meadows, 1993). These processes can be seen in children's progression over time. For example, in learning to read, many children need the support of the phonetic approach, sometimes laboriously sounding out individual phonemes or blends, concentrating on parts. Fluent readers discard these processes and rely on fast processing, with the eyes skimming rapidly across whole words. (We may use the skills of de-coding when meeting a difficult, unknown or foreign word.) Similarly in play activities, a young child may spend a lot of time exploring a construction kit, discovering how to manipulate and connect the parts. Older children tend to focus more on what they intend to build, and have broader funds of skills and knowledge on which they can draw. The highly individual ways in which brains respond to experience may also help to explain differences in the ways we process information: for example, in numeracy tasks, children and adults have many different strategies for carrying out calculations and arriving at the answer. The highly social ways in which brains respond to experience may also help to explain gender differences in play preferences and behaviours, and the ways in which learners process social and cultural information.

The following vignette was recorded in a nursery and involved three girls, all aged three and a half to four years, and exemplifies playful minds in a playful context, and the ways in which play enables children to map their understanding of social phenomena.

Sophie comes into the home corner, alone. She speaks into a mobile phone: Going to bed now Mummy. It's night time. Got dolly. Goodbye. *Sophie lies down, pulls the cover over her and goes to sleep. Tasha and Beth come into the home corner. Tasha sits next to the bed.*

Tasha: I'm the Mummy. I'll read the bed time story. (*chooses book from shelf next to bed*)
Beth: I'll read the story.
Tasha: No, I'm the Mummy. You be the Daddy.
Beth: Daddy's can read stories.
Tasha: No. Mummies read stories.
Beth: Well MY Daddy reads ME stories.
(*Tasha reads a pop-up book showing different insects*)
Tasha: Now, let's see. Here's the naughty spider and he's popping out for some dinner.
Sophie: Don't read me spiders. I'll get bad dreams.

This short vignette shows the spontaneous development of a play script, which includes some metacommunicative elements, for example, negotiating roles and rules, reproducing cultural knowledge about bedtime routines, challenging gender stereotypes, conveying meaning through symbolic actions, understanding that print conveys meaning, and acting as readers (Wood, 2004: 27). Sophie's playful mind conveys the pretence of going to bed, and quickly flips into her real-world experiences such as fear of spiders and bad dreams. But can we make any connections between playful brains, playful minds and playful learning?

▓ THE PLAYFUL MIND

Many researchers in the field of neuroscience remain cautious about making connections and generalizations from how the brain develops to how children should be educated. But it is possible to at least explore some connections. Many of the examples given throughout this book show the human mind at play. So is play essential to the developing brain? Most theorists agree that children's natural desire to play arises spontaneously from their interactions with playful others, but whether play is an evolutionary necessity or a cultural phenomena is more debatable. While children are naturally curious, active and sociable from birth, the ability to transform their activity into play is usually learnt in conjunction with adults or more experienced others. Play activities are socially constructed and mediated. For example, the first 'peek-a-boo' games involve close interactions between the baby and the caregiver, with each interaction being contingent on their intersubjective responses: the caregiver stimulates the baby's interest, the baby responds with pleasure, thus stimulating further play. As the child comes to understand this routine over time, he or she may initiate the play, and develop the play with a favourite toy, which stands as a proxy for a co-player. This simple activity involves taking a role (hider and seeker), pretence and dealing with a paradox (knowing that the person is still there but pretending not to know so as to sustain the game). So from the earliest simple games, the playful mind transforms experiences and events, helps children to revise and restructure their knowledge and develop their own particular ways of interpreting the world.

Children develop new brain circuits in response to activities that they actively seek, and actively engage in with other people. They need a great deal of practice in order to develop, integrate and consolidate these new circuits. When we look closely at children's play, we can see that all the processes involved in playing, such as exploring, repeating actions, making connections, extending skills, combining materials, taking risks, appear to mirror exactly what the brain needs in order to grow and function effectively. Of course, these processes are evident in non-play situations, but the element of fun, enjoyment and motivation may be particularly significant in providing playful types of stimuli for the growing brain. However, play may have a special role in helping the brain to make novel connections or interconnections, and integrate its regulatory systems. Play may also contribute to unity of mind and personality through the development of self-systems (self-esteem, self-worth, self-image and self-competence) as well as cultural, gender and sexual identities.

Developments in neuroscience inform us that babies are brilliantly intelligent learners, and that grown-ups are devoted to helping them learn (Gopnik *et al*, 1999). Babies have in-built exploratory and explanatory drives, which help them to find out and then seek explanations for what is happening in the world around them. To some extent, play turns these processes topsy-turvy in that it enables us to attach invented meanings to objects and events – a child becomes an intergalactic warrior: a stick becomes a light sabre; a cardboard box becomes a star ship. The child's mind works on different levels: I know this is a stick but it signifies a light sabre, and I need you to know this in order to sustain the play. These processes work just as much with adults: when we see a play, dance or opera, the designer creates a different world, and the actors convey the words, moods, thoughts, feelings, actions of the characters. We suspend belief in order to accept the as if/what if transformations of a perform-ance. The act of playing requires us to access the power and flexibility of the brain by consciously engaging the imagination, attaching different meanings to familiar objects, and conveying these meanings to others. Children develop awareness of the play/non-play paradox, as shown in Joe's playful drawing of himself (Figure 3.1). Joe knows that he should only draw two legs, but chooses to draw four; he also knows that he has to let his teacher know that he is joking, otherwise she may well ask him to draw his picture again with the 'correct' number of legs. Joe has already developed a good theory of his own, and the teacher's mind.

The playful mind can also be a teasing, or mischievous mind: Anna (age three and a half) loved playing at hiding things, but usually conveyed what she had hidden, and where: 'I bet you don't know where I've hidden the chocolate bar. I bet you don't know I've hidden it in the drawer.' Anna became more mischievous when she hid the car keys, and wouldn't reveal the hiding place. She knew the keys were important, and seemed to enjoy her aunt's frustration as she rattled through the usual hiding places. Anna was also developing her own theory of mind – the ability to understand how one's own and other people's minds work, and how belief states can be manipulated.

■ SO CAN WE LINK NEUROSCIENCE WITH PEDAGOGY AND CURRICULUM?

The research evidence from neuroscience is both exciting and ground-breaking in terms of understanding how the brain grows and functions. However, there remain cautious implications for how we educate young children. Learning changes the structure of the young brain, by organizing and re-organizing neural networks and connections. Play activities may help children to develop and refine these networks. For example, in the development of memory, transfer from the sensory register to short- or long-term memory is dependent on the learner attending to different stimuli and using certain cognitive strategies to aid memorization, organization and internalization. Mnemonic (memory-assisting) strategies are cognitive activities that include perceiving, attending, concentrating, rehearsing, recalling and repeating, all of which impose some structure on what is being learned or experienced. Observations of children at play reveal how they use these strategies, both spontaneously and deliberately. They often remember quite accurately how to make a dumper truck, or

FIGURE 3.1   I'M ONLY JOKING

the details of play themes that are of current interest (as shown in the 'Disappearing pegs in the road' play described in Chapter 2). However, many children have difficulties remembering facts and figures, particularly if their learning is not situated in meaningful contexts. There appears to be a distinction between what is remembered spontaneously and what has to be memorized deliberately, which indicates that the brain needs different mnemonic strategies and experiences to assist learning. Wood (1998) and Meadows (1993) suggest that children can be taught these strategies as long as they are embedded in meaningful activities, which enable them to be practised, applied and transferred to different contexts:

> Simply asking a child ... to pay attention, concentrate, study, learn or remember is unlikely to bear fruit. Unless we embody the material to be learned and remembered in a task that makes sense to the child, one that involves objectives he can realize and that draws attention 'naturally' to the elements we wish him to take in, our imperatives to concentrate, memorize or learn are almost bound to fail. Young children can and will concentrate and remember but will often need the support of a more knowledgeable and intellectually skilled assistant. Such assistants act as 're-mind-ers'. At the same time, they provide living illustrations of the processes involved in memorization which eventually the child comes to 'internalize' and exploit for himself. Looked at in this way, the processes involved in deliberate memorization and contrived or formal learning situations take place first in external, observable and social terms before being internalized by the child to become personal, mental activities. (Wood, 1998: 61)

As the architecture of the brain becomes more complex, children progress in how they use their brain power. When learning something new, novice learners use a lot of mental energy in concentration, attention and perception. With practice, children attain increasing levels of mastery, which then releases energy for controlling processes and outcomes, and transferring knowledge across contexts. These processes can be observed in learning to do jigsaws. With their first inset trays, children typically select pieces at random and bang them on the tray to make them fit. More deliberate experimentation may follow, in which children learn to rotate the pieces, test them against the template, and develop spatial orientation. These skills are supported by trial and error, repetition, deliberate memorization and success. A more knowledgeable other may help children to develop the mental architecture and strategies for tackling different types of jigsaws: attending to the shape and size of each piece, using visual and tactile exploration, learning to use relevant language – back to front, upside down, wrong way round, straight/wavy edges, middle, top, bottom, fitting together – and encouraging deliberate efforts

- Positive emotional support.
- Secure early attachments.
- Sensory stimulation.
- Positive and supportive social interactions.
- Language-rich environments and interactions.
- Encountering novel challenges and problems.
- Active learning styles (hands-on and brains-on activity).
- Active participation and engagement with materials, resources and people.

FIGURE 3.2   CONDITIONS FOR BRAIN GROWTH AND DEVELOPMENT

to remember the sequences and appearance of the finished product. In modelling these strategies, the knowledgeable other helps the child to acquire the tools for thinking and learning which help to make learning more efficient. Whether rehearsal and repetition in play have any later impact on more formal learning processes has not been adequately tested or proven, but it is possible that these valuable formative play experiences may have some lasting effects on the ways in which the brain develops and the extent and efficiency of the neural networks.

We know that brain growth and development are influenced positively by a number of factors that are situated in children's social and cultural contexts, as listed in Figure 3.2.

The educational implications may be tentative, but nevertheless provide support for a curriculum that includes both child- and adult-initiated activities, promotes individual as well as shared exploration, enables the co-construction of knowledge and provides rich opportunities for learning. Although children's brains develop rapidly under positive conditions, the processes involved are complex, and it may be that one of the most important conditions that supports young learners is time to engage with these essential stimuli, rather than rushing them on to the next stage of learning in order to achieve arbitrary targets and defined outcomes. Time is also essential for children to become master players and learners: as the brain develops, basic skills become increasingly refined, enabling learners to develop advanced or 'meta' skills in memory, cognition and language.

META-MEMORY

An advanced form of memorization is 'meta-memory' – which is defined by Meadows (1993: 57) as knowledge of what memory behaviour is happening at the moment, and one's understanding of task difficulties;

one's own skills, abilities and deficits, and strategies that will enable one to perform a task satisfactorily.

Meta-memory also influences transferability – the deliberate transfer of strategies and skills between tasks and problems, usually involving deliberate reflection and organization. Young learners are considered to be deficient in this area because of their lack of experience. However, the foundations of these skills can be observed in play because they store a wealth of information gleaned from many sources, which they weave into different types of play. For example, in socio-dramatic play, children draw upon individual and shared memories, which are interpreted and organized to provide the script and content of the play. They use recall strategies in repeated play themes, drawing on experience and imagination to remind each other of previous actions and sequences as the following example shows:

> Ellie: You be the baby and I'll be the Mum.
> Jen: No, I want to be the mum, I be'd the baby last time.
> Ellie: No, it's my turn to wear the dress cos Helen had it yesterday and I was the mum but I couldn't wear the dress.
> Jen: OK then, you wear the dress but I'll be the mum as well and I'll have the baby and the pram. We'll be two mums.
> Ellie: Yeah, and we'll go down the clinic for a 'jection cos my baby's got the measles. Has your baby got the measles?
> Jen: No, my baby's had medicine cos she's sick. I had medicine and I was sick.

As in the episode with Sophie, Tasha and Beth, Ellie and Jen share their real-world experiences in a play context, and illustrate their abilities to memorize sequences and events.

METACOGNITION

Contemporary theories of teaching and learning indicate that a transmission–acquisition model is inadequate for building the flexibility and creativity demanded of children and young people in the 21st century. Instead, models of teaching and learning that actively empower children to become self-conscious and self-regulating learners offer far more promise for maximixing the potential of the human mind. An advanced form of cognition is *metacognition*, which is defined as the self-conscious participation and intelligent self-regulation in learning and problem-solving situations, including knowledge and awareness of what is involved in learning. We can extend this definition to encompass 'meta-play', which involves the complex processes described in Chapter 2, such as

- Recognizing the nature of the task and the demands it makes.
- Checking existing knowledge, skills and understanding.
- Planning strategies and actions.
- Predicting the possible outcomes of strategies and actions.
- Asking questions.
- Self-testing.
- Monitoring ongoing activities.
- Estimating.
- Revising and reflecting.
- Communicating ideas and clarifying understanding.
- Transferring skills and knowledge across different contexts.
- Making connections with existing knowledge and past experience.
- Making generalizations.

FIGURE 3.3   WHAT IS INVOLVED IN METACOGNITIVE ACTIVITY?

defining and orchestrating play activities; stepping in and out of play; solving problems as they arise; and communicating meaning through symbolic transformations (making one thing stand for another). Metacognitive skills and strategies can help children become master players and learners, and these are enhanced with the kinds of activity listed in Figure 3.3. There are key processes which help children develop metacognitive skills and strategies. These are listed in Figure 3.4 (Fisher, 1995).

The plan–do–review cycle is considered to be an empowering approach to learning because children are encouraged to become independent, and interdependent, learners and self-running problem-solvers. Figure 3.5 lists the skills involved. Many of the processes involved in learning to learn, and developing mastery, need to be learnt consciously and deliberately.

Practitioners play an important role in helping children become efficient learners by teaching them how to control their own intellectual activities, in adult- and child-initiated activities. Children need to use language about learning so that they come to understand what learning is all about, can describe their learning and explain the meaning of their representations and activities. These supportive interactions help to develop a co-constructive approach to learning and teaching, which will be explored in Chapter 5.

■ METACOGNITION IN PRACTICE

Different play contexts provide meaningful opportunities for children to use metacognitive skills, especially when they act as co-players and

- **Planning**: planning goals and sub-goals, operations and sequences, identifying obstacles and possible problems, knowing the process and predicting the outcomes.
- **Monitoring**: keeping in mind the goals, place in the sequence, possible obstacles and errors, knowing what to do when things go wrong or plans fail, knowing when the goal is achieved.
- **Assessing**: assessing the success of strategies and progress towards goal achievement, assessing errors and mistakes along the way, evaluating the whole process.

Planning skills can be achieved in three phases:

- **Direct instruction phase**: explaining to students about plans and planning, showing examples of plans and planning strategies involving students with recording or implementing given plans.
- **Facilitation phase**: explaining how plans can be created, showing how plans can be modified and extended, involving students in putting plans into their own words.
- **Self-generation phase**: explaining that everyone needs to be able to plan, showing examples of students' planning, involving students in making their own plans. (Fisher, 1995)

FIGURE 3.4   DEVELOPING METACOGNITIVE SKILLS AND STRATEGIES

- Speaking and listening in a group.
- Understanding the concepts of planning and making decisions.
- Being able to implement a plan.
- Selecting and knowing how to use materials and resources.
- Acting independently and collaboratively.
- Asking for assistance from peers or adults.
- Specifying the assistance needed to implement a plan or carry out a task.
- Paying attention to the activity.
- Creating, identifying and solving problems.
- Remembering how the plan was carried out.
- Reflecting on action – raising and answering questions.
- Representing knowledge and experience.
- Processing information and communicating the meaning and purpose of an activity.
- Conscious awareness of learning processes (metacognition).
- Making and sustaining relationships with peers and adults.

FIGURE 3.5   SKILLS FOR PLANNING, DOING AND REVIEWING

---

co-tutors. The following example shows how Andrew (age six) was aware of his knowledge and expertise and how he used it to assist Nigel (age five). The children used the plan–do–review approach.

ANDREW'S TRUCK Andrew chose to make a truck from the Fisher-Technik℗ construction kit. He had recently achieved success with making models from this kit, initially with a plan and adult help. Andrew did not ask for help and started to collect the pieces he needed from the kit. Nigel asked to join him.

> Andrew: This is good this is. I can make a lorry. I don't have to copy a plan because I can make it.
> Nigel: Let's see, can I help you? What are you doing?
> Andrew: You slide them in here, down the side here.
> Nigel: What, do you have to do it all the way down with all these?
> Andrew: Four, you get four. They go on like this . . . you slide them then you get these big pieces (*refers to axles*) down through there. We need big ones. We need four. Get me two more. Oh (*laughs*) we only need two, I thought four.
> Nigel: There's four wheels we need.
> Andrew: We only need two of these (*axles*) cos the wheels go like this (*shows Nigel*).
> Nigel: Better, better.
> Andrew: We put the wheels on now . . . there . . . (*demonstrates to Nigel*) you do that one.
> Nigel: It's hard isn't it, to put them on?
> Andrew: Push them hard (*helps Nigel*). Now we have to put these on (*wheel stoppers*) to stop them falling off, these little ones. Put the little ones on . . . go on. This is going to be a milk lorry.
> Nigel: Got that one right haven't I Andrew?
> Andre: That's right. Now we put the edges on (*means the sides*).
> Nigel: What, we have to put them on?
> Andrew: Yes.
> Nigel: Why?
> Andrew: So that's the edges so the people can't fall out. (*Andrew continued until the model was successfully completed.*)

Previous observations revealed that Andrew became easily frustrated, was often dependent on adult support and had a short concentration span. However, in this activity Andrew showed initiative and maintained concentration and perseverance until his goal was achieved. He also supported another child, worked independently and collaboratively, used reasoning and problem-solving skills, and used language to reflect, explain, answer questions and direct the action. The development of his confidence, motivation and self-esteem was evident and, at review time, Andrew explained how he taught Nigel to make the model. The teacher offered further support by reminding Andrew of the words 'axle' and 'wheel stopper', which he had forgotten (Attfield, 1992).

VERNON'S RACING CAR Vernon (age seven) and Alec (age six) were making a racing car from a Gymbo™ construction kit, and wanted to make it strong enough to take the weight of one child. Vernon identified a self-created problem and articulated his thinking and problem-solving strategies.

> Vernon: This is no good, if you sit on it it's gonna touch the ground.
>
> Alec: What shall we do? Take that bit off?
>
> Vernon: That isn't a good idea because all that'll happen is that your weight will push it down. (*They try various pieces of equipment and alterations to their design.*)
>
> Vernon: If you put that there it'll stop your weight from making it go down, then put the wheels on there. They do this. Test it, push on it ... Alec you've got it the wrong way, how are you going to put the wheels on?
>
> Alec: Oh, yeah, mm.
>
> Vernon: You can put them on there ... that's it ... just adjust that ... you can put your legs on the side there ... that's OK now.
>
> (*At review time, the boys explained how they made changes to their original design and how the needs of others had been taken into account.*)
>
> Vernon: We were going to have the seat there but we had to change it because the weight puts it down when you sit on it and it goes on the floor so we changes it so the wheels are higher than the bottom bits.
>
> Alec: We put these on (*wheel stoppers*) to stop the wheels falling off and that's for big people to put their feet on there.
>
> Vernon: Little kids can sit there. They can't reach their legs down there so they put them there so it's easier. (Attfield, 1992)

This activity involved coordinating and controlling deliberate attempts to solve problems and integrated the metacognitive skills outlined above – predicting, checking, monitoring and controlling. Vernon's input was skills-, ideas- and content-oriented, so that the play episode incorporated learning processes and outcomes. Their internal cognitive processes were externalized in their discussion, behaviour, activity and reflection at review time. The outcomes included a successfully completed model, as well as enhanced self-esteem, social competence and the satisfaction of having engaged in the play. The discourse in children's play, the nature of their activity and the outcomes are rich in meanings and provide insights into their thinking and styles of learning. As children become more experienced learners and players, they integrate cultural and social knowledge and, as the following example shows, demonstrate meta-awareness of other children's needs, as well as the rules and conventions of play.

MAKING A BOARD GAME Jenny, Betty, Lee and Paul (age between six and seven) decided to make a board game after discussion, initiated by the teacher, about the toyshop needing some more toys. The children went to a quiet area to discuss their ideas.

> Betty: Well we could have a race track.
> Jenny: Or we could have the first one to get home like a frog jumping on lily pads.
> Lee: In a jungle, in a jungle.
> Jenny: And you've got to go in your home in a jungle.
> Betty: Or you could have quite a big one and on one side have a race track. You've got to go round the race track the right way and then you get into the jungle.
> Jenny: Or what we could do is a little game for young children and put like sums on lily pads and they've got to add up the sums and they've got to jump on the next lily pad.
> Lee: I like Jenny's idea.
> Paul: It could be just like Jenny's but . . . you could go along with a dice and a counter and you throw the dice and if you land on a square that's got writing on then you've got to do what it says.
> Jenny: That sounds good, like forfeits.
> Betty: I think Paul's is quite good cos it's fun.
> Jenny: What happens if it's really shy children, they might begin to cry with forfeits.
> Paul: We could have easy sums like $1 + 1$.
> Lee: Easy peasy.
> Jenny: That's easy for you but not for little children.
> Betty: They put two fingers up and count with them.
> Lee: Why don't we have both ideas on it?
> Betty & Paul: Yes.
> Jenny: Why don't we have sums and forfeits? And what did you say about the jungle, Lee?

These children were skilled learners and communicators, using language for explaining their ideas, reasoning, reflecting, sharing information and explaining. When they presented their ideas to the teacher, she extended their thinking by helping them to reflect on further elements of the design.

> Teacher: Before you start, so you've got it clear in your heads what the players can and what they can't do, there's something you need to do. How will the players know what to do?
> Jenny: Rules.
> Teacher: Right, you need some rules. How many people can play?

With further discussion and teacher participation the children clarified their ideas and devised a format whereby the long explanatory sentences for the rules were abbreviated. In Jenny's list of rules (Figure 3.6) she is

1. The first person to the finish is the winner.

2. If you land on a lily pad with a foursits on

you read it and do it. 3 There will be easy and hard sums

to do. 4 If you can't read on do ask for Help. 5 Home is

the small ponds 6 2-4 people can play the same 7 you need diffrent

souler counters 8 If you get a sum near home go home 9 If you get

a sum right not near home go on the Answer. 10 If your on the same

pad as a nother player the frist player there moves on some

you have 2 counters each

FIGURE 3.6   JENNY'S LIST OF RULES

writing for a purpose, in a particular style, showing awareness of the knowledge that has to be communicated in order for the game to be successful.

The children decided to have a pond at the end of the game as 'home' and, in the next stage of the planning, hit another design problem.

> Betty: We'll stick the pond on the end here.
> Lee: Cut the pond about that big, turn it over and stick it here.
> Jenny: Yes, but what happens if the game breaks and that bit falls off and you can't find it and it isn't very nice in the game, you can't play it any more.
> Lee: Have it round here.
> Betty: Wait a minute. I think we should plan it before we draw.
> Lee: On this piece of paper. We don't have to put one enormous pond.
> Jenny: I know, we could have four ponds a different colour.
> Paul: Yes, red and blue.
> Jenny: The people with the green counters have to go to the green pond.
> Betty: Yes and red counters for the red pond, and yellow for the yellow pond and what's left?
> Lee: The blue one. (Attfield, 1992)

This episode shows that meaningful contexts are essential for fostering cognitive and metacognitive processes. The teacher provided intellectually skilled assistance at the right moment, in response to the problems identified by the children, so that the activity was co-constructive (children and teacher engaged in joint activity). The 'meta' qualities of this episode are evident in their awareness of their skills and knowledge, joint recall of previous games (successful and unsuccessful), knowledge of social rules and conventions in playing games, and their theories of mind (understanding the younger children's minds and feelings). Within the spontaneous flow of play, there was a great deal of orchestrated cognitive and social activity, with sustained shared thinking (Siraj-Blatchford and Sylva, 2004) between the teacher and children.

METACOMMUNICATION

All children need language-rich experiences which help them organize and make sense of their social and cultural worlds and develop their identities. Language and communication are used at different levels. Thought processes are a form of inner speech, which can vary from deliberate planned action to daydreaming. Communication between children, peers and adults externalizes thinking and conveys meaning and cognitive competence. Out-loud thinking is an extension of self-speech, both of which provide a means of regulating activity, reflecting on action, describing, articulating ideas and intentions, as the following example shows. Etta, age four, was playing alone with a doll in the home corner:

> Now it's time to go to sleep. No, don't cry. I'm going to put you in your cot. Now shush that's naughty (*angry expression and voice, points finger at doll*). It's time for bed. I'll come back in a minute. (*Puts baby in cot, then stands still for a few seconds. Goes back to doll.*) Are you still crying? (*Hands on hips, angry expression and voice. Picks up doll.*) I'll have to see what's the matter. Oh dear, wet nappy. Alright, there, there, I'll change you. (*Holds baby closely, gentle voice and relaxed expression.*)

Etta used metacommunication through dialogue and gestures to create and sustain the pretence. She shifted her emotional state in response to the baby having a legitimate reason for crying and immediately communicated this through her behaviour and attitudes. She conveyed emotion and reason through her self-speech, which directed the play. Such experiences help children make the transfer to paired or group cooperative play because they rehearse ways of communicating action, imagination and pretence, as demonstrated by Mark (age six), who was playing in the workshop role-play area, trying to mend a radio. He had access to some tools and a variety of old electrical equipment and was talking to another child:

> I can't think around which hole this screwdriver goes in. (*Tried screwdriver in each hole.*) Look, it goes in that hole there. I can't have this screwdriver. I think I'll have that big one over there. I think this one came from a robot. (*Picked up hairdryer.*) I wonder if we can get this working. Switch is still working. We'll have to take it apart then. I don't think this is the right screwdriver.

In both examples, play provided a context for developing transferability of knowledge and skills, and language provided a link between the child's thinking and action. Mark used logic, reasoning, deduction and problem-solving skills in pretending to mend the equipment. His language conveys the suspension of reality: he believed that the radio was repairable so his actions conveyed meaning in the context of the play. Etta and Mark used language to communicate their meaning of the activity. Spoken language is not the only medium for effective communication: much of what we want to convey in social contexts is expressed through body language, facial expressions and gestures. The use of Braille, Makaton and British Sign Language can have positive effects for children with language and communication difficulties, and can provide an inclusive approach for all children.

In exploring the 'meta' qualities of children's play, these episodes show children's minds and brains at work: they actively brainstorm problems and solutions, using out-loud thinking to externalize their inner cognitive processes, thus combining hands-on and brains-on activity. They play with knowledge, language, ideas, roles, rules and relationships in creative, inventive and flexible ways. In order to develop a more informed understanding of the relationship between playing and learning, practitioners need to be sensitive to the patterns, styles, dispositions, interests and characteristics which children reveal and represent in their play. The following section describes schema theory, which many practitioners find useful in extending their understanding of children's minds at work and play.

SCHEMA THEORY

Schema theory derives from the work of cognitive psychologists, such as Jean Piaget, who investigated how internal cognitive structures are formed, and how these are related to observable behaviours and actions. More recent researchers have explored the educational implications of schema theory (Athey, 1990; Nutbrown, 1999; Worthington and Carruthers, 2003) from infancy through early childhood. Schemas are defined as repeating patterns and actions that lead to the coordination of cognitive structures through connections and interconnections. Patterns and changes in thinking and learning can be accessed through children's representations, language, mark-making, symbolization and play. The practitioner's role is to identify children's schemas and support their development through interaction, language and the provision of relevant materials and worthwhile content in a supportive learning environment. Informed diagnosis of children's schemas should inform curriculum planning and enable practitioners to plan for extension and differentiation, particularly in the ways children use and transform materials and represent their thinking. Thus schema theory can inform practitioners working across settings, using the different policy frameworks.

Worthington and Carruthers (2003) drew on research conducted in their own classrooms with four- to six-year-old children, and identified the most frequently observed schemas, including envelopment, enclosure, transporting, connecting, rotating, containing, going round a boundary, spirals, trajectories and transformation. On the basis of their research, they identified patterns in children's schema journeys specifically in mathematics and many different forms of representation. With younger children, their early schematic patterns involved fragments of knowledge and ideas, for example putting numbers to objects but not necessarily in the standard way. Early random mark-making showed repetition of simple forms (vertical lines, crosses, circles, triangles, arrows) which children see in their everyday environment. These simple forms became the basis of more complex forms of symbolic representation in, for example, literacy, numeracy, technology (plans and layouts), geography (maps and models) and the creative arts (musical notation, communication through dance, drama and mime). Children's schematic activities do not just emerge spontaneously: progression from these simple random forms to more complex controlled forms of representation can be nourished and modelled by practitioners, for example by connecting children with forms of knowledge which are immediately meaningful to the children and relevant to their future lives. Worthington and Carruthers (2003) provide evidence of how these fragments gradually build towards more coherent and coordinated concepts and skills, how connections between schemas are associated with different disciplines, and how schemas progress over time. The following extract shows how literacy and mathematics were connected, based on the children developing the role play area as a library van (which had recently visited the school).

> During their play, the children arranged the books and pretended to stamp the date on them.
>
> Marina and Frances were especially concerned about library fines and wrote a number of letters demanding huge fines for overdue books, using paper, envelopes and stamps from the office. They used calculators to work out fines due on several books, and real money to give change. Their calculations may not have been 'correct' but the children were using tools and resources in appropriate contexts and for purposes that made sense. They remonstrated with readers who argued about the amount of fines and Marina spent a long time on the phone complaining to borrowers about overdue books: clearly this aspect of libraries had left an impression.
>
> Marie-Anne made a road safety poster which she attached to the front of the 'counter': in the city library she'd seen a road safety poster in the same position. The children filled in forms with titles of books and recommended particular books to 'parents', drawing on their own experience. They counted how many books each borrower took. One of the children instructed a 'new' borrower to fill in a form with her name and age in order to join a library (Worthington and Carruthers, 2003: 168).

This vignette also shows how literacy and numeracy are social and cultural practices that children observe in their everyday environments, and subsequently imitate in their play. The value of schema theory in practice is that practitioners and parents can develop informed understanding of individual and shared patterns of learning and activity, and the social contexts in which these are situated (Nutbrown, 1999). Identifying children's schemas demands an informed understanding of what each child brings to an activity so that practitioners can fine-tune subsequent interactions in the form of teaching strategies, input of new skills or knowledge, or the provision of materials. For children with learning difficulties, the practitioner's ability to identify small steps in learning, and small fragments of knowledge and understanding, can be fundamental to how they develop individual plans for learning and playing (Wasik *et al*, 2002). Practitioners can scaffold as well as co-construct understanding with children, by carrying out their own research on topics that are of immediate interest (Jordan, 2004), thereby extending children's schemas with worthwhile content.

Athey (1990) states that children's achievements need to be understood by practitioners at a conceptual and theoretical level, not just on the basis of what is perceived. They need to understand the meaning of an activity in the child's own terms, including the forms of knowledge and cognitive processes which are being developed or represented. These insights are particularly important in the context of play. If early childhood specialists make claims about the value of play, then these must be substantiated with evidence that can be communicated to parents, caregivers, other educators and policy-makers. In pre-school settings more time is usually available for play and other self-chosen activities, which enables the skilled practitioner to identify schemas and patterns of learning. However, from Reception onwards, the balance between teacher-directed and child-initiated activities, including play, tends to alter significantly (Wood and Bennett, 2001). If curriculum frameworks are used slavishly, practitioners may be more concerned with gaps in children's knowledge, as defined by teaching objectives and learning outcomes. As a consequence, they may miss important evidence about children's individual learning patterns and journeys.

SOCIAL COGNITION AND EMOTIONAL LITERACY

Theories of social cognition and emotional literacy explain how young children develop their social and emotional skills, and their understanding of themselves in relation to others. Weare (2004: 2) defines *emotional literacy* as:

> The ability to understand ourselves and other people, and in particular to be aware of, understand, and use information about the emotional states of ourselves and others with competence. It includes the ability to understand, express and manage our own emotions, and respond to the emotions of others, in ways that are helpful to others.

Social cognition is defined as the process of thinking about emotions, feelings and how people interact with one another in social and cultural contexts. Social cognition plays a critical role in:

- the acquisition of social skills

- the ability to engage in interpersonal problem-solving

- the development of empathy (understanding the perspective and feelings of others)

- the development of an inner locus of control.

These processes are integrated and interdependent and, as with other areas of learning, are developed in conjunction with more or differently knowledgeable others. Patterns of learning are socially and culturally determined from birth so that children are gradually socialized into forms of appropriate behaviour in different contexts. Adults provide a bridging role in assisting children, by giving social and emotional cues, modelling how to behave in different situations, using language for different purposes, and providing feedback on how the child is coping. Children respond actively, by giving further cues and feedback so that learning is a joint activity, not a one-way transmission.

Social cognition includes the development of self-concept, cultural and gender identities. How children come to perceive themselves is determined to a large extent by their success and competence, particularly in educational contexts. In coming to understand their place in the world, children need to understand and know themselves, their strengths and weaknesses, attitudes and dispositions; how to interact with others, form relationships and overcome their limitations in social and individual contexts. Play activities provide many opportunities for developing social cognition and emotional literacy. Children play with strong emotions such as fear, grief, anger, jealousy, love, hatred, guilt, anxiety, betrayal, rejection and injustice. By understanding the real/not real boundaries of play, these emotions can be played with in relatively safe contexts, such as being frightened of sharks and monsters in chasing games, giving out excessive punishments in cops-and-robbers play, or being a very strict and unfair teacher in school play. Because mood states determine behaviour, children who are anxious, ill or stressed may not play successfully: they may lack the motivation to engage, take risks, participate cooperatively or enjoy an activity. If children are not able to express difficult emotions in appropriate ways, these may be expressed through inappropriate behaviours (overt or covert) and may interfere with a child's ability to play, learn and interact successfully with others.

In play contexts children need a wide repertoire of social skills and emotional literacy in order to become successful players. Play provides many different opportunities for children to learn about social and cultural norms: appropriate and inappropriate behaviours, society's rules and conventions, roles and relationships, and boundaries. For example, as discussed earlier in this chapter, in making their board game, Jenny, Betty, Lee and Paul revealed knowledge about rules and conventions, as well as empathic understanding of the needs and feelings of younger children. They knew that some children would feel distressed if they were challenged inappropriately by too many forfeits, showing awareness of concepts such as justice and fairness. They understood the rules of interaction, turn-taking, negotiating, compromising and synthesizing ideas, as well as the paradoxical nature of play.

Teaching children to think about feelings and relationships can contribute to their empowerment, for example by helping them to recognize and deal with conflict, resolve disputes, care for others, take control of their behaviour and make decisions. The development of social skills and emotional literacy contributes to children's positive self-concept, realistic self-esteem and inner confidence, all of which underpin effective learning (Roberts, 2002). Play enables children to create their own rules, determine appropriate behaviours, define roles and test their own boundaries as well as those imposed by adults. The success of the play depends on children abiding by the rules: a child who behaves destructively or uncooperatively will eventually not be invited to play. Children play with 'not real' anti-social behaviour as a way of testing boundaries, but ultimately they cannot tolerate this for real, especially in pretend play, because it destroys the sequence and flow which are necessary for inclusion, success and enjoyment.

Children often exaggerate emotions and behaviours in their play for different reasons. First, exaggeration signals 'this is play' and defines the boundaries and rules of what will be accepted and tolerated. Second, children need to exaggerate and play with different emotions in a non-threatening situation in order to explore how it feels to be angry, frightened, abandoned, lost, powerful or powerless. The 'what if' and 'as if' characteristics of play give children permission to behave in different ways. Their behaviours may be rooted in real-life problems, dramas and ongoing emotional concerns, or they may just want to be nonsensical, absurd, zany, even anarchic. For example, young children are frequently observed being angry and even violent towards dolls, playing at smacking and shaking, with threats of excessive punishments. Usually children are playing out their developing understanding of the world and their place within it. However, in exceptional cases, repeated or excessive anti-social behaviours may be indicative of problems in children's lives.

Practitioners need to acknowledge the dark side of play, and the ways in which children can subvert play for negative purposes. Play is not always a pro-social activity from childhood through to adulthood, especially where it takes place away from the control of adults. Teasing can easily become bullying; flirting can become sexual harassment. Friendly rivalry between football supporters can be transformed into violence. Children, and adults, manipulate play situations to gain control, by including or excluding others, by sharing or not sharing, by bribing and threatening. For example, from the day that William started nursery he decided that everything belonged to him and was for his sole use. He recruited a fellow conspirator, Tom, to help him exclude other children from the activities they wanted to dominate. When playing in the shop they wanted all the money and goods, put them into bags and hid with them under the climbing frame. They prevented other children from playing in the sand and water trays. William was protective of his own space, but invasive of other children's space. This extended to hitting, thumping and pushing where he felt threatened. William dominated Tom, and was often aggressive towards him in the nursery and at home. His anti-social behaviours were persistent and, on occasions extreme, and led to William being isolated because the other children disliked his aggression and need for control. In order to overcome these problems, the teacher and educational psychologist developed a home–school programme, which involved play tutoring for William and his parents so that he received positive attention and reinforcement.

Children do not always 'play nicely': they need to develop a wide repertoire of social and emotional skills in order to help them become successful players. As with other areas of learning, children need ample time and opportunities to develop these skills. Practitioners need informed understanding of what socio-affective learning encompasses, how this can be developed through play and what opportunities exist in other areas of the curriculum for further learning. These themes will be explored in more detail in Chapters 6 and 7.

CREATIVITY AND IMAGINATION

Many early childhood specialists are concerned that creativity is being devalued in the current technical/rational curriculum, particularly with the emphasis on literacy and numeracy (Anning and Ring, 2004; Beetlestone 1997; Duffy, 1999). There are strong arguments for developing alternative curriculum models that empower children with tools for thinking, develop positive dispositions towards learning, and enable them to explore ideas, experiences, feelings and relationships (Abbott and Nutbrown, 2001; Broadhead, 2004; Anning *et al*, 2004). These principles are embedded in the Reggio Emilia and Te Whāriki approaches, which will be described in Chapter 5. Creativity and imagination are important to lifelong learning and playing because they embody divergent forms of thinking and lead to novel, innovative combinations of ideas and experiences. These dispositions are not exclusive to the creative arts, but are important in all subject areas. For example, a well-disciplined imagination is essential in history, as children have to go beyond the evidence available to imagine what life was like in another time, to understand people's motivations and aspirations, to make deductions about how they might have felt and why they acted as they did, and to reason about causes and effects (Wood and Holden, 1995). As Egan (1991) states, it is human emotion and thought that can bring to life the concrete content we want children to learn. While a disciplined imagination can be seen as a form of reasoning, fantasy is altogether a more wayward phenomenon:

> Education is the process in which we use rationality to show and discover what is real and true, and so fantasy, which ignores the boundaries of reality, is seen as the enemy which slips out of the constructive constraints of reason and runs mentally amok in unreal and impossible worlds ... In rational activity the mind is awake, about constructive work, in accord with reality, attuned to the logics whereby things operate; in fantasy there is mind-wandering illogic, dream-like indulgence of the flittering shapes of the idle mind, disregard of hard empirical reality (Egan, 1991: 11).

Egan argues that features of fantasy become 'constituents of a rich rationality' and represent a legitimate means for making sense and creating meaning. Cohen and MacKeith (1991) use the evocative phrase 'world weavers' to describe the creative and imaginative worlds created by writers, artists and performers. Children become world weavers in their play: they suspend reality in order to construct pretence, but at the same time use logic and reasoning to create the 'as if' and 'what if' qualities of

What does this object do?
Epistemic play

What can I do with this object?
Ludic play

FIGURE 3.7   PLAY AND CREATIVITY

play. They engage in novel forms of thinking and acting, and create their own internal logic based on negotiated rules and shared meanings which are often repeated, revised, extended and elaborated. Children continuously edit their actions and interactions, and transform their use of tools and artefacts as they play, thereby showing that imagination and reason are not in opposition. Hutt *et al* (1989) argue that there are two levels of play, as outlined in Figure 3.7.

Epistemic play includes acquiring knowledge and information, using problem-solving, discovery and exploration, in which children find out 'what does this object do?' (the term 'object' can include all the material affordances in the learning environment – resources, tools, artefacts, machines). Epistemic play is productive play because it promotes learning: children are often aware of what they are making or doing, and their activity leads to an end-state which is a higher level of competence. In *ludic play* children find out 'what can I do with this object?' Ludic play has symbolic/fantasy and repetitive elements, is characterized by pretence and is highly dependent on mood states. Hutt *et al* conclude that ludic play may promote learning indirectly, or may serve some quite different function, but they do not go on to speculate what this might be. The outcomes may be enhanced competence, control and mastery, which can also lead to feelings of self-efficacy, or 'can-do' dispositions to learning.

The creative processes involved in epistemic and ludic play involve transforming understanding of how tools can be used, and what tools can be used for. All environmental tools have the potential to support creative learning (see Figure 3.8).

The following episode describes a child's playful learning journey with technology, and exemplifies these concepts:

TOOLS FOR USE
(what does this do?)

Personal tools: cognitive, social, emotional, physical.
Cultural tools: symbol systems, artefacts, disciplined ways of learning e.g.
technology, literacy and numeracy.
Social and environmental tools: all the human and material resources that are
available to support learning and development.

TOOLS AND USE
(what can I do with this?)

FIGURE 3.8   TOOLS FOR USE, TOOLS AND USE

Navin became interested in the Roamer in his first term in Reception. At first, his teacher allowed periods of play and exploration to enable Navin to discover how to control the machine. Initially Navin punched in numbers at random but, with some input from his teacher, he gradually learned how to control the different functions. He planned a difficult challenge of making the Roamer go around a square and needed to learn the relevant spatial language as well as new programming skills. At first he made many errors and needed support to remember the sequence of the programming, and to talk about the errors he had made. His teacher remained in a supportive role and responded to Navin's self-initiated problems. Navin's sense of achievement was considerable when he succeeded in this task. He maintained his fascination with ICT and, by the end of Key Stage 1, became expert in his use of many different machines and computer programs. When his parents bought him a computer, Navin was the 'expert' teacher, and they were the learners.

In their study of children's drawing, Anning and Ring (2004) argue that *multi-modality* (using many different materials, tools, artefacts and resources, and engaging the senses) is the core to children's preferred ways of representing and communicating their growing understanding of their world, and their roles as active members of communities. The children in their study were 'world weavers', because they used drawing and other modes of representation in their play, and integrated everyday knowledge and experience. The development of creativity and imagination is dependent on children's engagement with multi-modal representations, and the involvement of adults at home and school to support emerging skills and interests.

MOVING FORWARD

The theories of learning and development reviewed in this chapter reflect a shift towards viewing children as capable, competent learners. Neuroscience offers insights into the immense complexity and plasticity of the human brain, and indicates that individual and collaborative activity generates development. From early infancy children develop naive theories about themselves and others, the world, and their place in it. Through play and other activities they acquire fragments of knowledge and understanding, which they represent in many different ways. These fragments become more organized and interconnected with maturity and experience. Young children's thinking may appear disorganized and idiosyncratic, but close observations reveal patterns and consistencies in what children play with, how they play, and how they represent their emerging knowledge and experience. Figure 3.9 lists ways in which playing and learning are linked.

Play activities function as an integrating mechanism for learning processes. Learning becomes more efficient if children become consciously aware of the processes that are involved in learning, and how they can gain control over those processes. Play also promotes 'meta' skills and competences in cognition, memory, language, communication and representation. These can be seen as higher-order thinking skills that enable children to make specific connections between areas of learning and experience. Learning is both recursive and incremental, so that children gradually develop flexibility and transferability. Learning involves gradual changes in skills, knowledge and competences as children act in and on the world, and participate in play activities in increasingly complex ways. Creativity and imagination are important elements in this process because they encourage divergent ways of thinking and reasoning and help children to make novel connections and interconnections between areas of learning and experience. The process is summarized in Figure 3.10.

In the following chapter we will provide more detailed understanding of how contemporary socio-cultural theories can underpin the relationship between playing, learning and teaching.

- Different forms of play incorporate cognitive, social and emotional challenges.
- Play provides the means for perceiving new connections and relationships between ideas, experiences, skills and knowledge.
- Play can facilitate learning by exposing children to new experiences, activities and ideas.
- Play allows children to construct meaning from experience.
- Play has cognitive consolidating functions because it incorporates practice, rehearsal, repetition, mastery and extension.
- Intrinsic motivation is an important aspect of playing and learning and enables children to develop problem-solving and sense-making capacities.
- Extrinsic motivation can support children's skills and dispositions as players and learners.
- Play provides valuable opportunities for discipline-based learning which connect children with distinctive ways of reasoning, understanding, controlling and making sense of the world.
- Play provides opportunities for children to use flexible, creative ways of thinking and acting.
- Play enables children to develop meta skills for thinking, learning and acting in social worlds.

FIGURE 3.9   *MAKING LINKS BETWEEN PLAYING AND LEARNING*

TEACHING AND LEARNING

involve

ACTION

COMMUNICATION

MEDIATION

INTERACTION

leading to

INTER-REACTION

FIGURE 3.10   *TEACHING AND LEARNING PROCESSES*

FURTHER READING

The following authors all take a creative approach to children's play and to the early childhood curriculum. They provide more detailed exploration of the themes covered in this chapter and include fascinating insights into children's learning, as well as guidance for practitioners. Gopnik *et al*

(1999) provide a highly readable account of the mysteries of the brain and mind.

Anning, A. and Ring, K. (2004) *Making Sense of Children's Drawings*, London, Sage.

Beardsley, G. and Harnett, P. (1998) *Exploring Play in the Primary Classroom*, London, David Fulton.

Beetlestone, F. (1997) *Creative Children, Imaginative Teaching*, Bucks, Open University Press.

Duffy, B. (1999) *Supporting Creativity and Imagination in the Early Years*, Buckingham, Open University Press.

Gopnik, A., Meltzoff, A.N. and Kuhl, P.K. (1999) *The Scientist in the Crib: Minds, Brains and How Children Learn*, New York, William Morrow and Company.

Hendy, L. and Toon, L. (2001) *Supporting Drama and Imaginative Play in the Early Years*, Buckingham, Open University Press.

Roberts, R. (2002) *Self-esteem and Early Learning*, London, Paul Chapman.

Weare, K. (2004) *Developing the Emotionally Literate School*, London, Paul Chapman.

Worthington, M. and Carruthers, E. (2003) *Children's Mathematics: Making Sense, Making Meaning*, London, Paul Chapman.

CHAPTER FOUR

Contemporary Socio-cultural Theories

In the previous chapter we explored some theories of children's learning and related these to play. However, we cannot assume that playing always leads to learning or that play is the only valuable means of learning in early childhood. In practice educators face a number of dilemmas in how they conceptualize and incorporate play into the curriculum. In this chapter we examine the idea of creating unity between playing, learning and teaching, based on a synthesis of the work of Lev Vygotsky (1896–1934) and subsequent developments in socio-cultural and activity theories.

Any discussion of Vygotsky's work needs to be prefaced by three important caveats. First, his premature death meant that many of his ideas were still being developed and had not been fully tested. What has become known as a socio-cultural model of learning is a synthesis of theories developed, extended and reinterpreted by his contemporaries and subsequent followers. Second, the essence of his work has been altered through the process of translation. Third, Vygotsky's ideas must be seen in their historical context: he was strongly influenced by Marxism, because its ideology penetrated all aspects of social, political, economic, educational and cultural life in the former USSR. Vygotsky was concerned with developing innovative psychological insights into the nature of development, learning, language, thought, concept formation and play. His work reveals many contradictions and inconsistencies, because he was still formulating his ideas up to his death. It has been left to others to interpret these ideas in the light of further research and advances in our knowledge of children's learning and development, and relate them to teaching and learning in schools.

In spite of these limitations, Vygotksian theories have important implications for teaching and learning in general, and for understanding children's play. The aspects of Vygotsky's work which we explore are selective and should be compared and contrasted with other theories. We have also drawn on contemporary interpretations and developments in socio-cultural theory, many of which have challenged Vygotsky's original ideas (Lambert and Clyde, 2003; Shayer, 2003). There is no single theory of learning, and hence no single prescription for teaching, which could adequately capture the dynamics of educating young children. Therefore the aim of this chapter is to provide a theoretical framework that will enable practitioners to think critically about their practice and achieve an intellectually deeper understanding of learning and teaching through play.

This chapter explores four key themes: Vygotsky's ideas about learning and development; the zone of proximal development; the relationship between development and instruction; and play. Key concepts and terms are highlighted, and illustrated through practical examples so that practitioners can make their own links between theory and practice.

LEARNING AND DEVELOPMENT

Vygotsky argued that no single framework of explanatory principles could provide an adequate explanation of the complex developmental changes that occur throughout childhood. Vygotsky defined development as evolutionary and revolutionary shifts with qualitative and quantitative changes in thinking, knowledge and skills. He argued that learning leads development – unlike Piaget, who argued that development leads learning. This is an important distinction which warrants further explanation: depending on which perspective is adopted, there are different implications for understanding learning, curriculum and pedagogy.

While Vygotsky did not reject Piaget's research into the development of logico-mathematical operations, he placed more emphasis on development as a *socio-cultural process* and considered that the social, historical, cultural and biological aspects of development work together. In a socio-cultural model, everything that happens around the child influences learning and development. Vygotsky's work therefore extends Piaget's ideas about the development of cognition as internal and individualistic processes. Whereas Piaget emphasized the actions of the individual child in constructing knowledge through actions on objects, Vygotsky regarded *social interaction* and *activity* between peers and adults as important in creating meaning, making sense and conveying culture within a shared context.

Vygotsky did not claim that social interaction automatically leads learning and development: it is more the means used in social interaction, particularly language, that are taken over and *internalized* by the child. He defined a wide range of *psychological tools* that assist in the learning process. These tools include language, various systems for counting, mnemonic (memory-assisting) techniques, algebraic symbol systems, works of art, writing, schemes, diagrams, maps, technical drawings, and all sorts of conventional signs (Wertsch, 1985: 74). These psychological tools are also cultural tools because they are used in specific ways in specific contexts. The subject areas of the curriculum represent important ways of thinking and can be seen as tools to assist learning and development because they include concepts, ideas, skills, beliefs, attitudes, emotions and language, all of which contribute to disciplined ways of knowing (Newman and Holzman, 1993).

Learners engage in many different *social practices* that are situated in *communities of practice* (Wenger, 1998). For example, literacy and numeracy are social practices, which children learn through *joint enterprise* and *participation* in a community where people use these tools for different purposes in their everyday lives (Carr, 2001a; Roskos and Christie, 2000; Marsh and Hallett, 1999; Worthington and Carruthers, 2003). The ways in which learners acquire and use these psychological tools create new capabilities, and transform their abilities to *participate* in different contexts. Thus socio-cultural theorists conceptualize learning as the *transformation of participation and understanding,* rather than individual acquisition (Fleer and Richardson, 2004). As learners become more skilled and more knowledge-able, they are able to participate more competently and more independent-ly in different social practices. These processes are equally applicable to play as children become more knowledgeable about what is involved in different forms of play, and how knowledge can be used in the context of play. Vygotsky considered learning to be revolutionary because each successive layer of understanding transforms the meaning of previous understanding. These ideas represent a challenge to some long-held assumptions about early learning. There has been a tendency to regard children's thinking as naive and simplistic, because in Piagetian terms it has been seen as an immature form of adult thinking. In a socio-cultural model, children's ways of knowing, thinking, representing and understanding are important in the immediate term, and as the foundation for more mature and more complex forms of thought (Anning and Ring, 2004).

An important part of these transformational processes is the educative nature of relationships between children, peers and adults. Interactions with *more (or differently) knowledgeable others* lead the child towards what Vygotsky termed 'higher ground' or the next level of cognitive functioning. Learning or 'higher cognitive functioning' takes place on two distinct but interrelated planes – *the interpsychological and the intrapsychological*:

> First it appears on the social plane and then on the psychological plane. First it appears between people as an interpsychological category and then within the child as an intrapsychological category (Vygotsky, 1978: 57).

These processes are situated in social contexts and practices that generate qualitative, internalized transformations in a child's knowledge, skills and understanding. Thus relationships between individuals, actions, meanings and contexts, as well as the child's own internal motivations, all influence learning (Hakkarainen, 1999).

In investigating the relationship between learning and development, Vygotsky stated that if we determine the child's level of development from observations of what she or he can do independently of others, then we are considering only that which has already matured. He saw this as an inadequate basis for instruction and argued that we need to consider both mature and maturing processes (Newman and Holzman, 1993). *Internalization* (the process by which the interpsychological becomes the intrapsychological) is not a simple transfer from external activity to preformed internal cognitive structures. Shared and individual activity creates and develops these internal cognitive structures through language, activity, social interaction and environmental tools. These processes reflect the models of learning and the development of the brain outlined in Chapter 3: new experiences stimulate new connections, refine existing connections, and prune out redundant connections. The child is not a passive agent in this process: *active involvement* and *mutual engagement* are crucial in enabling learners to transform what is internalized through *guided reinvention and co-construction* (Jordan, 2004). In other words, more knowledgeable others help learners to learn about what is 'out there' in the world, and what is inside their own minds (Bruner, 1996). Learning involves processes of change that occur as an outcome of the relationships between individuals, other people and their environment: learners co-construct new understandings and capacities. Learning is therefore never simply a process of acquisition, transfer or assimilation. Learning, transformation and change are interrelated and interdependent, based on active involvement, mutual engagement and participation in sense- and meaning-making processes.

▓ LEARNING AND MOTIVATION

It is a common assumption in educational practice that children need to be *motivated* in order to learn. Vygotsky took a different perspective and argued that children need to learn in order to be motivated. Furthermore, he believed that the only good learning takes place *in advance of development*. However, as Bruner notes, this poses an apparent contradiction – how can good learning be in advance of development if a child is not conscious of what is to be learned, and does not have mastery and control? Bruner arrived at his own theory of what Vygotsky might have meant by this:

> If the child is enabled to advance by being under the tutelage of an adult or a more competent peer, then the adult or the aiding peer serves as a vicarious form of consciousness until such time as the learner is able to master his own action through his own consciousness and control. When the child achieves that conscious control over a new function or conceptual system, it is then that he is able to use it as a tool. Up to that point the tutor in effect performs the critical function of 'scaffolding' the learning task to make it possible for the child, in Vygotsky's word, to internalize external knowledge and convert it into a tool for conscious control (Bruner *et al*, 1976: 24).

The metaphor of *scaffolding* has become central to contemporary socio-cultural theories, and warrants further discussion.

▓ SCAFFOLDING

Scaffolding describes the ways in which more knowledgeable others provide assistance to learners. However, there is some debate about what is involved in scaffolding, who takes the lead, and whose intentions are paramount. In their discussion of socio-cultural theories, Ortega (2003) and Jordan (2004) problematize this concept. They agree that scaffolding has been interpreted to imply a one-to-one relationship in which the teacher, expert, or more knowledgeable other remains in control of what is to be learned, and how the teaching will be carried out – essentially a 'transmission' model. However, contemporary interpretations of this concept include a focus on *joint problem-solving and intersubjectivity*: the novice and expert establish mutual understanding of motivation, abilities, goals, interests and dispositions. The following example shows some of the pedagogical strategies that might typically be used in scaffolding learning, and demonstrates the importance of joint problem-solving and intersubjectivity.

Daniel, age five, planned to make a table from Tactic® – a large construction kit. He selected the correct pieces and assembled them in the right order. However, he became frustrated and dissatisfied with the final product because it was too wobbly to stand up. Daniel did not know how to interlock the tubes into the joints and asked his teacher for help. He had created a meaningful problem but lacked the requisite problem-solving strategies. The teacher used a range of pedagogical strategies: she *intervened* sensitively to *discuss* the problem with Daniel and *identify* possible solutions. She *modelled* the task using the correct language to describe her actions. She *demonstrated* how to line up the lugs on the poles with the hole in the joint and twist it to lock it firmly into place. Daniel watched intently, repeating some of the words and phrases used. The teacher asked him to show her how to interlock the tubes to *check his understanding*, offering further support by *revising* the task and *praising* his new skills. Her interactions were *contingent* on Daniel's motivations and goals so that the episode involved *mutual contributions* to teaching and learning. Daniel showed determination, concentration and perseverance and was pleased to be able to show a successfully completed table to his peers at review time. He was observed later that week demonstrating this process to another child using similar techniques to those modelled by the teacher.

This example shows how learning can lead development in the context of play. The foundations for learning were already there in terms of Daniel's interest, existing levels of competence and his confidence to approach an adult for assistance with a self-created problem. The relationship between learning and motivation can be a two-way process. Daniel had the motivation to get so far, but needed to learn new skills in order to be further motivated to complete the task successfully. His interactions with the teacher created an *enabling scaffold* that assisted Daniel's existing performance and led towards a higher level of performance. It is debatable whether Daniel would have discovered those principles for himself without the assistance of a more knowledgeable other (although this could have been a child). He could easily have become frustrated to the point of de-motivation without skilled assistance. Because of this assistance, learning became more efficient and provided further motivation. There was a synchronous teaching–learning dynamic between Daniel and his teacher, because they were acting productively in a *zone of proximal development*. This is the second key theme that we will explore in the next section.

THE ZONE OF PROXIMAL DEVELOPMENT

Vygotsky's theories about the *zone of proximal development* (ZPD) have received much attention in early childhood education, and there remains considerable debate about the validity and usefulness of this concept. In seeking to explain teaching and learning processes, Vygotsky developed his ideas about the ZPD, which he defined as:

> *the distance between the actual developmental level as determined by independent problem solving and the level of potential development as determined through problem solving under adult guidance or in collaboration with more capable peers.* The zone of proximal development defines those functions that have not yet matured but are in the process of maturation, functions that will mature tomorrow but are currently in an embryonic state. These functions could be termed the 'buds' or 'flowers' of development rather than the 'fruits' of development (1978: 86, original italics).

The ZPD can be seen as the common ground between where the learner is, and where she or he might usefully go next, which provides a foundation for *joint activity* between the novice and expert (adult or more capable peer). By identifying a learner's ZPD, the teacher can lead the child ahead of her or his development. There is no set prescription for identifying a child's ZPD: Vygotsky did not specify the process. However, the following pedagogical strategies are relevant:

- Observation and assessment, to gain feedback about learners and learning (what are this child's patterns of learning, dispositions, preferences, and interests?)

- Professional knowledge and expertise to make informed decisions about curriculum content (what are worthwhile skills, knowledge and understanding for this child/these children? How can those be presented to learners in meaningful, accessible ways? How can I build on children's own learning journeys through play?)

- Professional knowledge about learners (what has the child mastered, what are the next important steps in her learning?)

- Appropriate pedagogical strategies (what techniques and resources will support this child, and how much control can she take?)

- Productive interactions with learners (what do I need to do – guide, direct, scaffold, co-construct, stand back?)

Within the ZPD the novice and expert take different levels of responsibility. Learning takes place when the novice is enabled gradually to take over responsibility until mastery of the new role, skill or concept is achieved and internalized. In Vygotsky's view, this style of interaction (which he termed *instruction*) awakens many different functions that are in a stage of maturation lying in the ZPD. Therefore, rather than a 'watching and waiting' orientation, skilled practitioners need to know when and how to interact with children, to support learning and development. The 'more knowledgeable other' *assists performance*, as shown by Daniel's teacher in the preceding example. The assistance should support confidence and motivation. Children should be able to tolerate some struggle, but not become frustrated and de-motivated. At the same time, assistance should ensure that children are not bored, or feel that they have no control in the activity. Vygotsky believed that what children can do with assistance today, they can do by themselves tomorrow: the aim is to achieve conscious control and a higher level of cognitive functioning, thereby increasing mastery and independence. The teacher needs to recognize the child's intentions and meanings as the foundation on which to scaffold and co-construct understanding. Learning is accomplished with the progressive narrowing of the gap between the actual and the potential level of development, so that learners can participate more competently in different practices. The process is summarized in Figure 4.1.

■ LANGUAGE IN THE ZPD

Language is a significant part of the teaching–learning process. Language is, in Vygotsky's view, an essential 'psychological tool' for thinking and learning. Children need language-rich environments and effective support systems from people and resources. The language used by adults should be finely tuned to the child's level of development and understanding. Any new skills or concepts may need breaking down not just into sub-tasks but into sub-explanations so that the language can be matched to the child's progress, thereby becoming part of the scaffold to support learning. This does not necessarily imply oversimplification. There is substantial evidence to show that, from birth, adults expand on children's speech, giving a model of correct meaning, sentence structure, tense, grammar and word order. They make specific inputs of knowledge, technical language or elaborated explanations in response to a child's prompt, request or need. As the following example shows, these processes and strategies are equally important in play as children often create their own problems and challenges which need the support of a more knowledgeable other.

Vygotsky's theory of the zone of proximal development

In the ZPD the novice moves from other regulation
(interpsychological)

with

skilled assistance from more knowledgeable others
(peers and adults)

in

an enabling environment

with

appropriate materials, experiences and activities

combining

social, cultural and historical influences

acquiring

tools for thinking and learning, knowledge, skills, dispositions,
sense-making capacities

leading to

self-regulation (intrapsychological)

FIGURE 4.1   LEARNING IN THE ZPD

A group of Year 2/3 children were using Tactic™ for the first time. They established quickly that they wanted to make a push-along trolley for the younger children to use as a transporter for soft toys. The teacher was familiar with the equipment and, with the support of the teacher's guidebook, knew the correct technical terms for the different constructional elements. The children were able to select the correct pieces, but needed help with thinking through how to make axles and a chassis and how to align the joints to build a supporting framework. As the design evolved, they had to consider strength, stability, rigidity and load-bearing capacity. The children learnt about form, function and design, and quickly picked up the technical language which the teacher used throughout the interaction. This was demonstrated at review time when they were able to recall what they had done and learnt. The children were able to pass on their knowledge to other children, referring to the guidebook, the teacher and each other for support. This successful play episode led to a further challenge as the children decided to make a go-kart, and test how much weight it could bear. This project extended over a week, as they weighed each child in the Reception class, and tested the go-kart's strength, working from the lightest child, and recording their findings on a graph.

As well as shared conversations, *self-speech*, or *'out-loud thinking'* are used to guide behaviour and actions (by both adults and children). Self-speech is a characteristic of children's play as they structure and act out roles, sometimes taking on a parallel role. Self-speech can serve many purposes, as a mnemonic device, retrieving information, a self-regulation system, and a conscious way of gaining control over unconscious thought processes. It is also an effective way of revising and rehearsing information which needs to be memorized, and forms the basis of more skilled communication through speech and writing.

▇ JOINT ACTIVITY IN THE ZPD

Through *shared conversations* and *joint activity* practitioners can model essential tools for learning, such as reflecting on action, posing questions, noticing cause and effects, talking through actions, requesting and offering further support or information. The more knowledgeable other needs to receive and listen as much as to give and talk, in order to ensure *mutual contributions*. Pretending not to know can also be a powerful motivator to encourage children to demonstrate their skills and knowledge. This strategy allows the teacher to monitor the child's progress, aids further identification of the next steps, and thus informs curriculum planning. Through *assisted performance* learners move towards higher levels of cognitive functioning as their abilities to think and reason are changed, and they develop the ability to regulate independent action and behaviour. As new knowledge, skills and processes are internalized they form part of the child's individual developmental achievement: tools can be used in new and creative ways, and learners can transfer knowledge across different contexts. Children engage in activities willingly and exercise conscious awareness, thus developing *metacognitive skills and strategies*. Independent and interdependent action are important aspects of the teaching–learning relationship. One of the weaknesses of classroom approaches that stress the importance of independence and autonomy is that false assumptions are often made about children's levels of conscious awareness of their activity and their ability to control and direct their own learning (Bennett *et al*, 1997). If children are to gain control of their own learning, they need to learn metacognitive skills and strategies that make learning more efficient. Furthermore, we cannot assume that children are capable always of taking control because they may encounter novel situations and problems that they cannot always manage independently, as the following example illustrates.

> Joanne, age three, selected a range of jigsaws from an open shelf. The selection appeared to be deliberate, starting with easy inset trays, which Joanne accomplished without difficulty. After completion, each jigsaw was returned to the shelf and another selected. Joanne graduated to four-piece tessellating jigsaws set in a frame, and again completed these successfully though not as quickly. Her next selection was a more complex twelve-piece tessellating jigsaw that caused her some difficulty. She used all the correct actions, rotating the pieces, testing them against each other and against the frame. However, the level of cognitive challenge was too high and Joanne replaced the pieces randomly in a pile and put the jigsaw at the back of the cupboard. (Joanne actually checked to see if anyone was looking when she did this, perhaps because she understood the nursery 'rules' that jigsaws should be finished before being put away.)

This example shows how Joanne appeared to be checking through her existing competences as though she needed recognition of these to spur her on to a further challenge. She began with safe, known tasks and applied her skills to the more challenging task, showing evidence of some metacognitive awareness. Joanne had created the problem for herself by selecting the difficult jigsaw; she had recognized and tried to deal with the problem but lacked a sufficiently wide repertoire of problem-solving skills to complete the task. Joanne appeared to be operating at the edge of a ZPD but could not progress because there was no 'knowledgeable other', either adult or child, to provide assistance. Without assistance Joanne was de-motivated. This reinforces the point made earlier that children need to learn in order to be motivated, and play can provide children with motivation to act (Hakkarainen, 1999).

▨ PROBLEMATIZING THE ZPD

We have concentrated on Vygotsky's theories about the ZPD in relation to the individual child. This finely tuned approach to teaching and learning raises many problems and presents many pedagogical challenges. Productive interactions within the ZPD demand:

- high-quality interactions

- a richly resourced learning environment

- effective ongoing diagnosis to ensure an accurate match between the task and the learner

- responsiveness to the learner's own interests, ideas and preferences

- reciprocity between teacher and learner

- mutual contributions by the teacher and learner to the activity

- overt modelling of thinking and learning strategies.

The concept of the ZPD appears to imply a one-to-one relationship. In a parent–child context this might be achievable, but for educators in school or pre-school settings the everyday practicalities of time, number of children, routines, space and facilities can act as constraints. In the context of play it is especially difficult to give the children the attention they may need, particularly in school contexts where other demands impact upon how teachers spend their time. In the study by Bennett *et al* (1997), the teachers all valued play, but often had to prioritize teacher-directed activities rather than playing alongside children. Their decisions were influenced substantially by expectations from parents, governors and the demands of the curriculum.

The ZPD remains a challenging concept because it relates to problem-solving skills and to performance in other domains or areas of competence – social, physical, affective, cognitive. Furthermore, there is no single zone for each individual child: she or he may be working in many different zones in these domains. There are cultural zones as well as individual zones, because there are cultural variations in the competences, skills and knowledge that are valued in different communities. The modes of social interaction vary across different social and cultural groups (Rogoff, 2003). While play is valued highly in some cultures, the notion that children learn primarily through play is not universally shared

(Rogoff, 2003; Brooker, 2002). The concept of the ZPD need not be taken exclusively as an individual or joint (two-way) process. Newman and Holzman (1993) have interpreted Vygotsky's theories to argue that the learning environment should be a zone for proximal development. Creating shared zones involves:

- structuring and organizing the environment to facilitate high-quality interactions between adults and peers

- providing resources which afford opportunities for problem-creating as well as problem-solving

- making time for shared thinking, conversation and interaction

- using a range of pedagogical strategies and interactions

- making time to understand children's learning, and following their learning journeys.

Creating shared zones is not a difficult concept: it is what good practitioners do all the time through their *pedagogical framing, techniques and strategies* (see Chapters 5 and 6). Children can be educated effectively and creatively within whole-class, group and individual contexts, as long as practitioners remain mindful of the need to combine adult- and child-initiated activities, including play, and opportunities for playful activities. Children create their own ZPD through their play and self-initiated activities, which enables them to express their interests, dispositions, motivation, ongoing cognitive concerns and play themes. The zones that children create may not always be approved by adults, because they create their own rules, games and ways of knowing. For example, children often learn with adults how to ride a bicycle: they learn personal and road safety, and the Highway Code. In collaboration with their peers, they may learn to do wheelies, jumps and skids, take-offs from ramps, and set each other challenges that are concerned more with risk rather than safety. Play changes the nature of power relationships within educational settings because children are in control, or may act subversively to take control. For example, Sam had his own ways of dealing with low-level demands in the Literacy Strategy:

Sam (age five years seven months, Year 1) was in the Red (high-ability) group for literacy. The activity given to this lively group of children was well within their capabilities, and they did not need the 20 minutes allocated. Sam was clearly an astute manager of classroom processes. The teacher was absorbed with another group, and trusted the Red group to get on with their work. At regular intervals, Sam left his table, crept quietly towards specific children (all boys) and was observed talking to them briefly. As he crept back to his table, he always checked on the teacher's gaze. Clearly some sort of conspiracy was going on. At play time, Sam gathered together this group of friends, and they all took various Superhero figures from their trays. Sam had used his 'spare' work time to organize their playtime. Out on the playground, the energy, involvement, skills and enthusiasm of these boys contrasted starkly with the demands made on them in the more formal, sedentary activities that took up the whole of the morning.

Displays of performance in such child-controlled contexts are often linked with their self-esteem and peer-group affiliation rather than pleasing adults. If children only learn within a ZPD that is controlled by adults as experts, they will never learn to contest or change existing knowledge: they will merely reproduce what is already validated and used in society (Lambert and Clyde, 2003). We can therefore argue that play and playfulness create the conditions where children learn beyond the zones of adult control. Children create their own zones in which their activities (psychological and social) are at different (and possibly more challenging) levels than the controlled interactions in an adult-led ZPD. Winnicot (1971) defines this as *potential space* – the possible range of the child's omnipotence in which children see themselves as more capable than they are in other contexts, and act accordingly.

For Vygotsky, learning is predominantly, though not exclusively, a transactional process involving many different types of interactions and teaching styles, including play. This leads us into the third of Vygotsky's theories which is important in developing our understanding of teaching and learning, namely the role of instruction in development.

THE RELATIONSHIP BETWEEN TEACHING AND LEARNING

Vygotsky regarded *instruction* as central to learning and development. His use of the term 'instruction' may seem instrumental and didactic: however, it encompasses a wide range of *pedagogical strategies* and does not imply a simple transmission model whereby the teacher instructs and the child learns. The social relationship, which Vygotsky referred to as 'teaching', is a one-to-one relationship between novice and expert, or teacher and learner. It has been left to others to interpret his theories more broadly in the context of education. Socio-cultural theories about teaching and learning challenge some long-established tenets in early childhood education. Piaget stated that each time one prematurely teaches a child something he could have discovered for himself, that child is prevented from inventing it and consequently from understanding it completely (Meadows, 1993: 336). This implies a high level of activity on the part of the learner, and a complex range of sense-making capacities. While a certain amount of struggle is necessary and desirable, too much emphasis on discovery learning means that children constantly have to reinvent the wheel. As we have argued, children are novice learners and may need skilled assistance even in their play, particularly where the context or materials create opportunities for challenge. We cannot assume that children, or even adults, are always in a positive state of equilibrium that enables them to make the best of their motivation and learning capabilities. Skilled learners also need the support of more or differently knowledgeable others to develop their expertise.

ASSISTED PERFORMANCE

Central to our understanding of socio-cultural theories about the unity between teaching and learning is the concept of *assisted performance*. This is defined as what a child can do using internal motivations and capabilities, but with support from more knowledgeable others and from the learning environment. The people and the resources around the learner can provide a *scaffold* which supports the transition from dependent to independent activity. In a Vygotskian model, teaching is most effective when assistance is offered within the ZPD, and is most responsive to enhancing the learner's performance. The assistance can be provided by a more knowledgeable, more skilled or more experienced 'other' which, as we have argued, can be an adult or a peer. Contemporary interpretations of Vygotsky's ideas stress the importance of the learner's own activity in seeking and using many forms of assistance in the learning environment, such as computers and other information and communication technologies, materials, resources and tools. Thus novices and experts can *co-construct* meaning, knowledge and understanding. For Jordan (2004), the concept of *co-construction* is a powerful extension of Vygotsky's ideas about scaffolding and the ZPD. The concept of *co-construction* emphasizes the child as a powerful player in his/her own learning:

> To co-construct is to construct with others [and] places emphasis on teachers and children studying meanings in favour of acquiring facts. Studying meaning requires teachers and children to make sense of the world, interpreting and understanding activities and observations as they interact with each other (Jordan, 2004: 33).

In this model, assisted performance is *joint performance* and relies on the active participation of the child (*hands-on and brains-on activity*). Assisted performance involves learning to learn and learning about learning. Where more knowledgeable others assist performance they should not oversimplify the task. The task difficulty is held constant but the child's role is made simpler, or more complex, by means of *graduated or mediated assistance* from the adult. For example, Laura, age three, wanted to help her Dad make a new shed for the garden. She insisted on using the real hammer and nails and would not be fobbed off with child-sized, safer alternatives. Her Dad demonstrated how to use the hammer correctly by knocking in the nails part of the way and allowing Laura to finish them off. He also realized that Laura's interest and skills could be developed further by having access to wood and tools, which led to many other episodes of designing and constructing.

Oversimplification of tasks and materials can be patronizing to children and can result in unchallenging learning environments. Children can act as more knowledgeable others and, in some contexts, can be more knowledgeable than adults. They may have more accurate or detailed knowledge about an event or topic, particularly in relation to their home and community experiences. Worthwhile activities can be adult- or child-initiated. In the former, the practitioner needs to use a complex range of strategies to inspire or maintain the child's interest and involvement. Even in a play-based activity the child may be task-oriented, as shown by Daniel (making a table in an earlier example) and Laura. Sayeed and Guerin (2000) highlight the importance of *mediated learning experiences (MLE)* in play, particularly for children with special educational needs, and from a range of cultural and linguistic backgrounds. In MLE, adults (or more knowledgeable others) use a wide range of strategies to support the child's skills, knowledge and performance (see Em's story in Chapter 8).

SUSTAINED SHARED THINKING AND PLAYING

In the government-funded studies on Effective Provision for Pre-school Education (EPPE) and Researching Effective Pedagogy in the Early Years (REPEY), the research teams have identified progress and achievements in relation to what happens in the settings in order to support children's learning (Moyles *et al*, 2002; Siraj-Blatchford and Sylva, 2004). They found that in the most effective settings, positive cognitive outcomes are associated with adult–child interactions that involve *sustained shared thinking*. This involves mutual engagement and involvement between the child and adult, based around potentially instructive content (something is being learned). The concept of sustained shared thinking requires practitioners to think about how they interact with children to support learning, and how they might engage in *sustained shared playing*, as described in Chapters 5 and 6. The nature and extent of adult involvement and assistance will depend on the learner, and the playing–learning–teaching context. This applies equally to the earliest games of peek-a-boo, as to becoming a skilled chess player. The child's intentions and motivations are important aspects of sustained shared thinking. As the interaction develops, the intentions of the activity may change. Changes may be initiated by the child in response to assistance from a peer or adult, or to the changing nature of the activity, as is frequently demonstrated in children's play. The practitioner may also influence the child's intentions by introducing new knowledge, skills or understanding. This does not imply that the practitioner should dominate or lead the activity. In sustained shared playing, the interactions should remain responsive to the child. As the child's involvement and expertise develop, he or she can help the practitioner to provide assistance by requesting specific support, assigning a role or activity to the more knowledgeable other and demonstrating a new level of performance. Creating unity between playing, learning and teaching involves *reciprocity* between the child's and adult's intentions: both are involved in co-constructing meaning and understanding.

■ SELF-ASSISTED PERFORMANCE

As children's experience and expertise develop, they become more capable of assisting their own performance. They develop *metacognitive skills and strategies* that enable them to make choices and decisions, exercise conscious control and awareness of their activities, and seek out help from other people, tools and resources in the environment. This is a progression in play activities that adults sometimes dread, because children are more likely to take risks, set challenges for themselves and each other, and test their own skills, strength and competences. At the same time, children's sense of their own mastery leads to positive self-esteem and 'can do' orientations to further learning. They may still need activities that involve practice and repetition in order to consolidate their skills, and develop the abilities to transfer these across different contexts.

TOWARDS INDEPENDENT PERFORMANCE

Through experience and activity, children internalize the rules, processes, skills and concepts necessary to independent performance. They experience quantitative and qualitative transformations: they know more, and they know differently. They can act more competently across the domains of learning – cognitive, psycho-motor and socio-affective. Children progress towards 'self-sustained take-off' and may act as more knowledgeable others in collaboration with their peers (as Daniel did in his construction activity). Learners remain interdependent but may become more selective and intentional in terms of seeking assistance based on their own motivation, goals and interests, and providing their own *self-scaffolding*:

> Ultimately this 'scaffolding' technique of teaching has been so well internalized by the learners that they can provide it for themselves in new learning situations; the learning child internalizes the teacher's actions and reflections, transforming them into his or her own way of solving that particular problem or doing that particular task, but also internalizing and developing more general tools – how to observe, how to imitate, how to analyse, how to scaffold one's own cognitive activity or another person's. These powerful 'metacognitive' activities contribute to making the learner into a 'self-running problem-solver' (Meadows, 1993: 344).

THE PROGRESSIVE SPIRAL OF LEARNING

Vygotsky considered learning as a lifelong process with no final rung in the ladder of competence. Bruner (1966) characterizes this process as a 'learning spiral' to indicate how learners achieve qualitative and quantitative transformations in their competence. The learning strategies outlined above are *recursive* (we may use them repeatedly in many different contexts) and *incremental* (we may use them more expertly). As children become increasingly skilled learners, they can use a range of strategies to revise, maintain or enhance performance. At the same time, they need qualitative and quantitative changes in the assistance needed to achieve their own goals, as well as those set by others. However, progression in learning is not seamless or inevitable. Young children frequently have bursts of energy, interest and motivation where they are willing and able to learn. At times they can appear to regress as though a plateau has been reached and they cannot cope with any further advances for a while. Children may regress if there has been some upheaval or stress in their lives, or if there is poor continuity of provision across phases.

VYGOTSKY'S THEORIES OF PLAY

Vygotsky wrote little about play and his theories are more evocative than definitive (Newman and Holzman, 1993). However, his ideas offer some challenging perspectives, particularly if we relate these to the three areas we have already explored. Play for Vygotsky is mainly role play. He was concerned with its function as developmental activity, and regarded play as the leading source of development in the pre-school years, but not the dominant form of activity. Thus we can link the concepts of play leading development and learning leading development to explore the processes which link playing, learning and teaching. Practical examples examine the implications for curriculum planning and the role of the adult.

Vygotsky challenged the view that play can be defined simply on the basis of pleasure since there are other things which may be pleasurable for the child and equally there may be some forms of play which are not pleasurable. The main characteristics of play are:

- imaginary situations

- subordination to rules

- liberation from situational constraints

- definition of roles.

Like all other higher psychological functions, play is social in origin, is mediated by language and is learned with other people (peers and adults) in social situations. Vygotsky believed that all forms of play have imaginary elements and that all play is necessarily rule-bound by the presence of these imaginary elements. In combining the 'what if' and 'as if' elements, children suspend real-world behaviour and rules in order to enter into the imaginary situation (although the imaginary situation may contain real-world elements and rules). A further characteristic of play is *semiotic* activity – the ability to dissociate the meanings of objects and actions from the real objects and actions (making one thing stand for something else), and to use signs and symbols to convey meaning. Play thus creates early experiences of complex, abstract thinking in which action increasingly arises from ideas rather than from things. Vygotsky's characteristics challenge Piagetian notions of stages and hierarchies.

Children's thinking and activity in play can be complex, and they engage in abstract forms of thinking from an earlier age than Piaget identified. The formats of socio-dramatic play are excellent scenarios for learning and development (Ortega, 2003).

For Vygotsky, the developmental course of play is characterized by the changing relationships between imaginary situations and rules in play. In free play, children create an overt imaginary situation with covert rules. These can be implicit, or explicitly negotiated at the onset of play, or during the development of a play sequence. Children establish rules about roles, props, actions and behaviours that may change as the play develops. The rules are usually dependent on the context and are the preconditions of successful play experiences. Play activities provide a *unifying mechanism* which gives *coherence* to activities, relations, objects and tools (Hakkarainen, 1999). Coherence is established through the negotiation of meaning and the co-construction of play themes and scripts, which involves:

- setting the scene (the psychological frame for the play)

- developing the plot (co-construction of events, sequences, characters, play themes)

- developing the script (joint construction of meanings and identities)

- sustaining the play (moving in and out of the play to monitor coherence and negotiate changes).

HOGWARTS WIZARD SCHOOL The following episode exemplifies these processes. It was recorded by Joanna Cook (2003), who carried out research on role-play in her Reception class. The children are in the role play area, which has been designed as Hogwarts – the wizard school from the Harry Potter stories by J.K. Rowling. Jake has taken on the role of the three-headed dog. Alice organizes roles for Richard and Lucy:

> Alice: You're Hermione and I'm Hermione's Mum and Richard is Hermione's Dad. I wonder why our dog has been so naughty. He's Hermione's Dad and you're Hermione's Mum. I'm looking after the dog.
> (*Alice fetched a wizard's hat and put it on. She bent down to Jake, gave him a pink sponge [food], then ruffled his hair and pretended to pat him.*)
> Alice: (*to Richard and Jake*) You two play about and eat sweets as bones. I need a doll.
> (*to Lucy*) Let's get our doggies.

> (*to Jake who is eating 'bones' [pink sponges]*)
> You've had enough.
> > (*Jake decides he is going to be the dad. He stands up and gives a piece of plastic cheese to Richard*)
>
> Jake: I've got some cheese.
> Alice: You're dogs. You just have to crawl. Give us our cheese back.
> > (*Both boys crawl back into their kennel and hide. They each have a bone and pretend to eat them*)
>
> Jake: This is our kennel in Hogwarts.
> Lucy to Alice: Richard's turned into a dog.
> Alice to Lucy: But he can't.
> Richard: (*from inside the kennel*) I'm a doggy.
> Alice to Lucy: No, turn him back into Hermione's dad. We want someone to marry.
> > (*Alice and Lucy pick up wands and start chanting to the boys*)
>
> Marry me, marry me. Abracadabra. Make Richard turn into a boy. Abracadabra.
> > (*Richard comes out of the kennel, and starts running around the role play area with the girls chasing him and waving their wands. Lucy sits down – she has lost interest in the chase*).
>
> Alice to Lucy: Hey Lucy. There's a big surprise for you. These wands will turn Richard into a grown up.
> > (*Alice and Lucy wave their wands over Richard who is now standing in front of them*)
>
> Alice to Richard: I've got off his doggy hair.
> Richard: I've put on real hair.
> Alice to Lucy: He's standing up like a real person. (Cook, 2003)

Alice and Lucy are determined to set the rules for this game: when the boys try to step out of their assigned roles, Alice changes the rules in order to maintain control and flow of the play. The players accept the rules: they use language to communicate their understanding of their roles, and signify changing from one role to another (dog to a grown-up). Making and changing rules are also part of the process of co-construction of meaning and activity in play.

In contrast to free play, games have overt rules with a covert imaginary situation. Vygotsky used the example of chess, where players have to abide by clearly defined rules but at the same time imagine that the pieces move in specified ways and signify certain actions (1978: 95). Similarly, when playing football children assign their positions according to the established rules of the game but often decide which of their favourite players they represent. They act in the role of their current sporting heroes, exaggerating injuries, disputing the referee's decisions and reacting ecstatically to goal scoring. Play is linked essentially to the fulfilment of the child's needs, motivations, incentives to act and affective states.

Vygotsky considered that a full understanding of play can be achieved only when these factors are taken into account (Hakkarainen, 1999).

In contrast to Piaget, who distinguished between practice play, symbolic play and games with rules, Vygotsky linked play and imagination with rules in terms of gradual, qualitative shifts from an emphasis on the imaginary situation to the dominance of rules. As we have seen in the Hogwarts episode, rules stem from the imaginary situation:

> 'Let's pretend we are in Hogwarts.'
> 'Let's act as if we are certain characters.'

The children then created rules around the characters, and their interpretation of how their characters could act and what they could say. Newman and Holzman (1993) have argued that Vygotsky's theories about rules have created a paradox in our understanding of play and its role in development. On the one hand, imaginative or free play liberates children from everyday rules and situational constraints. At the same time, the play episodes created by children carry implicit rules that are necessary to establish and maintain the imaginary situation. Vygotsky argued that these rules of imagination both liberate children from everyday constraints but also impose other constraints. Children know implicitly that they must control their desire to act spontaneously outside their assigned roles in order not to destroy the play sequence. As in the Hogwarts episode, they may change or renegotiate their roles, but if too much disagreement occurs the play is likely to disintegrate. Equally, if children cheat or ignore rules in game play, such as Snakes and Ladders, part of the meaning and pleasure of the game is destroyed. It appears that subordination to rules and restraining spontaneous action are a means to pleasure and success in play. Both derive from inclusion, negotiation, cooperation and the co-construction of shared meanings.

The concept of subordination to rules is intriguing in the context of early childhood. Often children create quite elaborate, clearly defined rules to sustain and develop play and they will, for the most part, abide by these rules for the pleasure gained from inclusion, a sense of agency and control. They often use sophisticated (and sometimes quite ruthless) self-determining and self-maintaining strategies. In contrast, teachers sometimes have to wage a continuous battle to maintain externally imposed rules such as lining up, not running indoors, sitting still for a story. Perhaps this tension between resisting externally imposed rules and subordination to self-imposed rules tells us something about the anarchic nature of childhood and the ways in which children view themselves in relation to more dominant and powerful others. Play gives children the opportunities to act more knowledgeably and more powerfully, and to exercise control in an adult-dominated world. Play can change the nature of power relationships within educational contexts as the locus of control is with the children rather than with the adult. This perhaps explains why play, especially free play, is difficult to accommodate and manage in educational settings.

▓ PLAY AND MOTIVATION: REAL-LIFE PLANS

For Vygotsky the value of play is related to both cognitive and affective development through the fulfilment of a child's needs, incentives to act and motivations. The maturing of new interests and motives for action is a dominant factor in development:

> Action in the imaginative sphere, in an imaginary situation, the creation of voluntary intentions and the formation of real-life plans and volitional motives – all appear in play and make it the highest level of pre-school development. The child moves forward essentially through play activity. Only in this sense can play be considered the leading activity that determines a child's development (Vygotsky, 1978: 102–103).

The notion of the formation of 'real-life plans' is interesting, particularly in the context of imaginative play. Children do not step from the real world into an imaginary world but maintain a continuous dialogue between the two. Play thus reveals the unity of children's development, the varied sources of knowledge they draw upon and the novel, creative contexts they co-construct. Therefore in order to understand play we need to understand the special character of these needs, inclinations, incentives and motives, as demonstrated in the following Fire Station episode.

FIRE STATION ROLE PLAY The following episode was recorded by Sheena Wright, an early years advisory teacher, in a Year 1 class (age five to six). The role-play area was a Fire Station, which had been designed collaboratively between the children and the teacher. The resources included:

> Wellington boots, wet play clothes, walkie-talkies, two telephones, whiteboards, musical instruments, uniforms and helmets, fire engine, keyboard, tables and chairs, plastic bottles, selection of tools, torches, tubing and hoses, ladder, flashing blue light, wall chart showing the rota for the 'watches', coils of rope, notepads, tape-recorded messages, large bricks, large noticeboard covered in children's paintings of fire engines, signs and symbols (for example, Keep Clear, Emergency Exit, Fire Station, No Entry, Fire and Rescue Services).

The children had visited a fire station, and had learnt about 'watches' – the firefighters' pattern of shifts. They drew substantially on knowledge gleaned from a children's cartoon – *Fireman Sam,* and from a popular (adult) television drama series called *'London's Burning'*. Five children were in the role play area (two girls and three boys).

> What can I be? (*getting dressed*)
> I'm a fireman
> I'm chief
> OK
> Can I have the black hat?
> Where's the chief's hat?
> You can wear the red watch.
> (*In office/control centre*)
> Number 98 – there's a fire down town.
> What do we have to do today? (*using walkie-talkie to ask chief*)
> See if the road is busy.
> *Playing the triangle and bells to alert to the fire. Writing on the whiteboards*
> Number 2 fire. House number 2.
> Yes but what street?
> *Pushing the fire engine along (cardboard box). Two children are wearing hats and tabards. Two children use plastic bottles as oxygen tanks tied to their backs. Back in the office/control centre the chief has stayed with the typewriter – singing to himself and feeding in a sheet of paper. Types, rings the bell and shouts:*
> Ring the jingly bit.
> This is officer Bradley. Fire Fire.
> There's a baby locked upstairs.
> I'll get it.
> You didn't get it.
> Ssssss (*putting fire out*)
> Fire's gone. I've saved the house.
> *Children extend the play beyond the role play area into the classroom. They pass a pretend baby into the fire engine. One child is getting out his tools:*
> I've got the baby out, put it in the cot.
> *Back in the control centre the chief is reporting:*
> OK a robber has blown up the house.
> We definitely need to go.
> Go Go Go. We have to put our fire coats on cos we're the ones going in.
> And a safety hat (*selects one with a visor*)
> Boss am I late?
> We need you on a job.
> I need a safety thing (*harness*) so I don't fall over.
> (*fire bell ringing again*)
> Dog stuck up a tree.
> Jobs not for me – I go at night times. I'm blue watch.
> This is a burn seed – fire pops out. See that? (*backdraft*)

> You need your oxygen so you can breathe.
> (*Chief writing on the whiteboard*)
> I can do a hundred sentences (Wright, 2002).

This episode exemplifies many of the socio-cultural theories explored in this chapter. The teacher was instrumental in supporting the play, as evidenced in her pedagogical framing (visit to the fire station, developing the role-play area with the children, providing opportunities for children to make choices and develop their own ideas). The children were skilled players, and set the psychological frame for the play (assigning roles, ascribing meaning to objects). They quickly flowed into the play script, drawing on real-world knowledge (they understood the concept of a burn seed, the pattern of watches, and the many uses of literacy in the fire station). They used language, tools, objects and symbols in imaginative ways to convey pretence and meaning. Thought was separated from objects: for example, the washing-up bottles became oxygen tanks. They understood the real/not real paradox in their creative transformations of objects, roles and actions, showing abstract thinking and actions. Their cognitive activity included logic, reasoning, memory, recall of factual knowledge, communication, organization and the ability to negotiate shared meanings. The richness and quality of the play were influenced by self-restraint and self-determination. This episode shows how imagination and creativity are related to cognitive and affective development. Action arose from ideas, which allowed the children to act as if they were fire officers in real-life situations.

Play is a powerful vehicle for learning (and for learning leading development), thinking, generating ideas and communicating. Play thus creates potential spaces in which 'a child always behaves beyond his average age, above his daily behaviour; in play it is as though he were a head taller than himself' (Vygotsky, 1978: 102).

These activities demonstrate the interaction between socio-cultural influences (interpsychological) and internal processes (intrapsychological). Through play children manipulate and change their relationship with reality. This presents another paradox of play: children play to escape from reality, but at the same time they get closer to reality, particularly in their role play. In acting out roles they can experience what it is like to be a Mum, Dad, police officer, pop star, superhero; however, these roles are rule-bound because they are dependent on their interpretations of real-life behaviour. Thus imagination in play is not trivial or frivolous because it is linked to the development of consciousness and awareness of reality. Vygotsky stated that the relationship between realistic thinking and imagination is complex and can lead to higher forms of cognition. Skilled, experienced players free themselves from the need for props and often improvise:

> Bobby and Jamel were regular, experienced play partners who repeated similar themes based on karate-style play-fighting. One morning Jamel was waiting for the nursery to open and saw Bobby approaching some distance away. They both immediately adopted a karate position and gradually advanced towards each other using these movements. As they drew nearer, they circled each other with karate chops in mock aggression. There was intense eye contact, but no body contact and no dialogue other than sound effects for the karate chops. The play became more energetic and Bobby intentionally fell to the ground in a defensive position to signal his 'defeat'. Jamel placed his foot lightly on Bobby's abdomen and raised both hands in a victory salute – both boys were smiling at this point. Bobby then got up, dusted himself down and said 'OK, what shall we play today?'

Both boys were intensely engaged in this episode and blocked out all the activity going on around them. Bobby and Jamel could literally play with their play: it was so well practised that intentions could be communicated through symbolic gestures (mime, drama and movement) rather than verbal negotiation.

In play children are capable of abstract levels of thinking and often reveal themselves as keen observers and intuitive interpreters of other people's actions, characteristics and behaviour that goes far beyond simple mimicry and imitation. Teachers often report that young children playing school can represent teacher behaviours with alarming accuracy and some dramatic licence. Although Vygotsky did not eulogize play, he did invest it with profound significance for children's learning and development. However, he also noted a familiar problem with play which has dogged early years practitioners and theorists alike, namely that play bears little resemblance to what it leads to, at least in its most productive forms.

> Deep play is playing with fire. It is the kind of serious play that tidy and even permissive institutions for educating young children cannot live with happily, for the mandate requires them to carry out their work with due regard to minimizing the chagrin concerning the outcomes achieved. And deep play is a poor vehicle for that (Woodhead *et al*, 1991: 270).

Newman and Holzman's (1993) interpretations of Vygotsky's theories regard play as revolutionary activity because it involves imaginary situations and is concerned with meaning-making which is often novel and creative. Play involves transformational processes in children's knowledge, skills dispositions and understanding, thus enabling them to move towards higher levels of performance. In spite of positive valida-tions for play, practitioners still face a number of tensions in their practice. Deep play is serious and significant; however, it is difficult to control or assess in terms of outcomes. Vygotsky's theories indicate that outcomes are not immediately visible through what we might term surface features, but can be accessed through internal analysis. This is an important issue, and will be explored fully in the following chapters. Profound internal analyses of play, by academics and practitioners, have begun to delve beneath the surface actions of children's play to reveal their learning, patterns of thinking and understanding. Although Vygotsky warned against a pedantic intellectualization of play, research is demonstrating the relationships between playing and learning in different settings and contexts, and the efficacy of play for all areas of learning and develop-ment.

One further perspective has challenged our own thinking about play and has informed some lively debates with practitioners. Newman and Holzman (1993) have argued that play can be seen as revolutionary activity because it is concerned with learning leading development and meaning-making, in individual or collective zones. This has led us to question whether play is sometimes undervalued (as discussed in Chapter 1) because its significance is not fully understood, and because practi-tioners are wary of its revolutionary nature. Practitioners find it difficult to manage play because they cannot always predict outcomes or interpret the educational significance of different forms of play (Bennett *et al.*, 1997). This presents a dilemma: play can be limited if practitioners strive to control outcomes through structures that constrain deep play and revolutionary activity. Unchallenging environments can be disempower-ing for children and fail to harness the educational potential of play. Therefore the concept of a co-constructed curriculum is particularly relevant in order to enhance the quality of learning and teaching through play.

In summary, it is interesting to note some distinct changes in the theoretical discourses in early childhood. In the 'secret garden' metaphor, children were likened to growing plants, and needed nurturing conditions in which to flourish. The image of the child as unfolding and blossoming into maturity fails to capture the complexity of learning and development or the fundamental role of adults. The dominant contemporary metaphor is learning as building, participating and co-constructing. On the basis of the theories explored in Chapter 3 and in this chapter, we consider that social-cultural perspectives on playing, learning and teaching demand a reconceptualization of how play/learning environments are organized and, in particular, how practitioners might develop their roles in play. In the following chapters we will examine the practical implications of these theoretical perspectives.

FURTHER READING

These texts are more theoretical, and present contemporary perspectives on researching, theorizing and understanding play. They will be of interest to readers who are working on their own research or who want to develop their understanding of the theories explored in this chapter. Anning *et al* (2004) is strongly recommended because it provides excellent theory–practice links, based on contemporary research from leading early childhood specialists in the UK, New Zealand and Australia.

Anning, A., Cullen, J. and Fleer, M. (2004) (eds) *Early Childhood Education: Society and Culture*, London, Sage.

Hakkarainen, P. (1999) Play and Motivation, in Y. Engeström, R. Miettinen and R-L. Punamaki (1999) (eds) *Perspectives on Activity Theory*, Cambridge, Cambridge University Press, 231–249.

Lambert, E.B. and Clyde, M. (2003) Putting Vygotsky to the Test, in D.E. Lytle (ed.) *Play and Educational Theory and Practice, Play and Culture Studies*, Vol. 5, Westport, Conn., Praeger, 59–98.

Ortega, R. (2003) Play, Activity and Thought, Reflections on Piaget's and Vyogotsky's Theories, in D.E. Lytle (ed.) *Play and Educational Theory and Practice*, Westport, Conn., Praeger, 99–116.

Reifel, S. (2001) *Theory in Context and Out, Play and Culture Studies*, Vol. 3, Connecticut, Ablex.

Roopnarine, J.L. (2002) *Conceptual, Social-Cognitive, and Contextual Issues in the Fields of Play, Play and Culture Studies*, Vol. 4, Connecticut, Ablex.

Saracho, O. and Spodek, B. (2002) *Contemporary Perspectives in Early Childhood Curriculum*, Connecticut, Information Age Publishing.

CHAPTER FIVE

Developing Play in the Curriculum

The first four chapters have provided a detailed exploration of play, drawing on multi-theoretical perspectives. The following chapters focus on improving the quality of play in practice, while continuing to make connections between theory and practice. There is much useful theory and practical guidance from research studies, but what really matters in educational settings are the theories, values and beliefs of practitioners, and their ability to build their personal knowledge and understanding through observation, discussion, reflection and ongoing professional development. This chapter examines how practitioners can make informed choices about curriculum design and pedagogical approaches in their settings, based on sound theories and principles. The approaches advocated here respect some of the tenets of the ideological tradition that we explored in Chapter 1, but at the same time provide a secure justification for play that is informed by evidence from research and curriculum models from other countries. This chapter explores five key themes: understanding the processes that link playing and learning; examining different curriculum models; exploring the plan–do–review approach to integrating child- and adult-initiated activities, designing a curriculum that incorporates play, and planning for progression and continuity. The following three chapters focus on the linked themes of developing a pedagogy for play, improving assessment practices, and enhancing practice through professional development.

PROCESSES THAT LINK PLAYING AND LEARNING

Practitioners can develop informed understanding of play through examining the processes that link playing and learning. This can be achieved by a critical analysis of children at play, which includes observing what is happening in play-learning contexts (behaviour, language, actions and interactions, use of tools, signs and symbols), understanding the child as player/learner and reflecting on the quality of provision. By tuning in to play, practitioners can ensure that their provision is tuned in to the needs and abilities of all children in the setting. In addressing the following questions, we will refer back to the theories and research evidence explored in previous chapters, giving examples to illustrate key ideas:

- What is the child doing in the play activity?

- What is play doing for the child?

- What is happening inside the child's mind?

- What learning processes can we identify?

- How can we use this information to inform and guide our practice?

We have identified three levels that can be used to understand the relationships between play, learning and development. First, at a broad level, play is seen as contributing to the holistic development of the child, including the three domains of development – cognitive, affective and psycho-motor (Figure 5.1).

Macintyre (2001) describes how play-based activities contribute to children's learning in each of these domains, and integrate learning across the domains. She provides skills-based observational checklists and a developmental record to enable practitioners to track children's learning and identify areas of difficulty.

At a second level, we can look at play in relation to curriculum models: the Stepping Stones, the areas of learning in Foundation Stage, the National Literacy and Numeracy Strategies and the subject disciplines in the Key Stage 1 curriculum. Other curriculum models can be useful in informing and developing practice (Figure 5.2).

Play supports children's discipline-based learning, adding depth and detail to intended, possible and actual learning outcomes. Disciplined ways of knowing and understanding contribute to children's growing mastery of their social and cultural worlds. Skilled practitioners understand the important pedagogical idea that young learners can be introduced to complex skills and concepts as long as these are presented in appropriate, meaningful ways. Children actively seek knowledge and skills that are within and beyond their current level or zone, so that teaching and learning are co-constructive processes rather than a one-way flow.

- *Cognitive:* All the skills and processes involved in learning, thinking and understanding. Self-concept and identity, language and communication skills, positive attitudes and dispositions towards learning, developing mastery and control in learning. Developing different forms of intelligence – visual/spatial, kinaesthetic, aesthetic and creative, musical/auditory, linguistic, logical/mathematical, interpersonal, intrapersonal, physical, scientific/technological, intuitive/spiritual, social/emotional. Social and intellectual well-being.
- *Affective:* All the skills and processes involved in learning a repertoire of appropriate behaviours, making relationships, social interactions, expressing and controlling emotion, developing a sense of self, understanding the needs of others. Emotional well-being.
- *Psycho-motor:* All aspects of physical development including
  Fine motor skills – use of hands, fingers, feet, hand/eye, hand/foot coordination.
  Gross-motor skills – large body movements such as sitting, turning, twisting, balancing, controlled movement of head, trunk and limbs. Brain–body coordination, spatial awareness.
  Loco-motor skills – large body movements involving travelling and an awareness of space such as crawling, running, climbing, walking, hopping, skipping, jumping. Brain–body coordination, spatial and rhythmic awareness.
  Learning about the body, and gaining control of movement (body awareness). Communicating and expressing ideas through movement. Physical well-being.

FIGURE 5.1   DOMAINS OF DEVELOPMENT

- The four aspects of the Stepping Stones
- Foundation Stage areas of learning
- National Literacy and Numeracy Frameworks for Teaching
- National Curriculum core and foundation subjects
- High/Scope key experiences
- Te Whāriki: strands and dispositions
- Reggio Emilia: community, citizenship and creativity

FIGURE 5.2   CURRICULUM MODELS

At a third level, we can look at the cognitive processes that link playing and learning which are cross-curricular and cross-phase, summarized in Figure 5.3. These processes, skills and dispositions are essential to lifelong learning and playing, particularly as people need to adapt continuously to new technologies, and new opportunities for work and leisure. Looking across these three levels, play can be seen as an integrating mechanism, which enables children to move to and fro along the play-work

Cognitive processes and skills

- Attending, perceiving, observing, recognizing, discriminating, imitating, exploring, investigating, concentrating, memorizing, retaining, retrieving and recalling information, scanning for information, integrating knowledge and experience, categorization, classification, making connections and relationships.
- Making intelligent use of past experience to formulate a plan of action, reflecting on action, noticing causes and effects, using metacognitive skills and strategies – awareness and conscious control of one's own learning.
- Making choices and decisions, constructing knowledge, making sense.
- Communicating ideas, meaning, knowledge and understanding.
- Creativity, imagination, flexibility, making novel connections.
- Creating, recognizing and solving problems.
- Convergent and divergent thinking, practice, repetition, rehearsal, consolidation, retuning, accretion, mastery, interpreting.
- Communicating – through written and spoken language, gestures, mime, signs, symbols and artefacts.
- Making and testing hypotheses, predicting, innovating, combining, recombining, reasoning, extrapolating.
- Developing transferability, transferring knowledge and skills between similar and different contexts.

Attitudes and dispositions

- Curiosity and interest; motivation – intrinsic and extrinsic; open-mindedness, flexibility, engagement, involvement, enthusiasm, originality, creativity, independence, interdependence; willingness to take risks; ability to struggle, and cope with challenge and failure; perseverance, resilience, self-efficacy (can-do orientations).

Influences on learning

- Mood and feeling states; child health and family health; home and community cultures and experiences; parental pressures and expectations; social skills; learning environment – home, school and community; quality of relationships between children, peers and adults; child's and family's orientations to education, socio-economic status.
- Self-systems: self-concept, self-image, self-esteem, self-worth, self-efficacy.

FIGURE 5.3   PROCESSES THAT LINK PLAY AND LEARNING

continuum, and combine their real-world and play-world knowledge, skills and understanding.

As we have seen, learning and development depend on internal cognitive structures that are complex in their origins and subsequent evolution, and are intimately connected to children's social and cultural worlds.

Processes such as exploration, practice, repetition, mastery and revision are important in constructing, extending and connecting cognitive structures. Play activities enable children to impose some structure or organization on a task, make sense of their experiences and engage in ongoing rehearsal of these cognitive processes. Educators often express concern that children's play is sometimes repetitive but a closer examination may reveal subtle changes in play themes and patterns as children revise and extend what has previously been played at and played with. Where play is repetitive and stereotypical, the practitioner needs to find ways of stimulating new interests and ideas. Such interventions may be especially important for children with special educational needs who have the same rights to an appropriate curriculum that helps them to learn through well-planned play (Drifte, 2002; Macintyre, 2001).

The processes involved in playing and learning appear to contribute to building children's brain architecture: rehearsal and practice may lead towards pruning and editing existing connections in the brain, as well as making new connections. In play children develop exploratory as well as explanatory drives: they actively look for patterns, test hypotheses and seek explanations, leading to increased complexity in thinking, learning and understanding (Gopnik *et al*, 1999). These cognitive processes are socially and culturally situated and, through the subject disciplines, can become increasingly refined. For example, exploration and discovery are the building blocks of science: looking for patterns and relationships is fundamental to mathematics; imagination and empathy can lead to developing an informed historical imagination; technology and the creative arts involve planning skills as well as imagination, flexibility and spontaneity. Children's learning becomes increasingly focused through the distinctive methods of inquiry, key skills and conceptual frameworks which the subject disciplines represent. These disciplines provide learners with powerful tools for making sense of the world and incorporate distinctive, as well as interconnected, ways of learning. Although play is a process rather than a subject, many play activities provide opportunities for learning through the subject disciplines. As we argued in Chapter 2, children can be encouraged to develop playful orientations to learning (playing with ideas, rules, relationships, materials) within and beyond the subject disciplines.

These three levels provide a framework for curriculum design, which takes into account breadth, balance, differentiation, and progression and continuity across phases. The following example shows these processes in practice:

A Reception/Year 1 teacher was concerned about the early introduction of the Literacy Framework for Teaching, particularly the outcomes for writing and handwriting, and decided to carry out a small-scale action research study as part of a professional development module. She noticed that many of the children had difficulties with fine motor skills (especially boys). This affected their ability and motivation to write. Building on the research of a colleague on a previous module, she developed a 'fine motor skills carousel', which the children used for half an hour every morning. The carousel included different sensory and manipulative activities: threading and weaving; dough and Plasticine; tweezers and chopsticks for picking up small items such as beads and dried pasta shapes, with small containers to put them in; a washing-up bowl of water, with small scoops, spoons and egg cups. The activities were very popular with the children, and resulted in some tangible outcomes including: improved fine motor skills; concentration, engagement and motivation; persevering with challenge (especially becoming more accurate with tools), as well as satisfaction and pleasure. The teacher also noticed that these skills and dispositions transferred to adult-directed activities, especially writing, where previously reluctant boys became more motivated.

This example of evidence-informed curriculum development shows how the three levels described above can be integrated through play-based activities and can improve the quality of children's learning. The teacher also used her professional knowledge and experience to mediate national policy frameworks.

CURRICULUM MODELS

We have emphasized throughout this book that practitioners should use policy frameworks as a guiding structure rather than as a prescriptive straitjacket. This is a particularly important principle for children with special educational needs because they may need more time, more opportunities for practice and consolidation, and more finely tuned provision to support their learning. There has been much dissatisfaction with 'one size fits all' policy frameworks, with increasing interest in 'designer versions' of curriculum and pedagogy that are more in tune with children, local communities and the professional knowledge base within early childhood education. The curriculum that children experience extends beyond policy frameworks, because it involves everything that they experience in the setting, including the way they are greeted, how the environment is organized, how they are expected to behave towards each other, how adults behave towards them, and what behaviours are encouraged, tolerated, ignored or banned. By developing their own 'designer' versions, practitioners can draw on a number of models which are described in this section. Each has different features that can be combined or adapted to individual settings. All integrate play-based, playful and creative approaches to teaching and learning. These models have evolved and continue to evolve over time, in response to research, new theoretical understanding and wider changes in society. As such, they are not set in stone, but are open to mediation and skilful adaptation.

■ TE WHĀRIKI CURRICULUM (NEW ZEALAND)

Te Whāriki (New Zealand Ministry of Education, 1996) is the first national curriculum statement for New Zealand, encompassing children from birth to five in the early childhood sector. It is a bi-cultural curriculum that reflects the cultural heritage, beliefs and traditions of Māori communities, and is relevant to the country's multi-cultural society. Te Whāriki is based on socio-cultural theories of learning and development, and aims to move the sector away from the individualistic approaches to developmentally appropriate programmes, towards recognition of the fundamentally socially constructed nature of learning, and the importance of knowledgeable others in the setting, home and community (Cowie and Carr, 2004; Jordan, 2004). The curriculum has been envisaged as a *whāriki*, or mat, which is woven from principles, strands, goals and learning outcomes. The four principles are:

- ■ Empowerment: the early childhood curriculum empowers the child to learn and grow.

- ■ Holistic development: the early childhood curriculum reflects the holistic way children learn and grow.

- ■ Family and community: the wider world of family and community is an integral part of the early childhood curriculum.

- ■ Relationships: children learn through responsive and reciprocal relationships between people, places and things.

- Well-being – *Mana Atua*: the health and well-being of the child are nurtured.
- Belonging – *Mana Whenua*: children and their families feel a sense of belonging.
- Contribution – *Mana Tangatta*: opportunities for learning are equitable.
- Communication – *Mana Reo*: the languages and symbols of their own and other cultures are promoted and protected.
- Exploration – *Mana Aotūroa*: the child learns through active exploration of the environment.

FIGURE 5.4 TE WHĀRIKI: STRANDS

The five strands are listed in Figure 5.4.

Within each strand there are a number of broad goals that relate to the overall learning environment, what the children learn and experience within that environment, and the ways in which practitioners make links between the home, community, the setting and other early childhood services.

The curriculum framework provides further specification of learning outcomes (knowledge, skills and attitudes) in the five strands, along with examples of experiences that help to meet these outcomes. Staff are encouraged to think critically about their overall provision and their everyday routines and practices in relation to how the outcomes are being achieved, and the overall quality of their provision. Each of the strands links with the learning areas and essential skills of the New Zealand Curriculum Framework for primary education. The curriculum provides a strong focus on children and their learning. Spontaneous and structured play are valued as key learning experiences. Curriculum planning is based on children's ongoing interests so that skills, knowledge and understandings are embedded in activities and experiences that reflect their cognitive, emotional and social concerns. Family involvement is encouraged through shared assessments across home and the setting, with family members contributing to children's documented learning stories (Carr, 2001a). The following vignette shows how these principles work in practice:

Vini, aged four, tells the teachers that his mother needs new slippers. He makes a pair for her (with much measuring and gluing and decorating), and when the teachers write this up their assessment emphasizes Vini's developing identity as a 'caring' and

> thoughtful person. His mother contributes a comment to the assessment folder that adds a reference to the technical expertise that this work illustrated: she writes that the slippers Vini made were 'unbelievable in terms of thoughtfulness and technical perfection for a little child' (Cowie and Carr, 2004: 98).

The outcomes in Te Whāriki are broader and more process-oriented than those in the Curriculum Guidance for the Foundation Stage (CGFS) and Stepping Stones. For example, in the Exploration strand, children develop:

> Spatial understandings, including an awareness of how two- and three-dimensional objects can be fitted together and moved in space in ways in which spatial information can be represented, such as in maps, diagrams, photographs and drawings (New Zealand Ministry of Education, 1996: 90).

The outcomes are holistic in the sense that they transcend subject boundaries. In contrast, the Stepping Stones in the CGFS are more specific and hierarchical in terms of knowledge, skills and understanding within each of the discipline-based areas of learning. These two orientations reflect fundamental social and political assumptions about children and childhood, and about what early childhood education is for. In England, early childhood provision has been influenced strongly by instrumental approaches to learning, with an emphasis on school readiness, and providing a head start into literacy and numeracy. In order to ensure 'curriculum coverage', whole-school plans often include a rolling programme of topics. The socio-cultural orientation of Te Whāriki places more emphasis on the early childhood centre or classroom as a community of learners: learning is a co-constructive process that involves the child acting in context, with increasingly competent forms of participation (Carr, 2000, 2001a, b).

Building a curriculum around children's interests does not imply an individual approach. In Vini's slipper-making activity, the emphasis is on his individual interest. However, Carr (2001b) provides an example of collaborative interests that were stimulated by a hat-making activity. The activity took place in the construction area, which provided access to paper, card, cardboard boxes, scissors, staplers, glue, paint, rollers, brushes, pens and materials for collage. Children had free choice in using the materials and deciding what kinds of kinds of hats to make (for example, tiaras, birthday hats, sun visors, and hats for babies and cats). This open-ended activity created a problem space, or ZPD, for the children. They persisted with difficulties, created and solved a wide range of technological problems, such as measuring, cutting, fixing, aligning and joining, drawing on support from peers as well as adults. Hat-making skills developed over a period of time, providing opportunities for tackling technological challenge and acquiring knowledge and skills in transformation, redefinition of function, representation and engineering. The context also afforded opportunities for social challenge and participation, and the acquisition of knowledge and skills in making and maintaining friendships. Carr's research demonstrates how these opportunities for learning were situated in the pedagogical framing of the play/learning environment, the materials and resources that were made available, the use that children made of the environment and the resources, and the existing knowledge, expertise and skills that each child brought to the activity.

In New Zealand, there are ongoing debates about 'interests versus skills', particularly with reference to children with special educational needs (Cullen, 2004), which reflects similar issues in the wider early childhood community. Within a predominantly interests-based approach, it is challenging for practitioners to identify specific learning needs of individual children. Within a predominantly skills/content-focused approach, too much atomization and specification of learning outcomes is equally problematic. If literacy and numeracy are privileged over other areas of learning, practitioners may neglect holistic approaches to integrating knowledge and experience (Adams *et al*, 2004). In creating their own designer versions, practitioners need to evaluate and combine both approaches. A common area of agreement across international contexts is a view of the child as competent, powerful and strong. This is also reflected in the Reggio Emilia approach, which has similar implications for curriculum organization.

▓ THE REGGIO EMILIA APPROACH (NORTHERN ITALY)

This approach developed in Reggio Emilia in the years following the Second World War. From being unique to the area, this approach has gained international recognition and respect for its ethos, pedagogy and curriculum provision. Central to this approach is an image of the child, which is expressed eloquently by Lawrence Malaguzzi, the founder of Reggio:

> Our image of children no longer considers them as isolated and egocentric, does not see them as only engaged with actions and objects,

> does not only emphasize the cognitive aspects, does not belittle feelings or what is not logical and does not consider with ambiguity the role of the affective domain. Instead our image of the child is rich in potential, strong, powerful, competent, and most of all connected to adults and other children (Malaguzzi, 1993: 10).

The approach is founded on key principles (Edwards *et al*, 1993) about how educators view children. These principles are itemized in Figure 5.5.

The 'hundred languages of children' can be expressed in many different ways, using a wide variety of materials, tools and resources:

> Drawing, painting, mark-making, printing, writing, signs and symbols (including Braille and Makaton), dance, mime, drama, facial and body gestures, puppets, shadow play, plans, maps, buildings, designs, photographs, sculptures, blocks, construction materials, natural materials, computers and ICT . . . and many more.

The children engage in authentic activities with skilled assistants: for example, making a sculpture garden, growing fruit and vegetables, cooking, involvement in community projects. They learn to use tools correctly in order to support their skills, creativity and expression. The 'hundred languages' principle contrasts with the narrow focus on reading, writing and numeracy skills in the British system, and reminds us that children should be empowered to use all modes of representation and to engage themselves intellectually and emotionally in their work and play (Anning and Ring, 2004). The freedom to use different modes of representation is especially valuable for children with language and communication difficulties, and those with English as an additional language. Imagining 'a hundred languages' enables practitioners to think creatively about inclusion and involvement for all children.

SO WHAT CAN WE LEARN FROM THE REGGIO EMILIA PRINCIPLES? Practitioners in the UK who have visited Reggio settings are often impressed by the quality of the material resources, the design and layout of the spaces, the provision of art specialists and the quality of children's representations (Abbott and Nutbrown, 2001). The child-centred approach is neither woolly nor sentimental, because educators build on experiences and activities in ways that nurture the child's interests through relevant and meaningful curriculum content, and by encouraging different modes of representation. However, practitioners need to question the extent to which the Reggio experience can be generalized, and whether versions of good or effective practice can be built from the nuts and bolts of other models. By evaluating and reflecting critically on different models, practitioners can create their own designer versions, which are

The child as protagonist: children are strong, rich and capable. They have readiness, potential, interest and curiosity in constructing their learning. They use everything in the environment to help them. Children, teachers and parents are the central protagonists in the educational process.

The child as collaborator: children grow up in communities of practice which include *more* and *differently* knowledgeable others. Learning takes place in social contexts, using the resources (material and human) within the environment. How children learn, and how their identities are formed, are intimately connected with their social worlds.

The child as communicator: many different forms of symbolic representation are valued – written and spoken language, movement, drawing, painting, building, sculpture, shadow play, collage, dramatic play, music. These 'hundred languages' enable children to represent and communicate their thinking in different ways, including what they know, understand, wonder about, question, feel and imagine. An *atelierista*, or trained artist, enables these processes.

The environment as third teacher: the design of the learning environment (indoors and outdoors) supports educative encounters, communication and relationships. Specific learning spaces are provided, with equipment and materials which may change over time as projects develop. Choice and independence are encouraged through access to materials and the opportunities that children have to combine and explore. The environment is a motivating force in creating spaces for learning, and creating a sense of well-being and security.

Teachers as co-constructors: Teachers work collaboratively with children, developing and extending themes and interests. They work on short-term and long-term projects which are designed and planned collaboratively. Teachers interact in supportive ways, by listening, observing, talking and documenting children's learning journeys. In the *atelier*, or art studio, the children work with the *atelierista* on projects. By discovering children's interests and agendas, teachers can help them to make further discoveries in and about their environment.

Teachers as researchers: by developing collegial relationships, staff engage in continuous professional development, based on documenting and discussing children's progress and achievements. They draw on established theories and build their own working theories about their provision.

Documentation as communication: in common with Te Whāriki, documentation is shared with the staff, other adults in the setting, and parents. Documentation panels (displays) and books provide evidence of children's learning through photographs, representations, transcriptions of their language, and comments by practitioners. Documentation conveys information to parents about the overall provision, and the children's progress and achievements, and conveys to children that their work is valued.

Parents as partners: participation is actively encouraged, including two-way communication about the child's experiences. Parents offer ideas and suggestions to support the child's learning and development, and contribute their skills to the setting.

FIGURE 5.5   REGGIO EMILIA KEY PRINCIPLES

built on personal as well as shared principles and practices. Practitioners who are empowered will be able better to mediate the increasing standardization of curriculum and pedagogy that is imposed through policy frameworks. If we regard children as strong, competent and rich, it follows that practitioners should be seen in the same terms: to have the support and resources to provide a curriculum that supports children's richness, and that is informed by the professional knowledge of the community. Being strong in their principles, competent in their provision and rich in their professional knowledge may also help practitioners to resist pressures for inappropriate practices from politicians, colleagues, parents and the media.

■ THE HIGH/SCOPE CURRICULUM

The High/Scope curriculum originated in the USA and was based originally on Piagetian theories and developmentally appropriate principles about teaching and learning. Detailed guidelines describe curriculum content, planning, routines, and strategies for assessment and record-keeping. Various revisions have been carried out since the original version of the 1970s, with more emphasis being placed on socio-cultural theories and the proactive role of educators (Bredekamp and Copple, 1997). Curriculum content is based on key experiences, which represent the eight areas of learning listed in Figure 5.6.

Active learning is the foundation of the High/Scope approach: learning is initiated by the child. The curriculum is planned around children's needs, interests and ongoing cognitive concerns and can be adapted to different age groups and settings, to children with special educational needs and from different ethnic groups. Adult-directed activities are valued, and focus on teaching specific skills and knowledge across the eight areas, and

- active learning
- language
- representation
- classification
- seriation
- number
- spatial relations
- time

FIGURE 5.6   AREAS OF LEARNING IN THE HIGH/SCOPE APPROACH

providing resources to support children's interests. The approach incorporates plan–do–review, which involves children in setting their own goals and choosing their activities within a structured, well-resourced environment. Children carry out their plans individually, in pairs or in groups. This element of choice does not embody a *laissez-faire* approach because practitioners structure the indoor and outdoor environments to provide key experiences in the eight areas of learning, and to encourage as much independence as possible. The role of the practitioner is to facilitate learning, support the children's decisions and plans, and monitor their activity. The support should be tuned into what the children are doing but, at the same time, encourage challenge and extension.

There is an underlying assumption in this model that what children choose is what they need. However, feedback from practitioners suggests that some caution should be exercised here. Research has shown that some children repeat what is safe and known; they may not have the knowledge, confidence or expertise to use materials and resources differently, to try out new activities, and push their own boundaries (Bennett *et al*, 1997). They do not always have the social skills or confidence to join a group of players or engage successfully in more complex forms of play (Broadhead, 2004). In a socio-cultural model of teaching and learning, communities of learners co-construct learning through joint activity and guided participation, and responsive interactions based on the learner's activity. Practitioners need to have a clear idea about what areas of learning can be accessed through areas of play provision such as construction, role play, or sand and water. Drifte (2002) provides detailed guidance on ensuring that all the working/playing areas of the setting are accessible to children with special educational needs, thus supporting their choices and plans.

■ PLAN–DO–REVIEW (PDR)

In PDR activities, children are allowed to combine materials and resources according to their intentions. The PDR approach can be used effectively in practice (Bennett *et al.*, 1997), and has the potential to provide an empowering curriculum model. Review time is seen as an important element of High/Scope where children come together to discuss what they have done, made or learned. They are encouraged to ask questions, share information and think about future extensions. When used effectively, review time can encourage the development of metacognitive skills and processes. At its worst, it can degenerate into a repetitive, tedious ritual.

The effectiveness of review time depends on the size of the group and the practitioner's expertise in guiding the discussion, modelling questions, prompting and praising, and encouraging children to engage in out-loud thinking about their learning and activity.

Julie Fisher (2002) draws on the underlying theory and principles of PDR, and provides detailed guidance on how practitioners can teach essential skills and competences. Many practitioners report that Fisher's book has become their 'bible' because it is both pragmatic and aspirational in terms of developing approaches that value children's play and self-initiated activity. Some of the key ideas are revisited here, with the recommendation that readers refer to Fisher's work for more detail.

FISHER'S GUIDANCE ON PDR

What does the teacher plan?

- What does each child need to know now? (concepts/skills/knowledge/attitudes)

- How is this best learnt? (differentiation = activity/process/outcome/grouping)

- What support does the child need?

- How can I include the spontaneous interests of the children?

- Which activity will be teacher-intensive?

- Are other activities planned so that the children can be independent learners?

- What kind of support/intervention do the other activities need?

- Have I planned to revise both teacher-initiated and child-initiated activities?

What can the child plan?

- What work do I want to do today?

- What work do I need to do today?

- In what order shall I do my work?

- With whom shall I work?

- What resources/equipment do I need?

■ What do I want to do with my finished work?

How can children be involved in making decisions?

Involving children:

- ■ gives opportunities for real-life problem-solving
- ■ encourages them to maintain something that they have planned
- ■ enables them to have an element of control over their own learning environment
- ■ leads to the development of organization as a life skill
- ■ gives them a sense of responsibility/self-esteem
- ■ encourages cooperation and collaboration between them and adults
- ■ enables the teacher to see things from the children's perspective.

Children can be involved in planning and arranging:

- ■ the use of space
- ■ the naming of work areas
- ■ the selection of resources
- ■ the categorizing of resources
- ■ the sorting of resources
- ■ the labelling of resources
- ■ the location of resources
- ■ designing and mounting displays.

Children can be involved in:

- ■ selecting themes and topics
- ■ designing role-play areas
- ■ designing outdoor play areas
- ■ designing props and resources for play
- ■ planning research and investigations

- planning PE sessions – use of apparatus
- deciding how to represent their ideas and outcomes of activities
- managing some of their time
- planning to follow their own interests
- identifying pairs or groups for collaboration
- school councils
- negotiating rules and sanctions
- monitoring the implementation of rules and sanctions
- identifying problems and generating solutions
- taking responsibility for their behaviour
- taking responsibility for using and clearing away resources.

Reflecting on planning and implementation . . .

- What can each child tell me about himself/herself as a learner?
- What does each child already know/understand?
- What learning skills and strategies does each child use?
- How does each child work with others?
- What is the child interested in?
- Have I planned to observe teacher-intensive, teacher-initiated and child-initiated activities?
- Have I planned to involve the child in self-assessment?
- What is the focus of my assessment of the teacher-intensive task?
- Will I observe or participate?
- Have I identified the evidence on which to base my assessments?
- What strategies have I established for recording unplanned observations and conversations?

- How will I use all the evidence collected to inform future planning?

In order to be implemented successfully, the PDR approach involves teaching children the tools for thinking and learning, helping them to use metacognitive skills and strategies, and assisting transfer across contexts. Planning in collaboration with others helps to develop social and communicative skills; in mixed age groups, older children can act as models of planners, doers and reviewers. Ideally, PDR should be implemented throughout a school so that children develop increasing levels of competence and mastery, building incrementally on 'can-do' orientations to learning.

WHAT PLANNING SKILLS DO CHILDREN NEED TO LEARN?

- Speaking and listening in a group.

- Understanding the concepts of planning and making decisions.

- Being able to implement a plan.

- Selecting and knowing how to use materials and resources.

- Acting independently and collaboratively.

- Asking for assistance from peers and adults.

- Specifying the assistance needed to implement a plan or carry out a sub-task.

- Paying attention to the activity.

- Creating, identifying and solving problems.

- Remembering how the plan was carried out.

- Reflecting on action – raising and answering questions.

- Representing knowledge and experience in different ways.

- Processing information and communicating the meaning and purpose of an activity.

- Using conscious awareness and control of learning processes.

- Making and sustaining relationships with peers and adults.

interacting, participating, listening, observing, responding, directing, redirecting, demonstrating, modelling, questioning, praising, encouraging, advising, guiding, suggesting, instructing, imparting new knowledge, diagnosing, extending, discussing, reflecting, prompting, enriching, assisting, mediating, explaining, enabling, . . .

FIGURE 5.7   PEDAGOGICAL STRATEGIES

Originally the High/Scope model was designed for an adult:child ratio of 1:8, so implementation with larger groups can be problematic. Practitioners who have experimented with PDR have reported that planning with large groups takes up too much time (up to 20 minutes) and often results in children becoming restless. Some have reported that they use small planning groups on a daily basis so that during the course of a week all children are able to experience greater choice, autonomy and independence (see Amanda's story in Chapter 8). Practitioners need to give support for children's planned activities, drawing on appropriate pedagogical strategies such as those in Figure 5.7.

Practitioners are sometimes unsure about how to use review time constructively so that children can feed back what they have been doing in their self-initiated activities, including play. Reviews can be carried out in different ways:

- 'in the moment' reviews, in response to a child's immediate success, challenge, problem-setting or problem-solving

- at the end of a session, either within a small group (with key workers, classroom assistants or other helpers) or feeding back to a larger group

- at the end of the day

- at the end of a week

- at the beginning/end of a topic (for example, brainstorming and mind-maps).

Plan–do–review serves important purposes for children and practitioners:

- Children can value their own and others' work.

- Children can develop a sense of agency and mastery because they make decisions, identify and solve problems as they arise.

- Practitioners can shift the balance of power in classrooms, enabling children to take responsibility for their own learning.

- Practitioners can build some of the curriculum around children's self-identified interests.

- Practitioners can use review time to understand what and how children are learning, and plan further provision accordingly.

- Practitioners can value the learning that arises from children's own interests and motivation.

The PDR approach can be integrated successfully with the learning outcomes defined in the policy frameworks. For example, in the Stepping Stones, Becoming a Competent Learner includes finding out about people and the environment, and being resourceful. Becoming a Skilful Communicator involves describing, questioning, representing and predicting, and sharing thoughts, feelings and ideas, so that children are increasingly aware of their own competence and capabilities. In the Key Stage 1 curriculum, PDR is integral to design and technology, and to citizenship education. Children can also design their own tasks and problems in literacy (for example, writing a play script for a well-known story) and numeracy (planning menus and food to celebrate Diwali).

■ KNOWLEDGE BASES FOR TEACHING AND LEARNING

This brief review shows how current international trends emphasize the importance of the practitioner's role, and the complexity of the knowledge bases that underpin their practice. Practitioners need a good understanding of the structures of the subject areas of the curriculum – the concepts, skills, tools for enquiry and investigation, and ways of thinking and reasoning. They also need to understand the cross-curricular nature of teaching and learning, how connections can be made, and what connections children make through their own activities. Although practitioners may prefer to view the curriculum as integrated from a child's perspective, they can plan and evaluate activities in terms of the subject areas. Professional knowledge encompasses shared as well as individual values, principles, visions and beliefs that influence the ethos of the setting, and everything that happens there. For example, the belief that children are powerful learners underpins the High/Scope, Te Whāriki and Reggio Emilia approaches and influences the quality of the learning environment, the children's experiences and activities, and the quality of relationships. Envisioning children as powerful learners enables practitioners to support children's choices and decisions, as well as nurturing and stimulating their learning. Professional knowledge is not static: skilled practitioners reflect critically on their planning, provision and children's learning journeys, and are willing to improve their practice. They use evidence from their own evaluations, from their peers and from research studies to support development. Although settings differ widely in their aims and orientations, the practical ideas outlined in this chapter can be adapted and applied by all practitioners so that they can create 'designer versions' rather than a 'one size fits all' approach to their practice. The following section focuses on integrating play into the curriculum, building on these ideas.

CURRICULUM DESIGN

All curriculum models reflect a set of beliefs and values about what is considered to be educationally and developmentally worthwhile in terms of children's immediate needs, their future needs and the wider needs of society. Knowledge is not value-free. The models described here give status to different funds of knowledge, ways of coming to know, and modes of thinking. Practitioners make informed decisions about curriculum content, and how that will be presented to young children through adult- and child-initiated activities. They also need to be aware of how the curriculum is received and interpreted. Play itself does not constitute a curriculum, but should be an integral part of the curriculum because it provides potential spaces for learning and development. So how can practitioners support good-quality play?

PEDAGOGICAL FRAMING AND STRATEGIES

The twin concepts of pedagogical framing and pedagogical strategies are helpful for thinking about how practitioners can support child- and adult-initiated play. *Pedagogical framing* involves making informed decisions about the structure and content of the curriculum (see Figure 5.8).

Within this overall structure, practitioners use a wide range of pedagogical techniques and strategies which support learning, such as working and playing alongside children, observing and assessing, introducing new themes and ideas, and demonstrating skills (MacNaughton and Williams, 1998). Curriculum design should be based on a co-construction of practitioners' intentions and children's intentions (Figure 5.9).

Planning: Defining aims and objectives, including planned and possible outcomes in play. Building on previous outcomes from play.

Organization: Indoor and outdoor environments: space, resources, time, daily routines, activities, what adults do, what children do.

Implementation: The ways in which adult-initiated activities and tasks are presented in order to support intended and possible learning outcomes and build on previous learning experiences and interests. The ways in which adults allow time for and follow play and child-initiated activities.

Assessment, documentation and evaluation: Understanding patterns of learning, interests, dispositions. Identifying learning outcomes from adult- and child-initiated activities. Documenting learning in order to provide a feedback loop into planning. Using evidence from all adults in the setting to evaluate the quality and effectiveness of the curriculum.

FIGURE 5.8 PEDAGOGICAL FRAMING

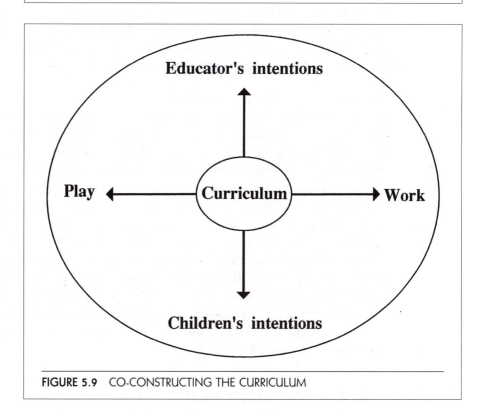

FIGURE 5.9 CO-CONSTRUCTING THE CURRICULUM

At the planning stage, practitioners frame aims and intentions, which can be long-, medium- and short-term. Pedagogical framing does not put the adult in control of everything that happens in the setting. In a co-

constructive curriculum, practitioners' intentions can include responding to children's intentions and meanings as well as allowing for unplanned developments. At the organization stage, practitioners decide how the learning environment (both indoors and outdoors) will be set out, what resources will be available, where they will be located, how much choice children have, and whether materials and activities can be combined. How the day, or session, is structured also influences the amount of time available for play. At the implementation stage, practitioners decide where and how they will spend their time, which should allow opportunities to follow children's own learning journeys. This approach was exemplified in Chapter 4 in the two examples of Hogwarts Wizard School (Joanna Cook) and the Fire Station (Sheena Wright). Cook (2003) describes a continuum between adult- and child-initiated activities. For example, in science, the children learned how to make an electrical circuit using leads, batteries, bulbs and crocodile clips. The teacher's input focused on scientific and technological skills, knowledge and understanding. In their role play, the children decided to make illuminated magic wands. The teacher responded to these ideas by supporting children in using and applying their new skills in a play-based problem-solving context.

Awareness of children's intentions can only come about through a curriculum model that encourages them to express their intentions and follow their own learning journeys. Practitioners should be sensitive to the meanings that children communicate in their play and use these to inform the next cycle of planning. Practitioners therefore need a dual perspective which involves understanding the meaning of play activities in the 'here and now' and deciding what are the next significant steps. In practice, this dual perspective may shift the emphasis more towards short-term planning so that the curriculum is responsive to learners and supports co-constructive planning (as in the 'magic wands' example). Children's interests and ideas may also form the impetus for planning a short topic or informing adult-initiated activities. Such an approach can be enabling and empowering for children and practitioners, particularly where there is a continuum between work and play, and between adult- and child-initiated activities.

■ THE PLAYING–LEARNING ENVIRONMENT

Practitioners should create an environment that supports unity between playing, learning and teaching, and ensure access and inclusion for all children. This involves taking into account human (children and adults) as well as material resources, and the relationships between them. The quality of material resources available, where they are located and how they can be used influence the quality of children's learning experiences. For example, in a day-care setting, the practitioners had a rotating pattern of resources that were put out for the children on a daily basis. The children could not choose other resources or move them from one area to another. After attending an in-service course, the leader of the setting realized that they were constraining children's learning opportunities. She acknowledged her own 'obsession' with tidiness, and was concerned about the mess that would be created, and how long it would take for the adults to tidy everything away. Following some staff development work, the practitioners decided to allow the children more freedom to choose their own resources and use them in different areas (using the PDR approach). They were taught to take responsibility for tidying up and taking care of the resources. By monitoring these new approaches, the practitioners identified the richness of children's symbolic activity and their creativity. Combining small-world resources with large construction equipment extended the children's imaginative play: they were more likely to create scenarios with hollow blocks (towns, zoos, parks, space ships) and act out stories with play people. Small construction equipment was used in many different ways in role-play activities: Cuisenaire rods became chips in the cafe; small blocks became gold and jewels in the pirate ship; play people were used in the sand and water trays in dramatic scenarios of flooding, burying, drowning, getting lost and being rescued. Thus the changes made in this setting afforded new opportunities for playing and learning, which also extended the cognitive and emotional richness of the children's activities.

■ THE CONCEPT OF AFFORDANCE

Carr (2000) uses the concept of *affordance* to describe the relationship between the learner and the setting. Affordance refers to the:

- perceived and actual properties of resources in the environment (objects, artefacts and tools)

- how these are used (this links with the idea of *tools for use*)

- how these might be used (this links with the idea of *tools and use*)

- how these may help or hinder learning.

This concept links with the socio-cultural theories outlined in Chapter 4. Carr (2000) discusses the importance of the 'more knowledgeable/ competent other' in teaching children how to use the tools and resources of the community, providing children with optimum levels of challenge as they become more experienced and more expert in their use of resources, and considering the accessibility of resources (whether resources encourage individual or collaborative activities, and whether they can be used by children across the ability range). In the Reggio Emilia approach, the specialist practitioner (*atelierista*) helps children learn how to use authentic 'tools of the trade' in, for example, design, architecture, planning and a wide range of arts and crafts. The underpinning philosophy is that children should have access to 'high affordance' resources and learning opportunities. Following a visit to Italy, Parker (2001) describes how she used familiar resources (overhead and slide projectors) in different ways to support children's learning. These resources afforded opportunities to support and extend children's thinking, creativity with representation and mark-making, and particularly their language: talking, exchanging ideas, reflecting on home-based experiences, making connections between areas of learning, and playing with words and concepts. In the hat-making activity described earlier in this chapter, Carr (2001b) demonstrates the importance of children having access to good-quality tools and resources, including scissors that cut, and glue that sticks. Practitioners also need to understand how they can extend the affordance of activities and resources for children with special educational needs in order to support access and inclusion (Macintyre, 2001; Sayeed and Guerin, 2000; Drifte, 2002). Drifte (2002) outlines how the affordance of everyday resources may need to be changed or extended. For example, Dycem mats can be used in the role-play area and tabletop activities to provide a secure, non-slip base. Some musical instruments can be hung on the wall so that children with physical difficulties can hit them using one hand. Visual props and puppets can be used to dramatize stories and encourage children's role-play activities.

Learning environments that have high-affordance tools, artefacts and materials can support children's skills and abilities as they become real-world mathematicians, designers, artists, technologists and scientists. Therefore children need

- to learn how to use resources safely, correctly, and with increasing competence

- time to play with resources so that they learn to use them in creative ways

- time to create their own problems and challenges

- tools and resources that are varied, of good quality, and are maintained or replaced regularly (for example, blunt scissors).

The following sections provide some practical examples of pedagogical framing and strategies in early childhood settings, and demonstrate how practitioners can create unity between playing, learning and teaching. The examples are also related to the subject areas and learning objectives of the curriculum frameworks, but at the same time illustrate the connectedness of children's experiences and activities.

PLAYING WITH LITERACY The links between play and literacy development have become more clearly established in recent years, and there is strong support in theory for planning literacy-rich play environments (Marsh and Hallett, 1999; Marsh and Millard, 2000; Roskos and Christie, 2000). Play integrates speaking, listening, reading and writing and provides contexts for meaningful literacy practices. Children use a wide variety of literacy-related skills, concepts and behaviours in their play and show interest in, and knowledge of, the many functions and purposes of print. When engaging in playful literacy, children are not just pretending to read and write; they are acting as readers and writers. This is a fundamental distinction which enables children to see the meaning and relevance of such activities. In Vygotskian terms, they are behaving ahead of their actual level of development, so that their competence is both situated in the present and anticipates future progress. In acting more competently, children also develop their confidence, as the following example shows.

Abigail (age four) loved reading. In this episode she demonstrated her knowledge about the functions of print, how books work, and her interpretation of learning contexts both in and out of school. She sat on a stool with a favourite 'Meg and Mog' book and announced to her grandma, mother and aunt that she was going to read the story. Because they were chatting she said, in a teacher voice, 'fingers on lips', and didn't start until they were all quiet. When her aunt put her hand down, Abigail said sternly, 'I don't remember telling you to take your finger off your lips. Put it back.' She read the title of the book and asked her audience what they thought the story was about. She held the book the right way up and turned the pages in sequence. On each page she asked questions such as 'And *where* are Meg's shoes? Are they *on* the bed? Are they *under* the bed? What do you think is going to happen next? Will Mog fall *off* the broomstick?' She picked out the words 'Meg' and 'Mog' by recognizing the capital M, but did not differentiate between them. She followed the words from left to right with her finger, and pointed at specific parts of the picture when asking questions. Abigail was behaving as a reader; she reproduced a schooled version of literacy by emphasizing the prepositions, using a teacherly voice. She was also demonstrating playful enjoyment of sharing books in a social context, making connections between learning at home and school.

Play, pretending and language are symbolic activities that support and share many characteristics with the development of reading and writing. Socio-dramatic play can be a particularly rich context for literacy development because of the connections between story-making and telling, and symbolic activity. The following example shows how a Year 1/2 teacher created a continuum between adult- and child-initiated activities, using a co-constructive approach which incorporated plan–do–review:

Nicola decided to develop the children's role play through stories. The children chose *Where the Wild Things Are* by Maurice Sendak, and wanted to divide the role-play area into two sections – one for the protagonist Oliver's house and one for the Wild Things' house. The children planned the area, making or bringing in props and resources. They made up names and characters for the Wild Things and represented their ideas through writing, drawing and painting. They extended the story by projecting themselves into different roles and scenarios and making up adventures. They talked and wrote about imagining the reaction of their parents to their absence, or what would happen if they brought home a Wild Thing to live with them. Salah described how he would teach him good manners and not to eat the cat. Jelika planned to make her own puppet, which she took home every day, and involved her family in writing stories and scripts that she shared with friends. One group made up a menu of Wild Things food, and then planned a party, which involved many mathematical activities. The children also used geographical literacy: they drew maps of the land where the Wild

Things live, and the routes from their homes. They acted out their stories in the role-play area, which the teacher extended in dance and drama sessions (moving and acting in the characters of the Wild Things, acting the 'wild rumpus'). In the writing corner, materials and resources were always available for free writing. The children made books to record their stories, which became a shared resource for the class. As the children's interests developed, the teacher provided stories and poems about mythical creatures and lands, which reflected the multi-cultural community. Teacher-directed and child-initiated activities were continuously integrated along a work–play continuum, with children having lots of opportunities for representing their ideas in different ways. The range of activities enabled all children to be included and to participate according to their abilities.

This example demonstrates how role play can count as authorship because children co-construct play frames, scripts and texts. Although this authorship is not of the formal, written kind, it nevertheless shares common features of plot, characterization, sequencing, scripting and editing the dialogue and interactions to direct the course of the play (Hall and Robinson, 1995). Such narratives are often complex, novel and detailed; children interweave reality and fantasy, drawing on their social and cultural worlds. Play narratives can be inspired by stories (both fact and fiction) that adults tell to children, as well as stories that children invent. Booth (1994) describes some of the essential qualities of drama and role play:

- sharing the creations of their imaginations

- using story elements to structure their ideas

- creating new worlds of meaning

- communicating meanings explicitly to others

- stimulating lateral thinking

- playing out problems and possibilities

- inventing, elaborating and extending themes

- combining experience and creating knowledge

- gaining new experiences
- making connections between written and spoken language.

These qualities are not mere by-products of play, but are situated within play, as the following example (Attfield, 1992) shows:

> Jerry and Joanna (both aged seven, Year 2) wanted to make up a story for television. Initially they learnt about cartoon drawing in the context of their favourite Walt Disney films. They decided to write the narrative for their story and draw the pictures to sequence the plot. The story integrated elements from adventure and fairy stories with cartoon characters, and showed a good understanding of plot and sequence in a condensed form. The children developed the story to perform as a play for the class. They wrote lists of the characters, drew cartoons to show the development of the plot, and used speech bubbles for the dialogue. They combined play with authentic activity – the children were behaving as if they were scriptwriters. They also changed the characters and story lines, occasionally challenging some of the gender stereotypes in Disney films.

Linking play and literacy involves imaginative planning, varied resources, and engaging with children to give their literacy status, provide an appreciative audience, and support their developing skills and confidence. Practitioners can extend children's understanding of the literacy events which take place in real-world contexts. For example:

- writing a menu

- reading a recipe

- filling out cheques, signing receipts

- reading brochures and filling out booking forms in a travel agency

- drawing maps and plans of journeys

- drawing plans for buildings, parks, playgrounds

- designing cards, posters, badges, clothes, book covers

```
telephone  messages

HeLo  it is
          So
Can you Fun
buy me at he bea
apPle
```

■ developing comic strips and story boards (drawing and writing)

■ using websites and other ICT.

Marsh and Millard (2000) provide a wealth of examples which remind practitioners of the importance of using children's popular culture in the classroom, including comics, magazines, websites, computer games, television and films, and popular music. For example, they argue that comics can provide a wealth of opportunities for supporting playful approaches to literacy, such as:

■ analysing story structure

■ understanding characters and how they change over time

■ identifying playful uses of language such as puns, alliteration, assonance and onomatopoeia

■ being critical of texts – identifying and challenging stereotypes

■ making links between comics, websites, games, and other 'spin-off' products.

For children with special educational needs, Drifte (2002) recommends providing books with different textures and/or incorporated noises that are activated by buttons, and that integrate different communication systems such and Braille and Makaton. Provision that has breadth and relevance to children's lives helps them to engage in reading and writing

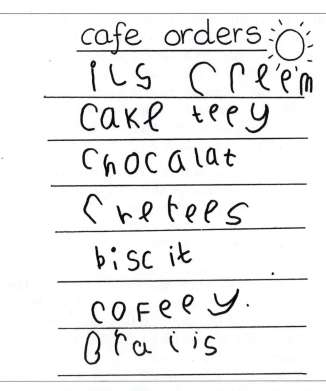

for a variety of purposes in authentic situations. Playing their way into literacy provides powerful stimuli for learning.

PLAYING WITH NUMERACY Children become real-world mathematicians by participating in everyday practices in different contexts – home, community and school. The amount of mathematical knowledge children have on entry to school is a strong predictor of their future progress. Before they start school, many children demonstrate a range of mathematical knowledge and competences, but this richness and complexity is not always recognized in pre-school and school settings. Children invent their own strategies that enable them to solve a variety of addition and subtraction word problems. They also develop their own systems for representing their calculations such as tallying and idiosyncratic notations (Worthington and Carruthers, 2003). These strategies are often evident in play contexts as children encounter problems and develop their own solutions (Peters, 1998).

Practitioners can build on children's invented strategies and create contexts in which they move through different stages of representation, learn the interrelationships among ideas, and link their own informal strategies to the more formal symbol system of mathematics. Like all the subject disciplines, mathematics has its own discourse – ways of thinking, reasoning, problem-solving; methods, rules, and procedures. Children's success in solving mathematical problems depends on their embedded-ness in familiar, everyday practices and related discourses. Exploration and discovery are integral to children's mathematics (what does mathematics do?): the more formal teaching of rules and routines enables children to think creatively within the discipline and helps them to solve problems independently and collaboratively (what can I do with mathematics?).

The policy frameworks for the Foundation Stage, Numeracy and Key Stage 1 mathematics validate creative and playful approaches. Play activities can provide a range of contexts for integrating mathematics into everyday practices that children encounter in and out of school, as the following example shows (Attfield, 1992):

> Seven-year-old Toby enjoyed mathematical problems. In a role-play area resourced as a cafe, he pretended to be a waiter, using his mathematical knowledge to take money and give change. He was able to add and subtract mentally, worked out change from 50 pence, and added amounts up to £2.05p. He was particularly interested in adding up the money at the end and solving other money problems as they arose, such as: sandwiches are 10 pence each, so how many can Helen have for 30 pence? In another example, Sally was playing as the assistant in the toy shop, with Oliver helping her to take the money and give change. A long queue of customers formed so Oliver asked them to make two queues, saying 'I can serve them quickly . . . my Mum gets cross if she hangs around.'

Toby used formal rules and routines, combining abstract thinking with concrete experience in a playful context. The imaginary setting provided opportunities for authentic mathematical activities. In the next example (Attfield, 1992), Mary and Peta construct a Lego-Technic™ battery-controlled car using a plan. Their play integrates skills and knowledge in maths, science and technology:

> After the girls constructed the car they decided to follow the teacher's suggestion of making a ramp and comparing how far the car would travel on a flat and sloping surface. This involved

comparing, estimating, counting and predicting. Teacher extension supported the girls in measuring and comparing the distances travelled by the car. The activity was observed by peers, who suggested using different lengths of ramps. This led to an investigation of different materials for the ramps, and whether this made any difference. Mary understood the concept of a fair test, insisting that they let the car go rather than pushing it, and the concepts of forces and energy: 'you don't have to have batteries to make it move'. She also noticed cause and effect: 'The Bauspiel ramp is too short. It crashes at the bottom because it's too steep. We need something longer.' It was decided to extend this activity on future occasions by making different vehicles and testing them for speed and distance travelled.

Play experiences can provide open-ended opportunities for children to use and apply their knowledge, skills and understanding across the curriculum (see Chapter 7, Helen's and Vernon's play).

PLAYING ACROSS THE CURRICULUM These principles can be applied across other subject areas of the curriculum. The following examples show some creative pedagogical approaches that enable continuity between work and play, and playful opportunities for children to learn skills, dispositions and knowledge.

Playing with ICT

Hannah had a degree in media studies: she was keen to use her skills in her mixed-age class (Reception, Years 1 and 2), and wanted to improve her provision for ICT. The project was animals; a visit was planned to a local farm, and the children decided that they wanted to bring in their pets. She videotaped the visits from the children's pets so that they had a record of the discussions, which often involved family members. The children were interested in the camera and wanted to learn how to use it. Hannah was surprised at how competent and responsible they were, and supported their idea for a 'Pet News' programme. This involved turning the role-play area into a TV studio, with children acting as reporters on the latest pet news. They wrote news scripts and carried out interviews with children and family members. The project encouraged high levels of motivation because the children were engaged in authentic activity.

> The older children provided more expert models of literacy and language for the younger children, so there was much peer interaction and co-construction, as well as support and enrichment from Hannah. The children used a wide repertoire of social skills, including allocating roles, sharing ideas, organizing presentations, and learning from each other about caring for pets.

Playing with History

> Julie, a newly qualified teacher, worked in a small rural school, which was planning centenary celebrations that involved the whole school in the theme of the Victorians. Julie did some research in the school's old log books and discovered a story about a strict teacher who was rather harsh with the children, but also very poor at spelling. The records showed that the teacher was subsequently sacked for her spelling (but not for her harsh punishments of the children). This story provided the impetus for some teacher-directed role play with a Year 1 and 2 class. Julie prepared her children for the role play by telling them the story of the teacher, and asked the children to come dressed in costume for a Victorian school day. She hired a Victorian costume from a theatrical shop, and began the day in role. She carried out hand and nail inspections, and planned her lessons based on rote learning and drill, with the children using old slates and chalk. She wrote some incorrect spellings on the board, which the children spotted. The head teacher, also in role, came into the classroom and sacked Julie for her poor spellings. At this point some of the children were a little unsure about the distinction between reality and fantasy and wondered whether they would get their teacher back.

PLANNING FOR PROGRESSION AND CONTINUITY

While there is clear validation for play in the Foundation Stage, there remain concerns about the transition to more formal approaches in Reception and Year 1, and the lack of continuity in curriculum and pedagogy (Adams *et al*, 2004). In a study of progression and continuity, Wood and Bennett (2001) found that in nursery classes, children had long periods of time in which to engage in play and self-directed activities.

In Reception classes, time for play was reduced significantly as children were introduced to the Literacy and Numeracy Strategies, often from the beginning of the school year. By Year 1, there was very little time for play as teachers struggled with content overload from the policy requirements. Just as children become more skilled in their play, opportunities for play are restricted. Policy-makers assume that young children need more challenging work, whereas research shows that they also need more challenging play.

The examples given throughout this book indicate that children's play preferences change and develop alongside their developing skills, knowledge and dispositions. Hughes (1991) identifies the major developments beyond the pre-school phase. The child's thinking becomes more orderly, more structured and more logical. Play becomes more realistic and rule-oriented and reveals a developing need for order, a need to belong and a need for industry. Children's play involves more cognitive activity (*epistemic* play – what does this do?) as opposed to sensory exploration and physical manipulation (*ludic* play – what can I do with this?). Children build knowledge about play and become increasingly skilled as players. As their play skills develop, they use abstract forms of thinking: in Vygotsky's terms, action arises from ideas and symbols rather than from concrete objects.

In their need for order, children show increasing levels of competence in how they organize, structure and perform in their play-based activities (see examples in Chapter 7). They may become less dependent on an adult for support because they are more confident about sharing ideas, allocating roles and defining rules within a group. In terms of the need to belong, older children orientate towards peer-group affiliations and away from the family unit. Increasingly they construct their identities in relation to their peers and enjoy demonstrating skills, expertise and talents, which define their status:

> The peer group is a major socializing agent in middle childhood. It is from their peers, not from parents or teachers, that children learn about the nature of childhood. Peers will teach children quite effectively, and sometimes very harshly, about social rules and about the importance of obeying them and establish a moral order which may differ from that established by adults (Hughes, 1991: 100).

Hughes (1991) states that the developing need for industry is apparent in children's work and play: they need to be productive, to achieve a sense of mastery and a feeling of accomplishment. These attitudes and dispositions are related to their social status because play can bring either positive or negative validation from peers. Play and work can be congruent as children work hard at their play, showing concentration, perseverance, determination and attention to means and ends. Developing conscious awareness of their skills and abilities leads to greater control of processes and outcomes so that play provides contexts for expressing their ideas, choices and intentions. Broström (1999) argues that older children demonstrate a growing awareness of the purposes of play, which influences its content and complexity. There is a gradual shift from play with objects to play that is more structured and rule-bound, and involves taking on a role. Where older children engage in socio-dramatic play, they are more likely to spend time negotiating the plot and story line, defining roles and directing the action. They gradually progress from spontaneous, unconscious actions towards more structured, conscious actions: their play becomes more like a performance that often incorporates well-rehearsed themes, rituals and actions. Broström (1999) argues that adults can be involved in planning the collective fantasy in order to support children's extended play skills. This involves helping children to organize the play environment, supporting the chosen theme with appropriate props, and interacting with children on their terms. Frame play can be constructed around children's 'real world' experiences, stories, films and popular culture.

Older children also enjoy games with rules such as board games and, increasingly, computer games where they compete against a partner or a character. They enjoy the success of winning, because this contributes to their self-esteem and status in their peer group. Increasingly, children's identity becomes defined by what they think they are good at, and what they are perceived to be good at by their peers. This can be observed in the context of rule-bound games such as football or chess, which demand specific skill and expertise. In an increasingly consumer-oriented society, children's identity is also defined by what they own. For older children, hobbies and interests often structure their play: these may be centred on collections of toys, games or spin-off products from the latest film and television characters. Children build collections of toys and other items that define their social status and can be used in bargaining and exchanges with their peers.

Children (and adults) do not outgrow play but their preferred modes of play change as they develop their skills and competences as players. Therefore, planning for progression in play needs to be considered within and beyond the Foundation Stage. The activities and experiences provided should continue to reflect a balance between adults' and children's intentions. For example, older children enjoy the chance to compete with adults and peers in rule-bound activities (such as board games), but may need assistance from a more knowledgeable other to master the rules and conventions. In constructive play, there are many opportunities for progression. Much of the constructive equipment now available is technologically sophisticated and, in some cases, can be linked to computer programs. Such equipment can continue to integrate playfulness and industriousness as children learn to use their skills and knowledge to solve complex problems and extend their creativity and imagination. Children draw increasingly on disciplined ways of knowing and reasoning so that play continues to provide contexts for extending and integrating subject matter knowledge.

Children's rates of development vary significantly, as do their abilities and preferences. Planning for progression in play should take into account differentiation for children with special educational needs (Macintyre, 2001; Wall, 2003). Play/learning environments, both indoors and outdoors, need to be designed to promote the optimum development of children's abilities. For example, Peter had cerebral palsy and had difficulty controlling his body movements. His physiotherapy programme included a lot of repetitive tasks to improve control and coordination. The teacher designed a variety of activities that supported Peter's development, providing adult assistance where necessary, and enabling Peter to plan some of his own activities, especially on the large equipment which he enjoyed. Peter was supported by specialist equipment, such as grippers for pencils and brushes, and Dycem mats to secure objects and materials, which enabled him to engage in writing, drawing, constructive and small-world play. Peter's message to his Nan (Figure 5.10) indicates that he was acting as a reader and writer, and understood writing as a form of communication.

Jenny was partially sighted and needed a sensory-rich play environment. Additional sensory activities were planned, and new resources were made or ordered (for example, sandpaper letters and numerals, fluorescent paints and crayons, and different tactile materials in play trays). The teacher reorganized the nursery layout to create more space between the furniture, and added additional spotlighting to the book corner. In both these examples, all the children in the setting benefited in their social skills: they learned to play considerately with Peter and Jenny.

By developing informed understanding of the relationship between play, learning and the curriculum, the status of play can be extended beyond

FIGURE 5.10   'NANNY, PLEASE BRING MIKEY TO PICK ME UP FROM NURSERY'.

the pre-school years and can continue to provide powerful contexts for both teaching and learning. To summarize, children need:

- time, space, and varied, good-quality resources

- a curriculum which is culturally diverse and relevant, includes a wide variety of play experiences and a balance between teachers' and children's intentions

- appropriately matched activities and experiences with opportunities for hands-on and brains-on activities

- opportunities for practice, mastery, consolidation and transferability

- opportunities to perceive relationships between areas of knowledge and experience

- the support of more knowledgeable others – peers and adults

- opportunities to make connections between learning and experiences at home and school

- opportunities to develop confidence and self-esteem

- to play considerately with others, and take care of their playing/learning environments

- to be valued, listened to and taken seriously

- to play and work alongside skilled, knowledgeable educators.

The following chapter examines how practitioners can develop a pedagogy of play, which links their pedagogical framing, with pedagogical techniques and strategies.

FURTHER READING

The following books provide a good theoretical underpinning for children's learning in the curriculum areas, as well as practical guidance for practitioners. Drifte (2002), Macintyre (2001) and Wall (2003) are strongly recommended for helping practitioners to ensure access and inclusion for children with special educational needs.

Drake, J. (2001) *Planning Children's Play and Learning in the Foundation Stage*, London, David Fulton.

Drifte, C. (2002) *Early Learning Goals for Children With Special Educational Needs: Learning Through Play*, London, David Fulton.

Fisher, J. (2002) *Starting From the Child?* (2nd edition), Buckingham, Open University Press.

Macintyre, C. (2001) *Enhancing Learning Through Play: A Developmental Perspective in Early Years Settings*, London, David Fulton.

Pound, L. (1999) *Supporting Mathematical Development in the Early Years*, Buckingham, Open University Press.

Rodger, R. (1999) *Planning an Appropriate Curriculum for the Under Five's*, London, David Fulton.

Wall, K. (2003) *Special Needs and the Early Years*, London, Paul Chapman.

Webster-Stratton, C. (1999) *How to Promote Children's Social and Emotional Competence*, London, Routledge.

Whitehead, M. (1999) *Supporting Language and Literacy Development in the Early Years*, Buckingham, Open University Press.

CHAPTER SIX

Developing a Pedagogy of Play

Mari, age three and a half, has been watching a group of children playing together, but does not have the skills or confidence to join in. She asks the teacher to join in her play:

> Mari: You come on my bus. I'm the driver, you're the Mummy. (*Sits in driver's seat and pretends to drive the bus. Holds imaginary steering wheel and makes engine noises.*)
>
> Teacher: Where shall we go?
>
> Mari: Shall we go to Portland?
>
> Teacher: Is that a long way?
>
> Mari: Not very far, it's not very far. I've been there, we go to the zoo.
>
> Teacher: That would be good. I'd love to go to the zoo. How long will it take to get there?
>
> Mari: I don't know, it's not very far.
>
> Teacher: Will it take a few minutes or half an hour?
>
> Mari: What time is it? You look at your watch.
>
> Teacher: Ten o' clock.
>
> Mari: It's not very far. We go to see pandas. Oh we're there, it didn't take very long. You can come in as well.
>
> Teacher: Do I have to pay any money to get in?
>
> Mari: Yes.
>
> Teacher: How much does it cost?
>
> Mari: (*crossly*) I don't know, you've got the watch. (*Mari then turned away and lost interest in the play.*)

We have opened this chapter on the adult's role in play with an example of what not to do and when not to do it. Mari had the confidence to approach the teacher as a play partner: she was able to assign roles, communicate the pretence and define the action, showing abstract and symbolic thinking. Unfortunately the teacher was more concerned with eliciting Mari's concepts of space, time, distance and money. The barrage of questions eventually left Mari cross and frustrated: the teacher was not a good player and failed to enter into the role, the flow or the spirit of the play.

This vignette illustrates some of the dilemmas that practitioners face when considering their role in play. Ideologically, practitioners often consider that children should have ownership and control of their play, and that play is their private world. Intervention may be seen as intrusive, particularly in role play where adults may limit or change the direction of the play in ways not intended by the children. In contrast, highly structured play, where resources and tools are used for specific purposes, may allow little space for the child's creative thought and self-initiated activity. Adult-initiated activities are often perceived as having different (usually higher) status, intentions and outcomes to child-initiated activities. Practitioners are more likely to be involved in the former than the latter, with the result that learning opportunities are missed. In the study by Bennett *et al.* (1997) the participating teachers identified many episodes of play where children would have benefited from adult involvement, because they did not always know how to enter a play situation or to solve problems as they arose. Activities sometimes broke down because children lacked the skills of negotiation, cooperation or conflict resolution. The teachers realized that they made assumptions about children's abilities to share resources, include their peers, sustain friendships and share their expertise. As a result of participating in the study, the teachers changed their beliefs: they acknowledged that if play provides valuable contexts for learning, then it also provides valuable opportunities for teaching. Therefore a key challenge is to create unity between playing, learning and teaching so that the flow and spirit of play are enhanced rather than disrupted. So what support can practitioners draw on in order to develop a pedagogy of play?

There is substantial evidence to support the view that a socio-cultural model of teaching and learning can help practitioners to improve their practice (Anning *et al*, 2004; Sayeed and Guerin, 2000). These theories are equally applicable to developing a *pedagogy of play*, which is defined as:

- the ways in which practitioners make provision for playful and play-based activities

- how they plan play/learning environments

- all the pedagogical techniques and strategies they use to support or enhance learning through play (Wood, 2004).

Practitioners have an important role in supporting children's learning and development through play, particularly where play is likely to be a leading form of activity (as recommended in Birth to Three Matters, and the Curriculum Guidance for the Foundation Stage). In Key Stages 1 and 2, teachers should build on early play experiences to support progression and continuity; more challenging play is as important as more challenging work. Becoming a master player is the height of developmental achievement for young children: skilful practitioners make such play possible, and continue to nurture 'can-do' orientations to learning across the play–work continuum (Jones and Reynolds, 1992). In Chapter 5 we outlined the importance of *pedagogical framing* in building a co-constructive curriculum which integrates child- and adult-initiated play activities. This chapter focuses on *pedagogical interactions, techniques and strategies*, and examines key characteristics of the practitioner's role. Practical examples are given in order to relate principles of effective pedagogy to contemporary theories of learning. We are not making the assumption that play is only valuable when it pays into the curriculum, or when practitioners are directly involved. The pedagogical techniques discussed in this chapter outline different levels of involvement and interaction, and are intended to inform practitioners' decisions and actions.

1. BE A FLEXIBLE PLANNER

One of the main challenges in developing a pedagogy of play is planning for child- and adult-initiated activities. But which comes first? There is no right answer to this question, because it depends on the flow of activities in the setting, the age of the children and the range of abilities in the class or group. Younger children may typically need a period of exploration of materials (what does this do?) before they can develop their own flow of activity (what can I do with this?). Older children tend to become absorbed more quickly into play but need time for challenge and extension. As the examples in the previous chapter demonstrated, practitioners can pick up on an idea or area of interest from the children, or they can introduce their own ideas and suggestions. Either way, they can infect children with enthusiasm (Boyce, 1946) for learning and playing by *sharing intentions*. Planning for a rolling programme of topics or themes is not best suited to young children because their agendas may not fit in with the set topics: their interests may change, some play themes last just a few days, while others may span several weeks. The play spiral (Moyles, 1989) provides a useful framework for creating unity between adult- and child-initiated activities, which combines free and directed play (Figure 6.1). In this framework, Moyles reinforces the notion that learning is recursive (children engage in a wide variety of activities, using many

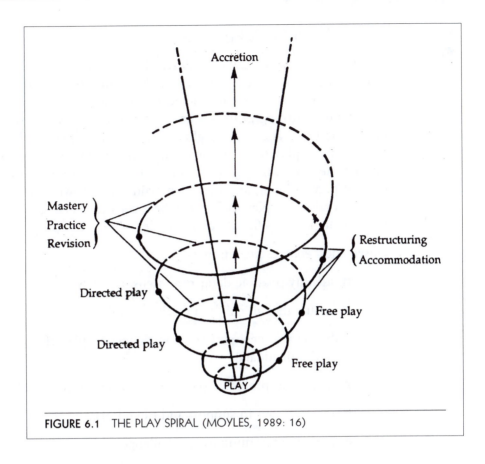

FIGURE 6.1   THE PLAY SPIRAL (MOYLES, 1989: 16)

learning processes) and incremental (learners become more skilled, knowledgeable, competent and confident). Different play activities provide opportunities for revision, practice and mastery, leading to further challenge and extension.

Practitioners plan for *intended learning outcomes* and allow for *possible learning outcomes* because in play activities, the two are not necessarily the same. In Chapter 5 we saw how pedagogical framing can enable practitioners to set up play–learning opportunities which make learning inevitable. At the same time, good assessment strategies (see Chapter 7) will ensure that practitioners are aware of the *actual learning outcomes* achieved by the children. By adopting a co-constructive approach to planning the curriculum, practitioners can ensure that learning experiences relate to, and go beyond, the policy frameworks (teaching, learning and playing can occur 'outside the boxes').

2. BE A SKILLED OBSERVER

Observation is an essential skill which is validated in all curriculum models. Being a skilled observer enables practitioners to tune in to children's play activities, understand the meaning of play in their terms, and identify learning processes and outcomes. However, observing play raises questions about the rights of children to play without undue interference – play often becomes more interesting when it takes place outside the controlling gaze of adults. Being a sensitive observer is an integral part of being an effective practitioner; knowing when to stand back and allow the play to flow can be a conscious pedagogical decision. So what are the benefits of being a skilled observer of play?

Observation enables practitioners to

- identify possible dangers and ensure safety

- ensure that all children receive attention

- be alert to new patterns and themes in play (for groups and individuals)

- be alert to problems (children being excluded or bullied)

- identify ways to support and extend play

- identify opportunities for challenge

- learn about individual children: their patterns of action and interaction, interests, agendas, dispositions

- learn about children's meanings and intentions

- show interest in, and value, children's play

- inform planning for individuals and for groups

- provide evidence to inform discussions about children's learning and share with others in the setting

- share experiences and inform discussions with parents, carers and other professionals

- provide evidence that stimulates reflection and evaluation of the quality of the curriculum offered, and what use children are making of the environment and resources (human and material)

- make links between theory and practice, raise questions and propose solutions

- support professional development.

Observation serves different purposes, and can be carried out in several ways. There is a difference between the spontaneous, ongoing observations that practitioners engage in on a day to day basis, and more planned, systematic observations. In the latter, practitioners need to decide:

- **Who** to observe: individual child, group, adult–child or peer interactions

- **When** to observe: beginning, middle, end or whole play session

- **What** to observe: whether to follow a child through one/many activities or follow different children at one/many activities

- **How long** to observe: a general 'sweep' of the area or classroom is always useful to check on what is happening in a group or in the room. Time sampling is useful for focusing on a child/activity/routine at specific times and intervals.

- **Where** to observe: indoors or outdoors, in a specific area such as role play, construction, sand, water

- **How** to observe: participant or non-participant

- **How** to record observations: written notes, digital photographs or video, checklist.

Fitness for purpose is a central concern. Observation techniques and strategies vary according to whether practitioners want to learn more about:

- a particular child or group of children (for example, boys/girls, friendships, ability groups)

- the effectiveness of the curriculum

- the effectiveness of specific activities

- the effectiveness of routines

- the actions and interactions of staff in the setting

■ the value of doing observations as a research or professional development activity.

Becoming a skilled observer takes time and practice. However, time is
often a major difficulty for busy practitioners. Therefore, play-based
observations should be planned as an ongoing part of the daily or weekly
routine. The aim is to capture the child as player/learner in the
playing/learning context. *Participant observations* can be carried out as part
of everyday interactions with children in play activities. A notepad or
checklist can be used to record information: for example, how a child
enters a role-play area; what skills, knowledge and competences children
are using in large construction; use of language and other forms of
representation. Digital cameras are also helpful for recording critical or
significant incidents. In participant observations, practitioners can maintain an active and interactive role with the children, which is useful for
tracking the effects of an intervention (for example, introducing new ideas
or resources into the play). In *non-participant observations*, the practitioner
is not involved in the activity, but will be placed nearby in order to record
information. Using a digital camera, a video with a good microphone, or
placing a tape recorder nearby, captures information that can be used at
a later date for reflection and discussion.

Although being a skilled observer is an essential characteristic of effective
practitioners, there are *ethical issues* involved in such activities. All
observations should be sensitive to the children: having an adult present,
or nearby, can influence the flow and spirit of play. Children may play
differently (in a more restrained or self-conscious way) or may not play
at all. Observation can impose an unequal power relationship in that
adults may intrude on aspects of play that children would prefer to remain
private. Practitioners should also be mindful of how they use recorded
information, particularly video and still images, and with whom the
information is shared. On the positive side, children often enjoy looking
at the photos and video recordings, and may offer additional information
about their actions and meanings. Video recordings are useful for tracking
learning and development for children with special educational needs,
especially where information has to be shared with other professionals.
Regular, systematic observations can sensitize practitioners to the ways in
which children master the cultural tools of school, home and society and
how these are integrated in their play. These insights can inform
documenting and discussing play with parents, and provide evidence that
play is a valuable tool for learning.

3. BE A GOOD LISTENER

Play activities provide flexible, open-ended opportunities for children to create their own sense and meaning. Play is multi-faceted and multi-layered, and the meanings that children construct are not always immediately visible to adults. Being a good listener enables practitioners to respect and engage with children on their own terms, within their own frames of meaning as they negotiate the real–not real boundaries in play activities. Respectful listening also implies emotional engagement, thus enabling practitioners to take an interest in every child. Being a respectful listener involves being alert to the different ways in which children communicate, and their definitions of reality within the play context.

Children use meta-communication – talking about their talk, their symbolization, and their actions. They speak and act 'as if' they are a different character, but at the same time communicate the action in order to manage themselves and others. They step in and out of the shared fantasy in order to structure, define, negotiate and direct the play sequence. This involves different modes of communication and perspective-taking as they separate the management of the play from the pretence. It is often the case that children who are perceived as having poor listening skills in adult-directed activities may have significantly better listening skills in play because they are more motivated and engaged. Children have to be good listeners in order to filter the complex flow of information that helps to sustain the sequence of the play activity. For example, actions, gestures, language and symbols may be combined rapidly in a play sequence, with children clarifying the meaning of tools and symbols as the play progresses. Practitioners can learn a great deal about the child's playful state of mind, and the ways in which children communicate 'what is happening inside their heads' and transform this into 'what is happening in the play'. Many forms of play involve sophisticated levels of abstraction and symbolism which practitioners need to understand in order to inform their interactions and subsequent planning.

4. BE A GOOD COMMUNICATOR

Being a skilful co-player involves communicating with children in many different ways. In play (especially role play), children often use exaggerated gestures, body language and facial expressions, all of which help to signal 'this is play'. They clarify the meaning of tools and symbols both verbally and physically. Adults need to pick up on and use these signals to indicate that they are also in playing mode. For children with special educational needs, visual and tactile modes of communication, including British Sign Language, Makaton or Braille, promote inclusion and stimulate playfulness. Being a good communicator involves shared conversations, rather than question-and-answer routines (what might be termed typical 'teacherly' behaviours). Commenting on action, using out-loud thinking, questioning and reasoning, pretending not to know, conveying emotions, are effective pedagogical strategies, especially where practitioners go with the flow and spirit of the play. Communicating approval, validation and enthusiasm are also important strategies: practitioners can give powerful messages that what children are learning and doing in their play is as valuable as their 'work'. Being a playful communicator involves responding to children's ideas, language and actions, for example, by taking on a role, by showing interest and becoming involved as a co-player.

5. INFECT CHILDREN WITH ENTHUSIASM

Many play scholars provide examples of practitioners inspiring and supporting children's play. Hall (2000) describes a curriculum development project in a Year 1 classroom, which focused on children's literacy development. The role play began with a visit to a garage, followed by the children making the garage area (a workshop and office), and providing props and resources. Hall goes on to describe a wide variety of literacy activities that reflected authentic practices, and inspired play, including:

- writing to the Town Hall planning department for planning permission to build the garage

- receiving objections to the planning application

- writing advertisements for jobs and job applications

- writing estimates for repairs and bills

- writing safety rules

- writing notices, using clipboards to make notes about the jobs.

Because these activities were open-ended, children across the ability range were able to engage at different levels. As a result of the teacher's involvement in the play (pedagogical framing), all children engaged in reading and writing with intensity and purpose, because their activities were situated in authentic contexts:

> The constant association with the socio-dramatic play meant that the writing experiences were meaningful, were used to make things happen, were means-ended, were linked to a past and future that had real significance, involved a wide range of audiences and purposes, was highly social, and reflected the children's beliefs and values about how to use literacy appropriately – in short, all the things characteristic of literacy use. (Hall, 2000: 204)

BOX OF DELIGHTS Inspired by Hall's research, Jacqui Bamford, a Year 1 classroom assistant, worked with the class teacher to develop playful approaches to teaching literacy. They were concerned to address the teaching objectives in the National Literacy Framework for Teaching, but in a more child-centred way. The objectives focused on fiction and poetry: stories with familiar settings, stories and rhymes with predictable and repeating patterns. They wanted to transform the teaching objectives into worthwhile learning experiences which would

- engage children's interest in reading and writing through play-based and teacher-directed activities

- empower them to make choices and decisions

- encourage them to be creative and imaginative

- enable them to use a wide variety of skills (physical, cognitive, emotional and social)

- make connections across a range of curriculum subjects.

Over a period of several weeks, the children were told traditional tales. They discussed the plot, characters, sequence and setting for each tale. The children were organized into ability groups and each group was given three boxes to transform into miniature puppet theatres to represent the beginning, middle and end of the tale. The practitioners provided assistance for the different stages of the task. The children planned and made the backdrops and scenery. Some characters were attached to the backdrop, and some were made as puppets on sticks so that they that could be moved across the stage. The scenes were set for dramas to unfold.

The children were encouraged to retell the stories and make up their own versions. The adults suggested writing frames, such as retelling the story with changes to the plot and ending; writing letters (for example, from the wolf to the three little pigs); and writing scripts (for example, what Red Riding Hood said to her Mum when she got home). The boxes also provided a setting for the children to develop role play around the characters in the stories, making up dialogue, developing and changing the stories. The involvement of practitioners as co-players was integral to this project: they modelled taking on the role of a character, retelling the story, and inviting questions from the children. In the role-play area in the classroom, links were made between adult-initiated activities and children's playful exploration of literacy and language. Gradually they developed their stories, using literacy and language for many different purposes:

- taking telephone messages from Red Riding Hood to her mother

- Goldilocks writing a letter of apology to the three bears

- writing a recipe for the Little Pink Pig to bake a peach tart

- directing their own play scripts and writing their own stories.

This example of a child's story, based on Little Red Riding Hood, shows detailed understanding of plot, sequence, script, and structure:

> First little red riding hode [hood] was plaing [playing] in her garden. Later on her mum calld [called] her can you take some flowers and some wine to your grandma yes she side [said]. So she got her basket and then she put her red coat on and out she went. Hello side [said] her grandma wut [what] is in ther [there] side [said] gran some wine and some flowers. Then she herd [heard] a noys [noise] saying let me out. Then she pulld [pulled] the cuther [cover] off grandma and then the big bad wolf gobard [gobbled] her up after that her dad heard a noys [noise] like a big fat wolf coming from grans house so he cwikly [quickly] ran ther and slamd [slammed] the door. Then her dad ran home and tolld [told] mum. Then mum ran to grandmas house and then thay [they] cried ther [their] eyes out. The end.

As a result of this integrated approach, the literacy teaching objectives were met in a more holistic way. The Box of Delights project was particularly motivating for children who were struggling with literacy because they could participate successfully in different ways and at different levels. The children read their own versions of the stories, and performed some of their plays for the whole school. The success of this playful approach was evident in the learning outcomes, which included:

- improvements in children's text and word-level work (children using phonic knowledge, and beginning to use punctuation correctly)

- willingness to have a go and take risks

- creativity, imagination and empathy

- improved motivation and participation across the whole class, but particularly for the lower-ability children

- higher levels of confidence in developing plot and sequencing

- using a more adventurous vocabulary (oral and written)

- collaborative peer-tutoring, and enhanced social skills

- creating and solving problems

- enhanced self-esteem.

The project also infected the children with enthusiasm across the curriculum:

- Design and technology: designing the boxes and puppets, physical and manipulative skills such as painting, joining, fixing, cutting out.

- Maths: scale and size of boxes and puppets; area; measurement; using mathematical language and concepts in storytelling.

- Personal, social and emotional education: collaboration, turn-taking, making group decisions; peer-group modelling and interaction; peer affiliation; empathy with characters in the stories; exploring moral issues through the stories; self-esteem.

6. SUPERVISE FOR SAFETY, ACCESS AND EQUAL OPPORTUNITIES

Effective practitioners are always alert to the safety and well-being of the children in terms of the physical, social and emotional environment. All educational settings should reflect the pluralist society in which we live, and should enable children to function effectively as active citizens in their present and future lives (Siraj-Blatchford and Siraj-Blatchford, 1995). Brooker (2002) emphasizes the importance of understanding and valuing children's home and community cultures, and ensuring that these are reflected in the resources of the school. The curriculum should not just reflect home and community cultures (for example, food, festivals, clothing and rituals), but should enable children to co-construct learning through activities that integrate all aspects of their lives.

Although we have taken a positive view of the benefits of play, it is important to remember that children demonstrate anti-social behaviours, especially where they play beyond the adult gaze, and engage in covert or subversive activities. Play provides a means by which children come to understand and master the plural cultures of home, school and society. At the same time, they may convey negative or stereotypical attitudes. Children play with powerful concepts such as strength and weakness, good and evil, justice and injustice, belonging and rejecting. Play enables them to feel powerful in an adult-dominated world, which has both positive and negative connotations. They may include and exclude others on the grounds of ethnicity, gender, physical appearance and capabilities, and can behave in quite cruel ways – teasing, bullying, name-calling and other forms of social aggression. Discriminatory or abusive comments can occur beyond the adult gaze. For example, Cook (2003) identified instances of individual children being excluded from play, and of boys excluding girls or disrupting their play. For older children, school playgrounds can provide ideal opportunities for bullying and aggression, especially where they begin to challenge all forms of authority and establish their place in the peer-group pecking order (Bishop and Curtis, 2001).

Practitioners need to intervene to resolve disputes and challenge anti-social behaviours and, where possible, encourage the play to continue with minimal disruption. At the same time, it is important to reflect on the reasons for 'managerial' interventions in play. In Cook's study, the play transcripts revealed some gender discrimination in such interventions. The boys' play was often energetic and boisterous, and sometimes strayed beyond the boundaries of the role-play area. Play themes included chasing, dying or being killed, rescuing and being rescued, naughty dogs, sharks and crocodiles. The teacher and classroom assistant were more likely to intervene in the noisy play of boys than in the quiet, domestic play of the girls, even where the latter was stereotypical and repetitive (cleaning, tidying and looking after the baby). As a result of reflecting on her observations, Cook realized that the boys' play was often rich in terms of their play scripts and dialogue, and deeply absorbing. As a result, she became more accepting of the noise levels and more tuned in to the dramatic quality and educational potential of their play.

Ensuring access to play is particularly important for children with special educational needs. For example, when Lina started in a nursery class, she was unwilling to speak; she had few social skills and did not know how to play. She had been neglected by inadequate parents who left her alone for long periods of time, with little stimulation. She was passive and spent a long time sitting and watching the other children. The teacher and nursery nurse embarked on a long programme to encourage Lina to participate in play and other activities. This involved some play-tutoring, first in a one-to-one context and then gradually involving other children. After a shaky start Lina gradually learned to communicate and began to interact on her own initiative. It took about a year for her to learn the social skills for being a co-player, such as joining a game, taking on and staying in a role, and being able to pretend. Children with special educational needs often take small steps in their learning and playing, and take more time to build their skills and confidence. Therefore practitioners need to ensure that play activities are appropriate and accessible across all levels of ability.

Practitioners also need to ensure that children feel emotionally safe. In Chapter 2 we discussed the benefits and challenges of superhero and rough-and-tumble play. Not all children engage in these forms of play, and practitioners struggle with the moral and ethical issues involved in play-fighting, especially where they strive to create a democratic, caring ethos in the setting. There are a variety of strategies to deal with these issues:

■ Set up discussions in which the children can state how they feel about superhero play and listen to each other's points of view.

■ Explain the realities of weapons, aggression and violence in society. Even pre-school children are aware of conflict, violence and war from the media.

- Establish what the problems are and where they are occurring – indoors and/or outdoors – and what behaviours are impacting on other children.

- Encourage the children to explore solutions to the problems.

- Encourage the children to share in the process of making decisions about what happens in the classroom and playground. This can be done as a part of circle time; if the problem is more serious, dedicated time may need to he allocated.

- Implement the agreed solutions and monitor their effectiveness. Be prepared to support the children by teaching conflict-resolution strategies, and developing awareness of their behaviour, and sensitivity to how it affects others.

7. BE A SENSITIVE CO-PLAYER

Jones and Reynolds (1992) argue that practitioners can help children to become master players. Therefore they need to consider appropriate pedagogical strategies that support learning and development but are not overly intrusive or domineering. Again this is a question of balance. In a predominantly *laissez-faire* environment children may miss out on adult support and guidance. In an over-structured environment, children will not learn to be resourceful or creative in their play. Figure 6.2 lists some pedagogical skills and strategies that can be used in children's play, with the guiding principle that all interactions should be sensitive to the child and to the play context. (It is also interesting to note that children use these skills and strategies in their play.)

---

observing, listening, being playful, using humour, questioning, responding to children's initiatives and directions, communicating, demonstrating, modelling, encouraging, praising, advising, guiding, suggesting, challenging, adopting a role, staying in role, playing on the children's terms, instructing, imparting new knowledge, prompting, reminding, extending, structuring, re-structuring, transforming, directing, re-directing, managing, monitoring, assessing, diagnosing,

---

FIGURE 6.2   PEDAGOGICAL SKILLS AND STRATEGIES

It takes time for practitioners to learn when to intervene in children's play, how to adapt to the play context and what strategies to use in different situations. Adult involvement in play is complex because the same activity can serve a variety of different purposes according to the age, skills and prior experiences of the children, and the nature of the activity. Therefore the critical questions are:

- When to be involved?

- How to be involved?

- With what intentions?

WHEN TO BE INVOLVED

Practitioners can be involved in planning and facilitating play, as discussed in Chapter 5. Sometimes the initiative or idea may come from the adult, sometimes from the child. We have already given several examples to show that children who are used to playful adults will readily ask them for support with a self-identified problem. With experience, children learn to identify the support they need, which shapes the nature of the interaction. Skilled practitioners carry a memory bank of children's patterns of learning and previous experience: they can remind children of previous themes and activities, and help them to extend their skills. They can also help children make connections between areas of learning and experience, thus facilitating episodes of sustained shared thinking (Siraj-Blatchford and Sylva, 2004). Because practitioners need to be alert to safety, it may be necessary to intervene directly to resolve a dispute, particularly if the child does not have the skills or confidence. The intervention may provide opportunities to help children to recognize the problem and learn conflict resolution strategies which they can use in other situations.

HOW TO BE INVOLVED

Practitioners adopt a variety of roles as co-players and, at the same time, can use pedagogical skills and strategies to enhance children's play and learning. Episodes of sustained shared thinking often arise through sustained shared playing. Modelling is an important pedagogical strategy because imitation is a powerful spur to learning in early childhood. Bruner (1991) calls this 'observational learning' and argues that it is much more complex than the term 'imitation' implies. The practitioner can actively model skills, strategies, attitudes, behaviours and learning processes by using out-loud thinking, questioning, reflection on action and feelings. This assists the process of guided reinvention in which children internalize or actively construct knowledge and acquire tools for thinking and learning.

Direct instruction is often skills-based, and can be appropriate as long as practitioners tune their interactions with the child's observed needs and interests. Direct instruction may also involve out-loud thinking, talking through the task, modelling skills for the child, then checking whether the child has internalized the new skills or processes. These strategies are relevant in constructive play, sand, water, art and technology where children may need support with using tools and materials, and creating new uses and combinations. Different types of play require different roles. For example, in constructive play many of the kits available today are quite sophisticated and need specialized manipulative skills, technical language and understanding of concepts related to design and technology. By teaching relevant skills, concepts and knowledge, practitioners can enable children to develop their skills and play with their own ideas. With experience, children can extend their skills in planning, designing and building which reflect many of the processes adults use in authentic contexts. They also become more confident in problem creating and problem solving as the following example shows.

Joe, Helen, Katy and Martin are discussing their ideas for renovating an area used previously as a bank. They have decided to change it to an art gallery and want to put up black wallpaper to show up the paintings. They have already stripped the walls, removed the staples, cleaned it out and are now talking about the door that is old and has several holes in it:

> Joe: We could take the old door off and make a new one.
> Martin: We can't do that Joe cos if we cut the old door off we won't be able to get a new one back on.
> Joe: We'll put some cardboard down cos there's holes in it.
> Katy: Mmm, yes, it would be stronger then.
> Helen: Yes, you can put string through the holes so it will open.
> Katy: There's too many holes to do that. You'll get tangled.
> Joe: There's a big hole in the actual door bit. You could put a door handle there.
> Martin: I know how to make a door handle. You could get those screws like you use on a bath. You could get a screw and screw it on through the other side then you'd have a handle.
> Katy: There's a lot of little holes. We could cover those up with cardboard and paint over them and the big hole could be where the handle is.

Helen: Yes, and you could use string to put round the handle and it
would hold the door back like the hall door.
(*After this task was completed successfully, the children moved on to
papering the walls.*)
Joe: We'll have to cut the shape there (*where the paper overlaps the door*),
it's too big.
Teacher: Don't cut it. Instead of cutting it fold the paper under and
staple it there. That will make the edges stronger than a cut edge and
the edges will be smoother. If it's too big you can always fold it, if
it's too small you can't make it fit.

Katy goes to stick the wallpaper up in the middle of the wall. The teacher
shows her how to place it up against the corner and outside edge. Joe
starts to measure the size of the paper needed by placing the metre rule
down the centre of the paper. The teacher shows them how to measure
the outside edge. The children have measured to find the size of the
wallpaper they have to cut from a roll. They measure and cut one piece
and stick it on. They need three whole pieces the same size for each wall.

Martin: Start at the next bit now. It's 1 metre 55 centimetres isn't it?
Teacher: That's right. How many pieces do you think we'll need for this
wall?
Helen: Two.
Joe: Um, three.
Teacher: Yes, three I think, you'll need the same piece of paper how
many times?
Joe and Helen: Three.
Teacher: How about this time then we cut the next piece, then roll out
the wallpaper again and lay this piece on the top, mark it and cut it
to the right size?
Martin: That'll be quicker.

The children are measuring another piece of wallpaper that has to be 1 m
20 cm long. They lay down a one-metre ruler and get another one to
continue measuring. The end of the second ruler gets caught on a nearby
cupboard.

Teacher: Do you think we need to measure the next bit with the metre
ruler? We've got 1 metre, we need our paper to be how much longer?
Katy: 1 metre 20 centimetres we said –
Joe: Twenty more.
Teacher: Yes we only need twenty centimetres more. Would it be easier
to use a smaller ruler? It has centimetres the same as the metre ruler.
Helen: They'd be the same wouldn't they? (doubtfully)
Teacher: Let's try.

Helen picks up the metre ruler and checks to see if her measuring is the
same as the teacher's and then uses the smaller ruler.

Joe: It will be the same, Helen.

Teacher: It's always a good idea to check if you're not sure.

The involvement of the teacher as mediator promotes the development of new skills, thinking and understanding using the children's existing knowledge. This activity also demonstrates the continuum between play and work: it was child-initiated and enabled the children to follow their intentions. The children were pretending to renovate the bank and create an art gallery but at the same time needed real-world skills and competences to sustain the pretence. They were transforming ideas, materials and their environment. The teacher acted as a more knowledge-able other by demonstrating skills, using out-loud thinking, and promp-ting the children's metacognitive activity. She was responsive but not intrusive and the children accepted her presence on this basis. The children also assisted each other in order to sustain the activity. They brought energy and motivation to this task because they knew that their peers were creating their own works of art to hang in the gallery. Play provided an integrating mechanism for their knowledge, experience and social skills and prompted further learning.

It is perhaps easier for practitioners to respond to children's activities in similar play contexts where there are visible, ongoing opportunities for interaction with a co-constructed agenda. Role play poses different problems because it is a qualitatively different form of play. The main motives for role play are the development of relationships and moral consciousness, and the exercise of will. Practitioners are often reluctant to intervene in role play because of its free-flow nature. Many report that they see good opportunities for adult involvement but are constrained by their beliefs that they should respect children's privacy and ownership. Or they have forgotten how to play and feel that they need to rediscover these skills in order to play on the children's terms. In order to be a successful co-player, practitioners need to observe the play and understand what the children are playing with and playing at. They need to be sensitive to children's ongoing themes, rules, conventions, groupings, play partners, preferences and their use of space and resources.

Reflecting on the socio-cultural theories outlined in Chapters 3 and 4, practitioners do have an important function in role play, even where the motives arise from the children and they carry out most of the negotiation and management. The adult should respond to the children's initiatives, largely on their terms, and not take over, direct or control the play to the extent that it loses its spontaneity and becomes teacher- rather than child-centred. This can be problematic for adults who are uncomfortable with a shift in power relationships, particularly where children subvert or challenge classroom rules. In the study by Bennett *et al* (1997), one Reception teacher (Gina) set up a role-play area as a shop: the children made and priced the goods, and she anticipated that they would use their mathematical knowledge in buying and selling. However, the children were more interested in playing cops, robbers and guard dogs, and their play was often boisterous, noisy and disruptive. Gina believed that children should have opportunities for free play, without adult intervention. However, she acknowledged that some intervention was necessary in order to understand and nurture this play. Rather than banning the cops, robbers and dogs play, she actively nurtured the children's interests during teacher-initiated activities. Gina encouraged the children to write story boards and cartoons of play scenarios which they subsequently developed in the role-play area. On reflection, it is hardly surprising that the children wanted to enliven their shop play with cops, robbers and guard dogs: their play was much more dramatic and emotionally engaging than merely buying and selling goods, and they drew on television programmes, cartoons and characters in developing their play scripts and scenarios.

OW, OW, MY POOR ANKLE The following example shows how a teacher entered successfully into role play (Attfield, 1992). Jenny (age seven years two months) is playing as a nurse in the role-play area which was a health centre. The teacher registered as a patient with an injured ankle:

> Adult: Ow, ow, my poor ankle, what shall I do nurse?
> Jenny: I think that you should stay in for two days and calm yourself down and stop rubbing it.
> Adult: Is it broken nurse? Can I sit down? Ow, ow.
> Jenny: Yes, you'd better sit here. I'll go and get the X-ray . . . no you have sprained it. I'm going to bandage it before I water it.
> Adult: You're going to water my ankle? Why are you going to water my ankle, nurse, it's not a flower?
> Jenny: No I'm going to dab it and then I'll put this bandage on.
> *(Begins to put the bandage on over the adult's shoe)*
> Adult: Ow, ow. Do you think I should take my shoe off?
> Jenny: Oh yes. Nurse come and help me (*to another child*) . . . you hold the safety pin and give it to me when I've done this.
> Adult: Can I walk on my ankle or should I rest it?
> Jenny: I'll give you some crutches and when you get home you've got to put it on a stool or table or something soft.
> Adult: Do I have to take any tablets for the pain?
> Jenny: I'll give you a 'scription (*asks for help with writing here*).
> *(Later – to another child who has had a car crash)*

Jenny: I'll put the bandage on your arm and you must never put it on the table like that or it'll get even more bad and you can still play football but try not to hit anyone with your hand and be careful you don't cut it when you're washing up. There now, come back in two weeks.

The adult's questioning prompts Jenny's wide understanding of a nurse's role and related activities. The role play continued for some time and enabled the teacher to make some detailed assessments of Jenny's skills, knowledge and understanding as the record sheet shows:

Emotional: Jenny is quietly confident and able to organize other children in role play. She showed perception of the caring role of a nurse and sustained this attitude throughout the play.

Social: Takes an organizing role, involves others in the play. Takes turns with equipment and demonstrates skills to others.

Attitudes: Motivated to write and continued in role for an hour. Much enjoyment evident. Sustained concentration throughout the play and was fully absorbed in her role.

Language: Used language for directing, explaining, talking on the telephone, questioning her patients in her role as a nurse. She listened to others before making decisions. Used writing for different purposes – making appointments and writing prescriptions.

Mathematical: Experience of writing appointment times with the help of an adult.

Scientific: Naming parts of the human body (pelvis, hinge joint), knowledge of X-rays and what they are used for.

Physical: Used props for bathing wounds (tweezers and cotton wool), fastening bandages, tying slings. Organized layout of health centre, set up equipment, led patients around.

Problem-solving: Organizing one or more play partners, involving other children to help, thinking about caring for the patients and seeing to their injuries.

The teacher noted that Jenny wanted to know more about X-rays and bones and how plaster is used to set broken bones. She needed to develop more confidence in writing for different reasons and in different contexts. This information provided vital feedback into the curriculum to support further learning.

JACK AND THE BEANSTALK Practitioners often find it quite challenging to go with the flow of children's ideas and interests and follow unplanned developments. However, this strategy can be informed by observation of the children's activities, and joint creativity. A Reception class teacher noticed that the home corner was used in a repetitive, stereotypical way, mostly by girls. She used the story of Jack and the Beanstalk to extend and enrich the children's play. They were involved in planning the new setting, designing and making some of the resources, making suggestions for representing ideas in the story. The giant's treasure chest was filled with milk-bottle tops and a variety of resources that the children brought from home. A three-dimensional beanstalk was made which wandered up the walls and across the ceiling. The teacher added many other resources such as different sizes of clothes and cooking equipment to contrast Jack's home with the giant's home. Because the children were involved in planning and decision-making, interpersonal skills were developed such as negotiation, cooperation, establishing rules, and taking responsibility for looking after the props and resources. Time and opportunities were made for adult involvement, though not as much as the teacher would have liked, and the children were encouraged to talk about their play, add further resources and develop the theme as they wished. This model was both enabling and empowering. It allowed children to have ownership of their play but at the same time the teacher felt that they were enjoying higher-quality play with many opportunities for learning that were embedded in a meaningful context.

8. BE A RESEARCHER

Effective practitioners are good researchers: they are alert to the complexities of children's learning, and have an enquiry-based approach to improving the quality of their provision and engaging in professional development. Children are complex, fascinating and often enigmatic. Working and playing with children raises many questions, problems and challenges which are not always solved in the everyday flow of activities. Being a researcher helps practitioners to become reflective, thoughtful and analytical. Many of the examples in this book are drawn from small-scale research studies carried out by teachers and other practitioners on advanced study modules. They often set out with burning questions, issues they felt strongly about, tensions between their beliefs and the demands of policy frameworks, and a genuine desire to better understand playing, learning and teaching. Studies that have engaged practitioners as researchers in their own settings have reported positive benefits:

- Taking time to stand back and look more critically at what is happening in their setting.

- Learning skills and strategies for observing, recording and analyzing their practice.

- Learning collaboratively in a community of practice.

- Reflecting on their evidence, and generating strategies for improvement (sometimes at whole-school level).

- Feeling empowered by developing their skills and knowledge.

- Being able to challenge taken-for-granted assumptions.

- Changing their theories and/or practices (Bennett *et al.*, 1997; MacNaughton, 2000; Broadhead, 2004).

These processes are exemplified in the following observations that were carried out by Charlotte Rowland in her Reception/Year 1 class. The research activity was planned in a module on Teaching and Learning Through Play. The participants were asked to carry out ten-minute observations on two children, a girl and a boy, and bring their evidence for shared discussion and analysis. Charlotte's first observation enabled her to understand the meaning of Paul's play in the context of his activity, and his explanation:

Observation one, child two

Name: Paul   Age: 5

Date: Wednesday 5th February 2003   Time: 2 p.m.

Context: Outside area, during free play. Four/five other children present but not playing with Paul.

Observation: Paul was sitting on top of the caterpillar (play tunnel) and watching children playing in the home corner. The children left the home corner area after two or three minutes and Paul immediately went over to this area. He picked up the play dustbin and started to fill it up with play food and plates that had been left on the floor. Paul carried the bin over to the caterpillar and leaned over the top of it to empty the contents of the bin on the floor behind the caterpillar. He went back to the home corner and filled the bin up, and emptied it, in the same way. Paul did this three more times until there was nothing left in the home corner.

He then walked away from the area with a smile on his face.

He came over to me so I asked him why he had done that: he replied 'It's bin day. I'm the bin man. It's all gone to the dump.'

This observation shows how the meaning and purpose of a child's activity (especially in solitary play) is better understood within the context of play over a sustained period of time. On reflection, Charlotte considered that if she had only seen Paul filling and emptying the bin, she might have thought he was being naughty. His activity made more sense in relation to his imaginary context, and to his real-world knowledge. The next observation exemplifies the significance of observational learning (discussed above). The paradoxical nature of this episode is fascinating: the children are real pupils in a real classroom, but are playing at being pupils, and playing with typical teacher–pupil interactions, rules and routines. In this case, it is the teacher's behaviours that have been carefully observed, and reproduced by the children:

Observation two, child one

Name: Helen   Age: 5.4 (Year 1)
Date: Friday 14th February 2003   Time: 2.05 p.m.

Context: In classroom during activity time. Helen is playing 'schools' with two other children. Using teacher's easel, pens, etc.

Observation: Helen has previously been observed playing schools on her own, with imaginary pupils. Helen asked the teacher if she could play schools. She then collected the items she needed and asked two children to play with her – Khalid and Ella. Abi joined in briefly towards the end.

He: Do you wanna play schools?
El: Okay can I be Mrs F?
Kh: I wanna be Miss R
He: No I'm Miss R!
Kh: Ohhh! But . . .
He: We could take turns.
Kh: Okay. (*Helen sits on chair and picks up pen and paper*)
He: It's register time so you need to use your ears to listen.
El: I'm Mrs F.
Kh: When's it my turn?
He: Be quiet and listen!
Kh: Yes Miss R.
He: Now we will start 'Good Morning Khalid'.
Kh: Good morning, Miss R.

He: Now we will do an activity together on the carpet. I want you to listen very, very carefully.

Kh: But who's going to be special helper?

He: Oh you can be!

El: I'm still Mrs F.

He: Yes I know.

Kh: Can I have my turn soon?

He: Mrs F please would you sit with Khalid because he keeps talking and he should be listening.

El: (*moves next to Khalid*) Yes, be quiet Khalid and listen to Miss R!

He: Now let's start. We are going to do some counting this morning. (*Abi comes to join play.*)

Ab: Can I play? I wanna be Miss R.

Kh: It's my turn next.

He: You be you, Abi.

Ab: No I'll play later.

He: Let's get on now shall we, listen Khalid! We'll count to twenty.

All: Count to twenty together. (*Wind chimes – tidy up time*)

Kh: I didn't get a turn!

He: You can next time.

In this episode, the children have astute understanding of pedagogical routines, power relationships between teachers and pupils, and the rules of classroom discourse. These short observations reveal the child as player/learner, and the child in the playing/learning context. They also provide valuable evidence for discussion and reflection regarding the nature and purposes of play, and the ways in which children co-construct their play themes. In addition to having practical value, such observations also have theoretical value, in that they can enable the practitioner-as-researcher to understand the culture of play and the systems of shared meanings that children construct in socio-cultural contexts (as discussed in Chapters 3 and 4). Being a researcher can also inform the processes of assessment and evaluation, which will be explored in more detail in Chapter 7.

SO CAN WE DEFINE A PEDAGOGY OF PLAY?

In summary, this chapter has shown that the practitioner's role in play can be multi-faceted and multi-layered. The guiding principle is that adult interactions and interventions should be tuned in to what is happening in the play, and should respect the flow and spirit of the play. Both adult- and child-initiated play can provide ideas and interests that can be developed and extended. Practitioners can infect children with enthusiasm for playing, which can have positive effects on their learning. This is not to claim that play is only valuable when it pays into learning outcomes, or that play always has to be structured and organized by adults. Spontaneous, playful interactions can occur in adult-directed activities, just as children can be deeply engrossed and 'workful' in their play. The concepts of pedagogical framing and pedagogical interactions, techniques and strategies provide some guidance on how practitioners can think creatively about their roles in play, and help to create unity between playing, learning and teaching.

CHAPTER SEVEN

Assessing Children's Learning in Play

Vygotsky argued that we should not subject play to pedantic intellectualization, but at the same time he considered that only a profound internal analysis could contribute to our understanding of the meaning of play to young children. The aim of this chapter is to outline different purposes and forms of assessment, and provide insights into how assessment and evaluation can support teaching and learning through play. The focus is on assessment for learning: enabling practitioners to gather good evidence about children's progress and achievements which can inform practice and provision. Vignettes of children's play will show practical strategies for observing, documenting and discussing evidence of children's learning, and using individual play plans to support children with special educational needs.

THE PURPOSES OF ASSESSMENT

Assessment and evaluation are essentially at the heart of teaching and learning, and can be seen as complementary processes which enable practitioners to:

- develop their professional knowledge and understanding about how children learn

- make informed judgements and interpretations about children's learning, development, progress and achievements

- gather information about the effectiveness of the curriculum

- interpret the relationship between the planned curriculum, and how it is received by the children

- reflect critically on the quality and effectiveness of provision

- provide a feedback loop into curriculum planning

- build on, and extend, children's knowledge, skills and understanding

- make links between home, community, pre-school and school

- document information that can be discussed with parents, teachers and other professionals.

Ideally, assessment and evaluation should have a *knowledge function* and an *auditing function*. The *knowledge function* enables practitioners to develop informed insights into the patterns and styles of learning for each child, their needs, preferences, interests, friendships and identities. Practitioners also extend their professional knowledge about curriculum and pedagogical processes. Assessment should be useful to the child, the practitioner and other professionals. The *auditing function* enables practitioners to provide summative information about the child's competences and achievements in relation to curriculum objectives and learning goals, and includes baseline entry assessments, the Foundation Stage profile and Key Stage 1 SATs. There are ongoing concerns about the political emphasis on measurement and accountability (Carr, 2001a; Cowie and Carr, 2004); in line with established early childhood principles, the knowledge function, rather than auditing function, should be prioritized in practice. The two purposes should be interdependent, and contribute to informed reflection and evaluation about the quality and effectiveness of provision and practice. These processes apply equally to play, because it is a leading source of activity that provides windows into children's minds, thereby revealing patterns and meanings that are not always evident in more formal contexts. Building knowledge about the child as player/learner, and the child in the playing/learning context, can help practitioners to:

- 'fine-tune' their play provision

- understand the meaning of child-initiated and play-based activities

- help children to become master players

- inform the co-construction of the curriculum through joint activity.

FORMS OF ASSESSMENT

There are six forms of assessment, which serve different but complementary purposes:

- **Formative:** Practitioners form opinions and ideas about children's progress and achievements, which should inform subsequent curriculum planning. Formative assessment serves an important knowledge function by helping practitioners to understand 'where the child is at', and planning the next steps in the learning journey.

- **Ipsative:** Assessments of progress and achievement are related directly to the child's individual learning dispositions, preferred learning style, behaviours and previous experience. This form of assessment is referenced to the child rather than to external norms and expectations, and can be particularly helpful for children with special educational needs who may appear to be underachieving or failing against developmental norms or defined learning goals.

- **Diagnostic:** A more detailed form of assessment which requires educators to observe children in specific contexts, record difficulties and challenges, and plan appropriate support and interventions (e.g. behaviour, social adjustment, early difficulties with literacy and numeracy). Interventions can then be carefully matched to the child's learning styles and existing strengths.

- **Summative:** An overview or snapshot of progress and achievements at a specific point in time, usually referenced to curriculum provision or specific learning goals. Summative assessments can be criterion- or norm-referenced (for example, Baseline Assessment, Standard Attainment Tasks, Early Learning Goals).

- **Evaluative:** Assessment information is collated to provide evidence of children's progress and achievements over time, enabling practitioners to review the effectiveness of the curriculum offered, and identify priorities for change and development. Assessment thus becomes a tool for professional learning and critical reflection through feed-back and feedforward.

- **Informative:** Assessment information is synthesised and discussed with parents, teachers and other professionals.

A CREDIT-BASED MODEL

Carr (2001a) emphasizes the importance of a credit-based (rather than deficit-based) model of assessment, which involves identifying and building on what the child can do (essentially a knowledge function). As a result of her research in the context of the Te Whāriki curriculum in New Zealand, Carr's credit-based model takes a holistic view of learning and development, which is based on tracking the child's dispositions, achievements, and progress over time:

- the purpose is to enhance learning

- the outcomes focus on learning dispositions

- the focus for intervention is credit-based – what the child has already mastered: disposition-enhancing is prioritized

- validity is determined by the focus on the child in context: interpretations of observations, discussions and agreements

- progression is identified as increasingly complex participation across a range of contexts; learning stories map progression and achievements over time

- the value to practitioners is communicating with four audiences: children, families, other staff and self (the practitioner).

Carr's alternative, credit-based model is informed by the socio-cultural theories outlined in Chapters 3 and 4: children learn by playing and working alongside differently knowledgeable others. They are able to participate in increasingly complex activities, drawing on a wider range of knowledge, skills and dispositions. While policy frameworks provide a statutory entitlement, these do not define all that is valuable to children's learning and experience. A credit-based model, which draws on the six forms of assessment, enables practitioners to map children's learning journeys within and beyond the curriculum-based 'tick boxes'.

THE ASSESSMENT PROCESS

The six forms of assessment are relevant to understanding children's play and communicating the outcomes and benefits of different play activities. However, there are a number of pedagogical dilemmas in assessing children's learning through play.

■ PEDAGOGICAL DILEMMAS

- Play may not be taken seriously if practitioners fail to realize its potential as a medium for teaching and learning. The assessment potential of play is lost if it is relegated to the margins of the school day, or is used mainly as a time-filler.

- Play bears little resemblance to what it may lead to, so practitioners need to understand the immediate benefits to the child.

- Practitioners need to demonstrate convincing evidence about the relationship between playing, learning and teaching, based on observation, interpretation and documentation of learning processes and outcomes.

- Because play can be chaotic and unpredictable, it can be difficult to make connections between learning intentions and learning outcomes.

- Deep and serious play is 'playing with fire' and is not easily integrated into school contexts.

- Children may not have the time to develop meaningful sequences of play that can yield valuable assessment information.

- Adults often make judgements about what constitutes 'good play' or 'bad play', and define what forms of play are educationally worthwhile (for example, rough-and-tumble play is typically banned, even though it can provide rich opportunities for learning).

- Practitioners find it difficult to make time for observing and interpreting children's play in order to understand the meaning and significance of their activities over time.

■ Practitioners need sound pedagogical knowledge to observe, interpret and understand the significance of play.

■ Practitioners should strive not to control children's play according to narrowly defined outcomes, and to use assessment information in co-constructive ways in order to extend play.

A key principle in early childhood education is that adults should pay attention to children's existing experiences, and build on what they know within the context of their family and cultural backgrounds. Failure to do this can result in mismatches between the learner and the curriculum, which applies as much to play as to teacher-directed activities. The problem of mismatch can influence children's subsequent learning journeys, particularly if their home experiences, languages and cultures are not recognized. But how can practitioners find out where children are, and understand the wide variations in children's previous experiences, which can be influenced by social class, ability, gender, ethnicity, family composition and stability? In her account of the experimental Raleigh School, Miss Boyce exemplified how practitioners need to be tuned in to the culturally situated nature of children's learning and experience in the home and community. She provided some interesting insights into children's home-based mathematical knowledge, which was also influenced by their social class. (In pre-decimal currency, 12 pennies made one shilling, which is the contemporary equivalent of five pence):

> Mathematics was easy for us to teach, since their home and street experiences were rich in mathematical content. Some children almost fed themselves on six days of the week. They had a free breakfast at a charitable institution; with a few coppers [pennies] bought their own dinner (this usually consisted of chips, cakes or a penny pie), coerced their parents into giving them another copper to buy cakes for tea, and finished with bread and margarine. They also brought a halfpenny to school for their daily milk . . .

> Even the more cared-for children heard a great deal about economic situations. They knew the day on which the rent was due and the means of avoiding payment. Most of them ran errands and were successful shoppers although the food was invariably bought in pennyworths. Every outing and all new clothes meant saving up or weekly payments. We had a penny bank into which the children paid their parents' savings in pennies and sixpences; they watched the procedure with interest and could follow the entries in their 'paying in' books . . . They took themselves, as well as their younger brothers and sisters, to the 'Penny Pictures'. These and other first-hand experiences gave them a

background of utilitarian knowledge which the child in the more comfortable home does not acquire (Boyce, 1946: 157–158).

Miss Boyce documents many play activities in which the children used their 'home and street' experiences, thus demonstrating the important principle that practitioners' understanding of children's learning should be socially and culturally sensitive. What is taught in school may not always be part of children's home and street experiences. A teacher on a professional development module wanted to know how much mathematical knowledge children were using in the role-play area, which was a supermarket. They had been working on the Numeracy Strategy objectives for money, and she assumed that children would transfer this knowledge into their play. Close observations and transcripts of the play revealed very little mathematical discourse, because the transactions were made using a credit card (the till had a facility for 'swiping' cards). The teachers in the group speculated whether children today (unlike Miss Boyce's children) hear and see fewer transactions that involve counting out payment or change, because these are done with cards and electronic displays. Technological tools also impact on children's home and street mathematics.

In determining the relationship between play, learning and development, the critical questions are: what actually happens inside children's heads when they play? How do they become 'master players' and successful learners? What are the children doing that is of value and interest to them in the immediate term, and may be of relevance in the longer term? We have seen that play is a complex activity which integrates many different processes and, potentially, has a wide range of possible outcomes. The challenge for practitioners is to use assessment effectively to make sense of playing, learning and teaching through careful analysis and interpretation of the children's contextually situated, play-based activities. Play-based assessment can be especially significant for children with special educational needs in order to ensure their rights to play, access to play, and accurate match between their play preferences and the provision. Individual play plans (IPPs) can be developed alongside individual educational plans (IEPs) (Sayeed and Guerin, 2000). Evidence-based discussions about children's progress and achievement can involve children, parents, caregivers and other professionals, and enable practitioners to make links between children's experiences in different contexts. Collecting evidence of learning in play can also demonstrate to colleagues and parents the value and purposes of play, and the children's learning outcomes. So what are the guiding principles for developing good assessment practices that support good-quality play?

GUIDING PRINCIPLES

The value of observation-based assessment is endorsed strongly in the Foundation Stage and other curriculum frameworks explored in Chapter 5. Therefore practitioners need to shake off the guilt they feel when taking time for observing, making sense of observations and reflecting on assessment information. The three levels of understanding play presented in Chapter 5 can provide a useful framework for looking at the processes and content of children's play. The aim is to develop a holistic approach to play-based assessment, which enables practitioners to understand learning processes and dispositions, identify patterns of interests and learning styles and identify actual learning outcomes (which may not be consistent with planned outcomes). Practitioners can analyze the nature of children's thinking and learning, their areas of strength and potential development, and their capabilities, interests, attitudes and dispositions.

For example, Peter, who had cerebral palsy, often made small but steady advances in his physical development as he struggled to control his involuntary movements. These small steps were immensely significant and represented a great deal of effort and concentration. When Peter was four, his child-development profile from the hospital revealed mainly what he could not do in relation to standardized assessments based on 'developmental norms' for 'typical' four-year-olds. This was a deficit model of assessment which was inappropriate for Peter because he was not a typical four-year-old. In contrast, his detailed nursery profile, supplemented by videos, gave a different picture of Peter's capabilities and documented his learning dispositions, including the strategies and willpower he used to overcome his difficulties. This was a credit model of ipsative assessment based on Peter's individual rates of progress and his achievements over time.

The strategies listed in Figure 7.1 may help to deal with the pedagogical dilemmas identified above. Practitioners should aim to focus on the child, the context and the curriculum.

Although learning is recursive and incremental, as shown in the play spiral (Moyles, 1989; see Figure 6.1), patterns of learning are not predictable. Children sometimes progress in leaps and bounds; they also have difficulties and setbacks, fallow periods, or may even appear to regress, especially if they experience illness or stress. Children progress at different rates across the curriculum, according to their own interests and preferred modes of learning. If the curriculum is inappropriate (too

- Look at the context for assessment. What types of assessment are going to be made?
- What is the best way to gather evidence of learning – through observation, interaction, video- or audio-recording, making notes, or using a checklist?
- What are the intended learning outcomes for the activity? Focus on these at first in order to assess if there is a match between intentions and outcomes, where appropriate.
- What are the possible learning outcomes? Be aware of the scope for divergence, for example in role play. Consider the type of play activity, and the prior experience of the child/children.
- How did the activity develop and what opportunities for assessment were presented as a result?
- Document evidence of learning across a variety of activities in order to check how the child is using, applying and transferring knowledge and skills between different contexts. Involve team members in these processes.
- Document evidence of learning over a period of time in order to understand play themes, patterns of learning and ongoing cognitive concerns.
- Discuss observations with team members, including helpers and students, to share, validate or challenge perceptions. Share observations with parents and caregivers.
- Use assessments for summative, formative and diagnostic purposes – where is this child at and what are the next possible steps? Plan flexibly for challenge, extension, consolidation, repetition according to the information gained.
- Use assessments to inform individual education plans, and individual play plans.
- Feed this information back into the next cycle of planning (short-, medium- and long-term).

FIGURE 7.1   ASSESSMENT TECHNIQUES AND STRATEGIES

formal, too much sedentary activity, too much teacher control), children may make a conscious decision to switch off, or change their pace in accordance with the demands being made. A critical question when considering the assessment process is – does it do justice to the children? And, in the context of play, does it do justice to their play and self-initiated activities? In order to answer these questions, practitioners can use participant and non-participant observations (see Chapter 6) across a range of play activities:

- when children are playing alone

- when they are playing together

- when they are involved with an adult.

They need to be sensitive to:

- how individual children are spending their time

- the children's interests, dispositions and attitudes to learning

- the knowledge, skills and understanding that the children demonstrate as they are purposefully engaged in self-initiated activities

- how children's play progresses over time.

When looking at play, it is difficult to be sure whether the play activity itself has stimulated new learning, whether it is providing a context for mastery and revision, or whether it enables children to reveal what they already know, can do and understand. Through careful observations, practitioners can become more tuned in to patterns of children's activities, and more knowledgeable about the value of different types of play across areas of learning and development. Because play progresses as children get older, good assessment practices should inform how progression through play can be supported. Many of the case studies in this chapter involve Year 1 and 2 children, and provide evidence of increased complexity in their play skills and knowledge.

DOCUMENTING AND DISCUSSING

Carr (2001a) argues that describing, documenting and discussing learning are essential to effective assessment practices, and should involve all team members. Strategies for documenting progress and achievements should be manageable and meaningful (Figure 7.2).

Documentation can provide children with a concrete and visible memory of their activities, and can build a profile of progression over time. In Reggio Emilia and Te Whāriki, projects are documented at all stages, along with 'fragments of dialogue' to show evidence of development and progress, not just the finished products. Practitioners use this evidence to support and extend learning, and inspire children to continue with their investigations. The active process of documenting learning involves children in the assessment process, and enables them to understand more about their own learning.

Practitioners have used a number of strategies for documenting children's learning (Figure 7.3).

> Practitioners should aim to:
>
> - collect evidence over a period of time
> - look for patterns, meanings, interests and ongoing cognitive concerns
> - identify learning processes evident in play
> - identify discipline-based learning
> - develop understanding of how these processes can be extended through a range of activities that challenge children's thinking and action
> - share these insights with team members, parents, caregivers and other professionals involved with a child
> - involve children in self-assessment (for example, through the plan–do–review process)
> - use these insights to design further activities and experiences
> - provide evidence for reflection, evaluation and curriculum/staff development.
>
> FIGURE 7.2 STRATEGIES FOR DOCUMENTING AND DISCUSSING EVIDENCE

Annotations of play (processes and outcomes) should document the significance of the evidence. Brief annotations can build into more sustained learning stories (Carr 2000; 2001a), which provide a meaningful narrative rather than a snowstorm of ticks in boxes.

> Jodie *investigated* the water wheel. She *discovered* that she could make it turn fast or slow with the amount of water poured. She *inquired* whether it would work with sand. She *tested* her idea and *described* to the group what she had *learned*.
>
> Kamal *decided* to *design* a board game. He *drew* a plan and *wrote* some rules. He *discussed* his idea with a friend and they *collaborated* to achieve a joint goal. They *decided* on appropriate materials and *planned* the sequence for making the game. They used pictures and writing in the game and to convey the rules to the players, *showing awareness of purpose and audience*. They *persevered*, showed *intrinsic motivation* and *concentration*. They *tested* the game, *evaluated* it and *revised* the design in response to suggestions from peers.
>
> Andrew *enjoyed* playing in the post office. He *pretended* to be the postman. He *sorted* the parcels into different sizes and *learned* how to weigh them. He *learned* that heavy parcels cost more. He *decided* to send letters to his friends and *requested help* with writing their names. He *referred* to the dictionary to help with spellings. He *stayed in role* throughout the session. He *identified a need* for a larger post box and *planned* to make one next session.
>
> Sean and Joanne *played cooperatively* with the playdough. They both rolled out sausages and *used comparative mathematical language* (fat/thin, fattest/thinnest, long/short, longest/shortest). They *transformed* the saus-

- Slips of paper or sticky 'Post-it' labels for writing down notes of significant events which are then put into a folder or on a display board and analyzed at the end of the day or week.
- A daily diary for the same purpose. In both cases, more detailed notes can be written into a child's profile or record of achievement.
- Short accounts of significant events and developments with an action plan to inform further provision.
- Selected examples of the 'products' of children's play – layouts, drawings, paintings, emergent writing, constructions, plans, photographs of dramatic and socio-dramatic play, both indoors and outdoors. These should be annotated to indicate their significance, and can be shared within team and family members. Examples can be collated in a child's record of achievement, in a display or in a large book to show evidence of learning over time.
- Audio and video recordings where possible. These can be particularly useful for children with special educational needs where detailed evidence is needed for further reflection. It can also be interesting for children to watch videos of themselves playing and to give their own account and interpretations. Again this information can be shared with parents and caregivers.
- Tick lists can provide a summary of what has been covered and achieved by each child. These should always be supplemented by written notes to provide more detailed evidence of the contexts in which children are able to use and transfer their skills, knowledge and understanding. Tick lists can identify any significant gaps in a child's experience to ensure breadth and balance.
- Records of planning to show how learning outcomes are integrated in adult- and child-initiated play.
- Children's planning books: these can be annotated to document how the plans were implemented and what were the outcomes. Children's comments can also be recorded.

FIGURE 7.3 EFFECTIVE ASSESSMENT STRATEGIES

ages into shapes – triangle, oblong, square. Joanne said 'This is a round'. Sean *told* her it was a circle. Joanne *applied* the word subsequently. They *transformed* the shapes into wiggly worms and *decided* to mould different sized 'houses'. *They matched* the worms to the houses and spontaneously *created* a story about them.

Describing children's learning in these terms can enable practitioners to avoid banal descriptions and to provide rigorous accounts of the breadth and complexity of children's learning and development through play. Play-based assessment should not be invasive or destroy spontaneity: sensitive practitioners respect children's rights to privacy. Observation can be intrusive and make children self-conscious about their play. Audio and video recordings may be useful in some situations as they extend the possibilities for assessment without the presence of an adult. Holistic approaches to assessment enable practitioners to make meaningful connections between adult- and child-initiated activities so that work and play are not seen as separate or differently valued. Many practitioners begin collating profiles in the Foundation Stage, and transfer them into the next class or school. Parents and caregivers can contribute to the profile, thus creating links between learning and playing at home and school. These links can help to sensitize practitioners to cultural preferences and can help parents and caregivers to value their role in children's play.

DOCUMENTING AND INTERPRETING EVIDENCE

This section provides insights into how evidence of children's play-based learning can be documented and interpreted. The evidence is drawn from a small-scale research study which focused on assessing children's learning in a wide variety of play activities (Attfield, 1992). The observations were carried out in a local authority funded play project in a nursery and infant school in the southwest of England. The observations were supplemented by tape recordings of children's play with and without an adult present. The record sheet (Figure 7.4) was designed to show evidence of learning in the National Curriculum because all the children were in Key Stage 1. The record also includes information in other domains of learning and development, which contributes to a holistic picture of each child. The teacher's notes on intervention and extension show the links between formative assessment and planning the next learning steps. In some cases, the original transcripts have been included to show the evidence on which the teacher's assessments were based.

VERNON (1)

Child: Vernon is seven years old, quiet, self-contained, knows the rules and works calmly and methodically. He considers problems thoughtfully.

Context: Play in the cafe with a group of Year 1 and 2 children. The teacher participates for some of the time. Vernon organizes the area, prepares food, serves customers, clears away and stays for the session (one hour).

Curriculum

Language: Initially very quiet. Responds to the teacher, joins in and begins to participate in talk. Needs encouragement to talk to customers and ask for their orders. Writes the menu competently.

Name:	DoB	Date

Child

Context

Curriculum
Emotional
Social
Language/literacy
Mathematical
Scientific
Physical
Manipulative
Problem-solving

Drama/role play
Attitudes and dispositions:
Concentration
Motivation
Curiosity
Imagination/creativity

FIGURE 7.4   DOCUMENTING LEARNING THROUGH PLAY

Maths: Very able and becomes animated when dealing with money. Adds and subtracts in his head. Makes sure transactions are correct, attends to all the money handling rather than serving the customers. Practises known skills. Teacher observation shows he can work out change from 50p in his head and add amounts totalling £2.05. Knows concept of half but unsure of quarters.

Science: Food preparation – cheese grating, noticed spreading, heating, melting. 'It's not easy to grate, it's a bit soft and squidgy.' Washing up – noticed bubbles and the effects of soap on grease which he discussed with the adult present.

Problem-solving: 'Sandwiches are 10p. How many can Helen have for 30p?' Gives correct answer. Teacher extends – 'There are three sandwiches left and four customers so what are you going to do?' Vernon answers 'Cut them in half.' Clearly enjoys money and mathematical problems.

Social skills: Vernon comes to the cafe alone and then is joined by two other children. Doesn't become involved with them and attends to tasks alone. Social interaction develops while preparing food with teacher and children, and when serving customers. Seemed to need the support of the teacher to become involved. Engages in role play towards the end when he takes on the role of manager at a child's suggestion.

Attitudes/dispositions: Well-motivated to organize the money and add up the profits at the end. Shows concentration by involving himself in the money transactions. Likes helping others with problem-solving involving money and is encouraged by the teacher. Shows curiosity about other foods – grating apples – 'they'd be hard'. Is well organized, independent, lays the table correctly and clears up afterwards.

Intervention and extension: Teacher participates and encourages social interaction, extends money/problem-solving/thinking skills directly from a meaningful context and in response to problems set by Vernon – 'If we cut a whole sandwich into four pieces we call each piece a quarter.' Needs further experiences in these areas, both child-initiated and teacher-directed.

VERNON (2)

Context: He chooses to play in the post office. The teacher participates for some of the time. He then becomes an assistant in the toy shop.

Curriculum

Language: Speaks clearly and confidently in role and out – 'You need more money than that for the cafe.' Listens to what customers say. Re-labels two parcels. Gives directions and explanations to Sally in the toy shop.

Mathematical: Experience of units of weight extended with teacher in the post office. Familiar with kilograms, needs help with accurate weighing of parcels – 'I haven't done this yet.' In the toy shop he adds up the total cost of four items in his head correctly to 23p, gives correct change from 50p. Can count in 2s, 5s, 10s. Enjoys giving change, counts on, shows Sally how to do this, then gets stuck with change from £1.

Problem-solving: Sally gets stuck with money skills and a queue forms outside the shop. Vernon first helps Sally, then asks customers to make two queues – 'I can serve them quickly . . . my Mum gets cross if she hangs around.'

Attitudes/dispositions: Vernon is well motivated. His maths skills are valued and praised by the teacher and other children. This makes him even keener to use them to help others. His concentration is consistent. Vernon remembers and recalls his own skills with money and uses these in a meaningful context. Able to connect his own knowledge of weight to a new context with teacher support. Shows curiosity about weighing parcels. He acts out the role of a shop worker but stays as himself. He organizes the area well, sorts money efficiently and plans space for a display of toys in the shop.

The following accounts are based on the observations carried out by the teacher, using the plan–do–review approach. The accounts can also be described as learning stories because they document the context, the relationships between peers and between children and adults, the activity or task at hand, and include an interpretation by the storyteller who knew each child well and focused on evidence of new or sustained interest, involvement, challenge, communication and responsibility (Carr, 2001a: 95). Learning stories can be used to build up a child's profile and can also be referenced to the Foundation Stage profile and other assessment frameworks in Key Stage 1. Each account captures the play–work continuum, and the engagement of the children as players and learners.

1. Account of play

Vernon and John choose to play in Mr Fixit's repair shop. They use screwdrivers to undo the top part of a record player and examine it, take the face and back off a clock and examine the cog wheels and gear teeth. Very enthusiastic and interested in movement. Teacher intervenes to continue the development of interest and knowledge about cogs, then directs them to a construction kit – Capsela™ – where the movement of the parts depends on gear wheels and cogs. Vernon and John explore the apparatus and make a simple model. They talk about this at review time.

Indications of understanding

The boys have some knowledge and experience of wheels and cogs. Vernon explained how the meshing of teeth created movement. Development of speaking and listening with extension of vocabulary. They designed their own model with Capsela™ and, through practical activity, gained experience of putting together a working model using cogs and wheels. Able to investigate:

Teacher: Why does the propeller on your model go round without touching it?

Vernon: The handle moves this wheel and the cogs are all touching it so it moves the next one. The teeth have to touch each other to make them move.

2. Account of play

Vernon plays alone with the construction kit 'Lasy'™. He is making a Thunderbird car. Alec asks to help. The collaboration of ideas leads to a large model that has many functions. They play with the materials, language and roles. Vernon and Alec become Thunderbird characters, transform the model to a spaceship, then become astronauts and pilots. The final model is a vehicle that they show at review time and explain its functions.

Indications of understanding
Development of language, speaking and listening skills. Free play facilitated exploration and experimentation with materials and development of creativity through language and representation. Vernon talked a lot, offered ideas, information, knowledge of materials, suggested alternatives, asked Alec questions, acted out fantasy situations. Showed competence with problem-solving, able to evaluate and adapt a design to suit a particular purpose. They both used mathematical terms – shape and size – confidently. Extension of vocabulary:

Vernon: This is where the lookout stands. He looks through a watcher.
Teacher: Do you mean a telescope?
Vernon: Yes, a telescope.

3. Account of play
Vernon makes a model car from Capsela™. His friend James has made one from Ludoval™. They push the cars along the floor to see which one will go furthest. The teacher participates to extend thinking and observe the investigation, to assess measuring skills and their understanding of the concept of a 'fair test'. They investigate which vehicle goes furthest. They are joined by two more children with different vehicles and discuss the outcomes.

Indications of understanding
Development of speaking and listening, explaining, reporting, discussing, questioning. Use of mathematical language in context including length, shape, size, weight, comparisons between vehicles. Vernon chose to measure in footsteps, James suggested cubes. The teacher accepted the non-standard unit of footprints but raised questions about whose footprints should be used and was it a fair test. This led to the suggestion that a standard metre rule should be used. Vernon indicated his understanding of a fair test and shared ideas about factors affecting the movement of vehicles.

The following transcript shows the evidence on which the teacher's assessments were based.

Teacher: Are you going to find out something?
James: We're seeing which one goes the further. Mine's a rocket car, it keeps stopping though, Vernon's just crashed.

Teacher: Let's go over here where there's more space. Now, which one goes the furthest? How can we be sure it's fair, do you think? Where shall we start them from?

Vernon: It's got to be the same place. They've got to be level.

Teacher: Yes, good, otherwise it wouldn't be fair, would it, if one started in front of the other? Shall we make a start line with something? . . . What would happen if I pushed it?

Vernon: It would go more further.

James: Cos you're bigger.

Vernon: Your hand's bigger, you can push harder.

Teacher: So would that be fair?

James and Vernon: No.

Teacher: How about when you push your cars? Do you think you push the same as each other?

James: Vernon's a bit bigger than me. I don't know.

Vernon: I know, I could push his car and he could push my car and then we could see.

It was decided that to get a fair test Vernon could push both cars and then James would do the same. They also checked they were using the same hands as they thought a left-hand and right-hand push might make a difference. The teacher then suggested that they test to see which car goes further starting off from a ramp.

Teacher: Suppose we run the cars down a slope this time and see which one goes the furthest.

James and Vernon: Yes.

Vernon: Make the board go up more. Mine will go a long way.

Teacher: Do we need to push the cars?

James: They go more longer.

Teacher: Let's just start by letting them go, then it will be fair because no one is using a push. Make sure the back wheels are at the top and just let them go down. Will that be fair?

James and Vernon: Yes.

Other children then joined in so that there were four different types of cars to see which one went furthest. Through testing, observing and talking the children suggested factors that might affect the distance the cars travelled.

Sally: Mine won't go straight.

Kevin: The wheel's loose.

Vernon: I think it's all the weight.

James: It's the clipper on the rockets at the back, they're touching the floor.

Vernon: Mine's got more weight.

Kevin: Sally's got faster wheels than mine.

Vernon: They're bigger . . . got more plastic.

James: This wheel's sticking out, it needs a stopper.

Vernon: Put the smooth tyres on.

Kevin: We could put a technic motor on then it would go furthest.

Sally: My Dad's Landrover's got bumpy tyres.

This activity continued for some time with the teacher extending the children's understanding of concepts of friction, forces and fair testing. The evidence enabled the teacher to make ongoing formative assessments, as well as a summative assessment which indicated Vernon's levels of attainment in the core subjects of the National Curriculum.

HELEN

Child: Helen is six years seven months.

Context: Street play – vegetable shop and cottage.

Curriculum

Language: Talked about money with Claire, the shopkeeper. Helen corrected Claire, who was overcharging her. Talked with teacher about parks for children and made a list of the play equipment she would like in the park.

Maths: Handling money, counting, giving change. This was extended by teacher intervention.

Science/design technology: Suggests ideas for making play equipment, relates to materials, safety and weather. Dresses doll appropriately for a cold day.

Problem-solving: Defines a need for a park in the play project where toddlers can play. Suggests areas that could be used and identifies suitable apparatus for making a climbing frame. Suggests that the park should be separate: 'Put flowers in pots around the edge so they don't fall over. People won't trip over them.'

Social/emotional skills: Did not seek a friend to play with. Interacted with Claire in the shop. Invited teacher into the cottage as she wanted to talk. Confident in her role as mother looking after the baby. Took on a caring role and showed awareness of the baby's needs.

Attitudes/dispositions: Well motivated to develop the idea for a park. Takes this back to the class and develops it further. Fully involved in the role play. Maintained enthusiasm, concentration and motivation to develop her idea further. Was keen to put her ideas into practice and to test if the climbing frame would work.

Manipulative skills: Dresses doll competently. Able to tie bows and fasten hooks and eyes.

Drama/role play: Started as mother then customer. Stayed in role. Came out of role when she instigated teacher involvement.

1. Account of play
Helen dresses up as a Mum, then dresses a doll in winter clothes to take her out in the pushchair to buy vegetables from the shop. She plays alone. Interacts with shopkeeper and teacher in the shop and invites the teacher back to her cottage. Tells the teacher that they need a park in the play project for toddlers. They discuss suitable materials to make play equipment, the effects of weather on the equipment, safety issues. Helen writes a list of possible safety equipment that she later develops in class.

Indications of understanding
Initially solitary play but this became cooperative through interaction with a peer and adult. She read the price list, corrected the shopkeeper, added up to 20 and needed help with change. Teacher interaction ensured she understood the concept of change. Helen can give change from 10p and from 20p and can add two amounts in her head. Invited teacher involvement which developed speaking, listening skills and identification of a need. Able to write a list and generate a design proposal. Adult involvement needed to extend thinking.

2. Account of play
Helen is playing in the cafe with a parent helper and two five-year-olds, Jane and John. She lays the table, prepares jam sandwiches, writes the menu and discusses prices. Clears away afterwards, washes up, replaces plates, cups and cutlery.

Indications of understanding
Social and cooperative skills. Used language to inform and direct other children, practised writing skills. Practical mathematical experiences – using and developing number skills, handling money. Required help from an adult with making amounts of money to 15p and giving change. Developed physical and manipulative skills with washing up and clearing away. Extension of vocabulary – talked about properties of jam, identification of halves and quarters when cutting sandwiches.

Helen: When your customers give you the money you have to be sure they give you 15 pence. What does 15 pence look like? Come and show me. (*Jane picks up a 50p coin.*)

Helen: That's 50. (*Jane picks up a 20p coin.*)

Helen: That's 20.

Jane: I can't find one.

Helen: It's less than 20.

Jane: Can we make it like that? (*Picks up 50p and 2p coins.*)

Helen: 52 that would be. Our sandwiches are going to be 50p aren't they? (*Helen picks up a 50p and 10p coin and starts counting on from 50. The adult intervenes.*)

Adult: We can make 15 pence from what we have here. (*Helen picks up 50p.*)

Adult: Is 50 more than 15?

Helen: Yes, so we don't want that. (*Picks up 10p coin.*)

Adult: Yes, 10, what else do we need? Is that 10p?

Helen: No and four ones, 10, 11, 12, 13, 14.

Adult: Is that enough?

Helen: There isn't any more here.

Adult: There aren't any more 1p coins so what can you use instead?

Helen: Take that one away and put the 2 pence there instead, 10p, 1p, 1p, 1p, 2p.

Adult: That's right, let's count it with Jane. (*They count from 10p.*)

Adult: There's another way of making 15 with the money. You could use a 10p and a 5p coin together. 10 and 5 make?

Helen: 15.

Adult: That's right.

The girls are engaged in an authentic situation, making sandwiches for children to 'buy' at snack time, which provides a meaningful, play-based context for using and applying a range of mathematical skills and knowledge. At first, Helen is playing with the role of the 'more knowledgeable other' but seems to lack the requisite knowledge to scaffold Jane's learning in the way she originally intended. Her interactions with Jane are confident and 'teacher-like'. The teacher intervened to focus Helen's thinking and model the processes of solving the problem of how to make 15p. Subsequently when the customers came to the cafe, the girls adopted their roles in serving the children but maintained the authenticity by counting out the correct money and giving change.

3. Account of play

Teacher-initiated based on the need to make some beds for the teddies. Fifteen-minute discussion with the teacher about the properties of the beds – they have to be firm, the right size for the bears, and have legs. Helen worked with John, Mary and Alison. The class teacher interacted with the group, observing and assisting. The construction of the bed was a success and provided motivation for future play. Helen identified that she wanted to make a bed cover next time.

Indications of understanding

Cooperative skills were developed to achieve a joint goal. Helen was able to listen to others and share her ideas. Developed language skills – reasoning to select size and shape as well as discussing the suitability of the materials and tools. Used language to describe her experience of beds. Discussed and predicted the results of their actions. Problem-solving, reasoning, judging, estimating. Development of manipulative skills.

4. Account of play

Child-initiated. Helen asked to make a bed cover and pillow for the teddy bear's bed with Alison. They collected materials independently, worked well together and did not ask for assistance. They succeeded in making a cover and pillow that they showed to the group at review time.

Indications of understanding

Cooperative skills, speaking, listening, reasoning, giving directions, following instructions. New vocabulary – the word 'valance' was introduced. Developed skills in selecting materials suitable for a task – their choice was successful. The girls were being challenged and had to work hard at thinking through strategies to solve the problems they had created.

Helen: I'll get the bear. Right, first test it on the bed. Give me the cover. Yippee it's good. Now put the bear in . . . it's not quite long enough, it doesn't go down the sides, we can add a bit on each side. Get the pillow. I think the pillow's still a bit high.

Alison: It isn't, it's just right.

Helen: Mmm. The cover . . . look at the other side. I think we should have made it a tiny bit bigger.

Alison: Oh no, we'll have to start all over again.

Helen: Not if you do my idea.

Alison: What?

Helen: We can make another two little ones like that, look, and stick them on the side to make them bigger. Yes?

Alison: With different material cos we're doing patchwork?

Helen: Keep it all white cos we're doing little squares with the tissue paper and doing little pictures, remember? And then you do lines round it in brown so it looks like stitching.

The children were evaluating their ideas as they progressed. Helen identified a problem and suggested a solution. They followed through Helen's idea and made extra frills that were attached to the cover to make it longer. Helen overruled Alison's idea for the patchwork, because she didn't think they would have time to sew it. They showed skill in selecting the appropriate materials to make the patchwork successfully by sticking on tissue-paper squares. They drew pictures on the top of the cover, and drew stitches with black felt-tip pen. They worked creatively and cooperatively to achieve a joint goal, showing evidence of thinking and learning processes. The success of this activity was determined by the availability of materials and extra time allowed by the teacher for the girls to finish their task.

This evidence shows that Helen is a confident child, bordering on the domineering perhaps. She directs the cover-making activity and overrules Alison's suggestion for the patchwork. Helen is a successful player and Alison accepts her suggestions. This activity may seem more like work than play but does fulfil many of the criteria outlined in Chapter 1: it was intrinsically motivated, provided satisfaction to the players, the goals were self-imposed, self-controlled and the activity was dependent on the active engagement of the players. The activity moved along a continuum from 'pure play' to 'non-play', and was essentially playful.

Vernon's and Helen's play both indicate how they moved along the play–work continuum. The episodes also provide evidence of progression in the form and content of play. These children are more goal-oriented in their play, more adept at using tools and materials, and more able to formulate and implement plans and predict the outcomes. As we noted in Chapter 5, play in older children tends to reflect a need for order, a need to belong and a need to become more industrious. Children's self-concept becomes defined by their skills and competences as players, organizers, tool users and their ability to play creatively and imaginatively. However, not all children have the skills and confidence to achieve this level of mastery without additional support. For example, a group of Year 2 girls decided to perform a show in a theatre and began by discussing their ideas in a quiet area away from other children. The children argued about the plot, ending with one girl in tears. The teacher helped to resolve the dispute by discussing cooperation, ways of recording ideas and listening to each other. She suggested using a tape recorder as an *aide-mémoire* for the group's ideas and plans. Two of the girls wrote a list of events and characters in the play (Figure 7.5) and the girls performed this later to a large group. The children realized the need for improved planning and organization, and clear speech and audibility while performing (Attfield, 1992).

This practice-based evidence shows that play is progressive, and that children's skills as players progress significantly, thereby providing convincing evidence to support the case for play in Key Stage 1 (and beyond). The episodes demonstrate the value of play: its open-ended, free-flow nature enabled children to integrate their knowledge and experience. Play acted as an integrating mechanism for learning across the curriculum, and enabled them to combine their real-world knowledge with their play worlds. The teacher was able to map her assessments against the learning outcomes in the National Curriculum for Key Stage 1. While this is not the only justification for play, the study demonstrates how children make connections between areas of learning and experience, and how they use, apply and transfer knowledge, skills and concepts between different activities. The Play Project created opportunities for creating unity between playing, learning and teaching, and provided a wealth of assessment information. The play activities revealed children's ways of knowing, reasoning and understanding, in a dynamic continuum between sense and nonsense, logic and absurdity, fantasy and reality. The children combined epistemic and ludic play, and used language, symbols, gestures and signs to communicate their meanings and intentions. The adults acted as co-participants and co-constructors: they gave immediate feedback to the children, and were integral to making suggestions, supporting their learning and problem-solving, setting challenges, and valuing children's self-initiated activities.

This practice-based evidence also demonstrates socio-cultural theory in action. In Vygotsky's terms, the play activities were zones for proximal development and revolutionary activity. The children raised the cognitive demands on themselves and on others, in collaboration with the teacher. Figure 7.6 summarizes the value of play-based assessment.

ASSESSING SOCIO-DRAMATIC PLAY

In Chapter 2, we outlined some of the benefits of dramatic and socio-dramatic play. Children may reveal levels of competence and

1 Sadie

2 wolf

3 Servent

4 Fairies

5 baby

6 wolf and Servant

7 Fairies to duck

8 Sadie and wolf

9 Fairies

10 Fairies calls Fairies.

11 Fairies go

12 wolf get Fairies

13 Fairies tap wand

14 Fairies to the Rescue

15 party

16 The End

FIGURE 7.5   LIST OF EVENTS IN SHOW

Play-based assessment can enable practitioners to:

- establish clear principles for valuing play as an integral part of the curriculum
- identify the processes of learning evident in play
- identify extension activities which challenge children's learning and thinking
- provide meaningful evidence for each child's record of achievement
- provide evidence about the quality and effectiveness of play across the curriculum
- obtain different perspectives on how children operate as learners in self-initiated activities
- ensure that activities are matched to the abilities and interests of the children across the play–work continuum
- understand the nature and effectiveness of adult interaction in children's play.

FIGURE 7.6 THE VALUE OF PLAY-BASED ASSESSMENT

motivation that are not evident in other forms of play or in adult-directed activities. As Broadhead (2004) has shown, from the age of three, children make rapid strides in their social skills, and in their ability to engage in social and cooperative play. Many of the examples in this book provide evidence of how children's play skills and mastery develop in Key Stage 1. Socio-dramatic play also shows how, in Vygotsky's terms, children often go beyond the current contextual frame and make unexpected, creative transformations. They can behave 'a head taller than themselves'. The following example of socio-dramatic play was recorded by Cook (2003), and demonstrates the value of looking closely at play in order to understand and appreciate its complexity. The role-play area in the Reception classroom is Noah's Ark. The main focus is on Callum, age 5 (the Target Child [TC]): the observation lasts 10 minutes, and provides an activity record (in italics) and a language record. SG denotes small group, Cg and Cb denote when Callum talks to a girl or boy.

NOAH'S ARK

Three children are in the role-play area (two boys and a girl). TC walked into the role-play area and looked inside.

TC-self: How many people are there? Three. I can play there. I can dress up.

Walked out of the area and found a friend.

TC-Cb: Toby, d'you want to come and play in the home corner?

No verbal response, but Cb followed TC. Both boys started to rifle through the dressing-up box for animal costumes.

Two other boys were already in role, but it was difficult to ascertain their theme. They were sitting high up on top of two cupboards. They had used a chair to get up there and were swinging their legs, watching TC and Cb enter the role play area.

Cb-TC: He's scared to jump off his bed because he thinks he land in someone's kitchen.

TC had found a dog head-dress, tail and two gloves. His friend helped him put these on.

Cb-TC: Hello doggy.

TC-Cb: Ruff ruff.

TC crawled away on all fours. No-one followed him so he started to take off his dressing-up clothes. Another Cb spoke:

Cb-TC: I'm going to be a Daddy.

TC-Cb: I'm going to be a bamboo. It's wild and very very fierce. It's like Tarzan and an elephant talks.

It later became clear that he meant a baboon . . .

TC tried to pick up the dog costume and put it all back on again. Spoke to SG.

TC-SG: I'm a fierce dog.

TC then ran around the outside of the screen, frightening a Cg in the process. She replied:

Cg-TC: Bad doggy. No, bad doggy.

TC continued to chase. Cg ran and hid under the bench.

TC-Cg: I'm scaring you.

TC took off his outfit and wandered over to another Cb who was putting on a monkey outfit.

TC-Cb: I'm going to be what you are. I'm gonna be a gorilla.

TC ran around beating his chest. Two girls and another boy joined the group and all the children decided to use a chair to get up to sit on the work bench area.

TC-Sc: Who wants to be Noah?

Cb-SG: Who wants to see what you look like?

TC-SG: We're looking for sharks. I'm going to save everyone.

Cb jumped down and followed TC holding a plastic asparagus.

Cb-TC: This is what kills sharks. I'm going to smack them on the head.

The two boys continue this theme on their own. TC and Cb pretend to swim around the side of the play area. Another Cb joins them.

TC-Cb: Anyone who can swim can kill sharks. Quick, there's a shark.

TC found a skipping rope and began swinging it around his head. He picked up a tea pot and spoke to the two boys.

TC-SG: Sharks hate tea. That's why I'm holding a tea pot.

TC pretended to pour tea everywhere.

TC-SG: I'll pour it all over the sea I would.

Cb-TC: I can't stand up on water.

TC-Cb: Let's fill it up again.

Cb found a plastic kettle and pretended to pour it everywhere.

Cb-TC: This one's full up.

TC-SG: There's a shark inside (*in a very loud voice*).

TC ran into the role-play area and hit the floor with his teapot (imagining a shark). All the children ran inside and jumped onto the bench.

TC-SG: The shark's eating your legs.
Cb tried to carry on a different theme and fell onto the floor.
Cb-SG: I'm a crocodile.
Cb-Cg: The crocodile's dead. Let's tickle him.
Cb-Cg: I'm alive.
TC tries to intervene and change the plot again.
TC-SG: I can hear a roar in that place. Can you help me find him?
TC picked up his teapot again and started making sweeping motions under the work bench.
TC-SG: Swipe swipe, I'm still looking for sharks. (*loudly*)
TC fell to the floor laughing to himself.
TC-Cb: You throw it and the sharks can't sleep. (*refers to his teapot*)
TC got up and ran around the outside of the play area, shouting to the SG.
TC-SG: There's some sharks down there.
He picked up a piece of cloth which was lying on the floor.
TC-SG: I'll use my dusters and then they'll go.
TC ran screaming back into the role play area.
TC-SG: Run. You nearly got blown up by that thing.
Under the work bench a girl was sitting holding a doll.
TC-Cg: I'm a goody.

AN ASSESSMENT FRAMEWORK FOR DRAMATIC AND SOCIO-DRAMATIC PLAY

So how can practitioners make sense of this rapid and complex flow of language and activity? A useful activity is to look carefully at the Noah's Ark episode and use the following framework to identify the skills, dispositions and competences that children demonstrate in dramatic and socio-dramatic play. The framework is not intended as a checklist or a hierarchy, but it may sensitize practitioners to the complexity of play and the social, emotional and cognitive demands that are embedded in play episodes. This can also be used to track children's progression in play.

PLAY SKILLS AND KNOWLEDGE

- Uses memory and recall strategies.

- Defines a theme – plot, characters and sequence (text).

- Negotiates a play frame and establishes rules (context).

- Uses own ideas and listens to others.

- Able to negotiate and cooperate towards agreed ends.

- Transforms objects, materials, environment and actions.

- Communicates through language, signs, symbols and gestures (representational thinking).

- Communicates the pretence, defines roles and actions. Conveys meanings and intentions (metacommunication).

- Steps in and out of the play (distancing).

- Rehearses roles and actions, directs or manages the play.

- Can be directed and managed by others.

- Can maintain and develop a role.

- Uses imagination and creativity to combine and recombine ideas.

- Empathizes/understands the perspective of others.

- Creates, identifies and solves problems.

- Reveals motives, needs and interests.

- Listens, cooperates, revises and extends ideas.

- Uses metacognitive strategies – predicts, monitors, checks, reflects, evaluates.

SOCIO-AFFECTIVE AND COMMUNICATIVE SKILLS AND PROCESSES

- Communicates with peers and adults in small and large groups.

- Engages in conversations with peers/adults.

- Conveys ideas, comments on actions, gives directions.

- Joins in a game or activity.

- Assigns roles, takes on roles, stays in role.

- Negotiates rules, abides by rules.

- Plays alone/in parallel/collaboratively in pairs/in groups.

- Uses props/assigns meaning to objects.

- Uses abstract thinking to convey meaning and pretence.

- Offers alternative suggestions.

- Manages self and others in play.

- Understands own and others' emotions.

- Regulates own feelings and emotions.

- Distances self to direct, negotiate, develop and extend the play.

- Establishes friendships – same and opposite sex.

- Uses conflict resolution strategies.

- Listens to others/understands perspective of others.

INVESTIGATION, EXPLORATION AND PROBLEM-SOLVING SKILLS AND PROCESSES

- Creates, recognizes and solves problems.

- Observes closely and carefully.

- Asks and answers questions.

- Uses sensory exploration in investigating the properties and behaviour of materials.

- Uses fine motor skills in investigating, controlling and manipulating materials.

- Uses a variety of tools to assist investigation.

- Notices and communicates causes and effects.

- Uses descriptive language to convey experience, feelings and ideas, to organize, persuade and report accurately.

- Represents ideas through different media.

- Uses specific terms to describe and analyse experience (e.g. mathematical, scientific, technological).

- Perceives and describes relationships.

- Perceives and describes classifications.

- Makes connections between existing and new knowledge.

- Makes predictions, tests ideas/hypotheses.

- Describes activities and conveys information.

- Collaborates with others towards agreed ends.

- Seeks help from peers/adults.

CREATIVE AND IMAGINATIVE SKILLS AND PROCESSES

- Understands the what if/as if nature of pretend play.

- Able to pretend, conveys pretence, develops the pretence.

- Distinguishes fantasy and reality.

- Combines fantasy and reality.

- Generates and communicates ideas and imagination through language and different media – drawing, painting, modelling, writing, collage, printing, constructions and layouts.

- Combines materials and resources.

- Transforms materials and resources.

- Enjoys sensory experiences.

- Takes risks, refines ideas, edits work/products.

- Conveys abstract ideas verbally and through different media.

- Responds emotionally to experiences and expresses emotions verbally and through different media.

DEVELOPING INDIVIDUAL PLAY PLANS

The Code of Practice for children with special educational needs (DfES, 2001) recommends that children should have Individual Education Plans (IEPs), which provide a clear statement of their needs, and how these can be met. Sayeed and Guerin (2000) have developed the idea of individual play plans (IPPs). They argue that practitioners need to ensure that their provision includes desirable play outcomes for children with special educational needs, based on:

- high expectations

- careful planning

- quality provision

- potential reached.

The practitioner uses play-based assessment to:

- establish new expectations for the child as player/learner

- identify specific needs and interests

- support long-term goals and short-term targets.

While these principles are applicable to all children, Sayeed and Guerin emphasize that those with special educational needs are likely to require more specific levels of planning and support. The vast majority of children with SEN have general learning difficulties: however, many will develop their play skills along the same continuum as their more able peers, but at a slower rate. Checklists tend to be based on developmental norms – what is typically expected for children of a similar age and background. The learning goals and outcomes in the policy frameworks embody a hierarchical concept of skills, knowledge and understanding, which is not relevant for all children. Therefore, it is all too easy for practitioners to develop deficit views about the progress and achievements of children with SEN, which may exacerbate their difficulties.

There is consistent support for the view that children with SEN are more likely to need appropriate input from adults, and more opportunities for practice, revision and consolidation (Sayeed and Guerin, 2000; Macintyre, 2001; Drifte, 2002). Therefore the concepts of pedagogical framing, techniques and strategies (Chapters 5 and 6) are equally applicable, alongside:

- more specialised knowledge of the child

- knowledge about specific syndromes (such as Autistic Spectrum Disorder, Down's Syndrome, Attention Deficit and Hyperactivity Disorder)

- knowledge about the nature and effects of any impairments (auditory, visual, speech, language, physical).

According to the nature of the child's difficulties, assessment information should be gathered from parents, caregivers and all professionals involved because communication and collaboration are integral to effective provision (Roffey, 2001). Play-based assessment (Sayeed and Guerin, 2000) can enable all those involved to contribute their observations and knowledge about a child, and to work together towards common goals (see Em's story in Chapter 8). Play-based assessment is also important for ensuring access and inclusion. If a child is having difficulty in a specific area of play, it may not be the child, but the context, layout, or nature of the resources that need to be evaluated. Drifte (2002) provides a valuable overview of ensuring access across the areas of learning in the Foundation Stage, focusing on practical strategies and pedagogical approaches. Similarly, Macintyre (2001) explores reasons why some children may find it difficult to play, and identifies further negative effects. For example, children with dyspraxia find it difficult to go with the flow of other children's plans. Because they have difficulties with motor skills, they may be left out of cooperative activities and games. Children with ADHD can be restless, lack concentration, and cause annoyance and disruption to others. They may not be seen as 'good players', and can therefore be rejected or excluded, causing social isolation and further anxiety. Adult involvement in play can have greater significance for children who have such difficulties, because they can act as more skilled co-players, help to sustain interest and involvement, and infect children with enthusiasm for play.

FURTHER READING

These books provide detailed explorations of assessment in early childhood settings, drawing on key principles, theories and guidance for practitioners. The books that focus on children with special educational needs are helpful for developing more specialised formats and strategies for assessment.

Carr, M. (2001) *Assessment in Early Childhood Settings: Learning Stories*, London, Paul Chapman.

Cowie, B. and Carr, M. (2004) The Consequences of Socio-cultural Assessment, in A. Anning, J. Cullen and M. Fleer (eds) *Early Childhood Education: Society and Culture*, London, Sage, 95–106.

Drifte, C. (2002) *Early Learning Goals for Children with Special Educational Needs*, London, David Fulton.

Macintyre, C. (2001) *Enhancing Learning Through Play: A Developmental Perspective for Early Years Settings*, London, David Fulton.

Roffey, S. (2001) *Special Needs in the Early Years: Collaboration, Communication and Co-ordination* (2nd edition), London, David Fulton.

Sayeed, Z. and Guerin, E. (2000) *Early Years Play: A Happy Medium for Assessment and Intervention*, London, David Fulton.

Wall, K. (2003) *Special Needs and the Early Years: A Practitioner's Guide*, London, Paul Chapman.

CHAPTER EIGHT

Improving the Quality of Play

Creating unity between playing, learning and teaching is essential to a high-quality, effective provision in early childhood education. Although play is not the only way of learning in early childhood, play activities provide diverse opportunities for children to be inspired, enthused and empowered in their learning. Play activities promote 'can-do' orientations and support the development of positive dispositions for learning. Throughout this book, we have provided many positive validations for developing a play-based curriculum and pedagogy, which integrate and exceed the policy frameworks. Suggestions for practice have been grounded in sound principles and a detailed exploration of contemporary theories about playing, learning and teaching. In this final chapter, the focus is on case studies of professional development by practitioners in a range of settings. The intention is to share authentic examples of change and development, based on practitioners identifying their own principles, and addressing problems or challenges in their practice. Each of the case studies is presented as a story, and can be used for discussion, reflection and improvement. These stories point up the importance of being a reflective practitioner in order to sustain professional development and improvement.

LEARNING TO PLAY: EM'S STORY

Em's story is taken from a research study carried out by Diann Cudmore (1996). Diann was home visitor with the Portage programme, which is an early intervention programme for children with special educational needs. The role of the home visitor is to work and play alongside parents, who are recognized as the child's first, and most important, teachers. Parents and Portage visitors work collaboratively to promote learning and development, and enable children to achieve their potential, whatever their difficulties, condition or syndrome. Learning and teaching through play are integral to the programme, and the children's individual plans will incorporate objectives that can be achieved through a wide range of play activities.

Diann decided to base her Master's dissertation on Em, a two-year-old girl with Down's syndrome. This decision was informed in part by Diann's dissatisfaction with the assumptions that children with special educational needs learn from self-directed free play. From her experience, Diann had noticed the role of the adult is crucial in helping children to learn how to play, and supporting their play-based learning. Em's story illustrates mediated learning experiences (MLE) (Sayeed and Guerin, 2000), in which the adult takes a focused and structured scaffolding role. Interventions and interactions remain sensitive to the child's observed responses, so that the adult mediates meaning and significance, feelings of competence, shared participation and control of behaviour (Sayeed and Guerin, 2000: 82–83). Em's story therefore exemplifies socio-cultural theories of learning, but with more structured rather than open pedagogical techniques.

Diann decided to focus on supporting Em's pretend play. She began her study with the understanding that children with learning difficulties are typically described as having developmental delay rather than developmental differences. This enabled Diann to look at Em in terms of her differences and potential rather than deficits against developmental norms. Em's difficulties were multiple: language, speech, hearing, memory, cognitive processing and physical coordination. Em, Diann and Mum were learning Makaton sign language, which combines a gesture with the spoken word, and helps children to communicate through acts of shared meaning. Diann also identified that Em needed lots of opportunities to practise and consolidate new skills, using sensory stimulation, and scaffolding strategies to encourage Em to become an active participant in her play. Episodes of joint play were video-recorded and were shared with Em's Mum to discuss progress and achievements and make decisions about future activities.

In the first episode, Mum introduced a doll to Em, and modelled the actions for putting the doll to bed and covering her with a blanket, drawing attention to her activities through language. Em imitated this activity, but then moved on to another activity. She took the doll out of bed, and dropped it in front of Mum with a face cloth (small towel). Mum thought that Em wanted to wash the doll's face, and modelled the actions.

However, Em had a different agenda, but found it difficult to convey her own meanings. She put the doll back on the bed, and covered her with the blanket and the face cloth. Later in the episode, a similar event occurred. Em picked up the doll's nappy and shook it at her Mum, who thought that Em wanted to put the nappy on the doll. Em immediately pulled the nappy off the doll, and used it as a cover.

Diann identified some pedagogical dilemmas in the early play episodes. Both adults used a range of resources and techniques to engage Em in pretend play. However, because Em could not verbalize her intentions, it was often difficult for them to tune in to her own play agenda. To support Em's learning, photographs were taken of play events such as washing the doll, brushing hair, feeding and drinking, and putting the doll to bed. One photograph showed a spoon, bowl and some chocolate buttons (Em's favourite sweets, which were given as a reward when she used signs to communicate with others). The photographs were laminated and put into a book as a shared resource to help Em with her Makaton signing, using the pictures as additional clues to convey meaning and intentions. Sometimes the photographs were helpful and at other times they were a distraction. In the second videotape, Em had made significant progress in her signing and communication skills, but occasionally became frustrated with the book. She pointed to the picture of the spoon, bowl and chocolate buttons, and seemed to indicate that she wanted some buttons to eat, thus distracting her from the dramatic play. This shows that even the best intentions for supporting learning can go astray. For Diann and Mum, understanding Em's meanings became a focus of their play activities, as they gradually shifted from their own agendas of what they wanted to teach Em.

Over a period of three months, Em made significant progress in her playing and learning. She communicated more easily as she learned to use signs in context, and to express her own intentions:

> During the following play session, there are several incidents where Em uses the sign for 'bed' . . . and signs 'drink' in imitation, followed by a more successful episode when Em pretends to drink herself, offers me the cup and then, with a prompt from me, gives the doll a drink. Other brief successes are when Em brushes the doll's hair in imitation, and washes the doll in imitation.

> Mismatches also occur; one specific incident showing Em's apparent refusal to switch her attention from the bedding she is holding and shaking to my asking her 'who is this' and showing her the doll.

> Although Em looks at the doll and looks at me she ignores my question. She persists in her own intentions, making it very clear that she wants the doll on the bed by vocalizing insistently and pointing to the bed vigorously, saying' bed' through her use of sign (Cudmore, 1996: 57).

These mismatches proved to be valuable learning experiences for providing insights into Em's patterns of learning, and highlighting effective interactions as well as breakdowns in communication:

> Problems arise for the adults during the play when attention-switching strategies fail to distract Em from her own intentions. Successful communication occurs most frequently when the adults follow Em's lead, matching their comments, questions and actions towards the toy or game that Em was already engaged with and that had been chosen by her (Cudmore, 1996: 58).

This practice-based evidence was valuable for challenging assumptions, designing effective play experiences, and informing more finely tuned interactions which could be used by Diann and Mum to support continuity of experience. The study also shows the value of *ipsative assessment* (Chapter 7), which enables adults to plan the next small steps in learning based on observed patterns and dispositions of the child (rather than on defined teaching objectives). On the basis of her research, Diann developed a dramatic play checklist which identified 30 different types of behaviour, across four stages:

1 self-pretending and object-person pretending

2 object pretending

3 sequence pretending action/objects

4 role play.

Diann and Em's Mum used the checklist, not as a hierarchy of skills and competences, but as a typical range of behaviours that could be identified in the context of playing alongside Em. This enabled them to show differences in Em's development, and to plan their activities in response to her interests and play style. While MLE can be a valuable pedagogical approach for children with special educational needs, a key principle for mediating play is maintaining a focus on the child's motives and intentions. For Em, mediated playing and learning experiences supported her communication skills, imaginative use of symbols and tools, and her skills as a player.

PLAN–DO–REVIEW: AMANDA'S STORY

Inspired by Julie Fisher's work (see Chapter 5), Amanda Kersey decided to use the plan–do–review (PDR) approach with her Reception/Year 1 children. As a newly qualified teacher, Amanda aimed to relate her own values and beliefs to her practice, and considered that PDR would enable her to support children's autonomy, independence and self-initiated activity. Because of other curriculum demands, Amanda decided that she could not use this approach every day with the whole class. It was too time-consuming, and, at a pragmatic level, she could not be sure that children would cover all curriculum areas in their planning. She used the class groups for developing PDR so that each group had a turn at planning each afternoon. Amanda organized an adult to be available to help the children with their plans and provide support. Review time was carried out with the whole group so that children could talk about and show what they had been doing. PDR is not an easy option in the early stages: the first half-term was taken up with teaching children planning skills and getting them into the routines and expectations. Amanda organized the layout of the classroom to ensure open access to good-quality resources (tools, materials and play equipment). For example, in the writing area children had access to materials for making books, which linked with Amanda's approach to teaching literacy.

Amanda decided to use planning sheets to record the children's plans and feedback. Later these were changed to planning books, which served as a record of the children's activities. The planning sheet enabled the children to plan two activities, and provided space for feedback to supplement discussion at review time. Perry's plans have been chosen to show evidence of progression in his planning skills over time, and to show how Amanda documented evidence of the children's learning.

PERRY – OCTOBER

At the beginning of the Reception year, Perry is able to represent his plans by drawing pictures of blocks. Amanda records his plan (Figure 8.1).

In March, he is able to write his name and has become more skilled at representing what he wants do in his plans (make a tower with the bricks and make a map of the bricks at the writing table – Figure 8.2). Perry made boxes, which he took to the writing table, and put in some plastic letter shapes. In review time, Amanda records his comments:

> I made a good tower. I used a flat piece of wood at the bottom so I could stand on it and make it taller.

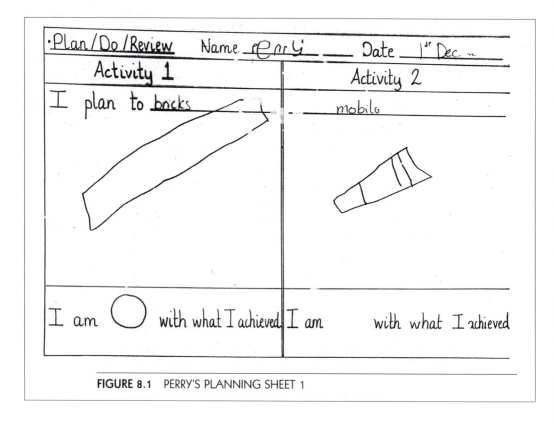

FIGURE 8.1 PERRY'S PLANNING SHEET 1

> Fine – I made a book. You had to find out what was in the boxes.

By the end of the year, Perry shows that he is more ambitious in his plans, and more sophisticated in his representation. Perry planned to make a puppet theatre with a friend. In his drawing (Figure 8.3), he shows them standing either side of the box, holding the pole that raises the curtain. Perry had seen a puppet show, and wanted to make the curtain himself. This was a self-initiated activity that involved some complex problem-solving skills: how to make the curtain, fix the pole to the front of the box, and raise the curtain at the start of the show.

After making the puppet theatre, Perry developed play scripts with his friends, based on the theme of Bears. At review time, Perry described their play:

> A crocodile came along and ate all the bears' food. The crocodile went upstairs and ate all their beds. The bears came home and saw the crocodile eat all their things. The bears whacked the crocodile on the nose with their paws. The crocodile went back to the water to swim away. Naughty crocodile!

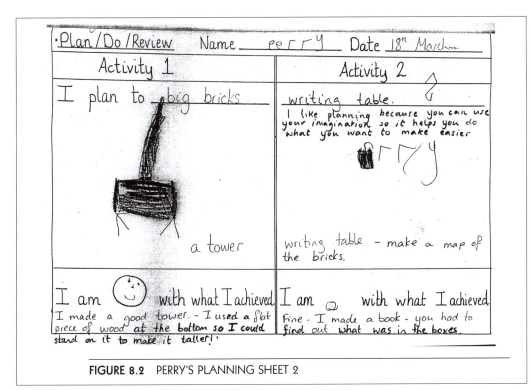

·Plan/Do/Review   Name___Perry___ Date _18ᵗ March___

| Activity 1 | Activity 2 |

I plan to __big bricks__

writing table.

I like planning because you can use your imagination so it helps you do what you want to make easier

perry

a tower

writing table - make a map of the bricks.

I am 😊 with what I achieved
I made a good tower. - I used a flat piece of wood at the bottom so I could stand on it to make it taller!

I am ☹ with what I achieved
Fine - I made a book - you had to find out what was in the boxes.

FIGURE 8.2 PERRY'S PLANNING SHEET 2

·Plan/Do/Review   Name___Perry___ Date _Monday___

| Activity 1 | Activity 2 |

I plan to __PUPPET show__   JUNK   model

I am 😊 with what I achieved   I am 😨 with what I achieved

FIGURE 8.3 PERRY'S PLANNING SHEET 3

Through this self-initiated activity, Amanda was able to make informed assessments of Perry's progress and achievements. His report of the story shows that he is able to sequence and structure a story, with a beginning, middle and end. He has a good understanding of plot, and makes novel connections between the story of the three bears, but replacing Goldilocks with the naughty crocodile. Perry creatively transforms the traditional tale and invents new meanings and roles.

Lucy, Kate and Kirsty also became involved in making books in the writing area, making puppets related to the theme of bears, and writing stories about them. Their feedback at review time provides evidence of their learning and activities, and some metacognitive skills.

LUCY MADE A BOOK ABOUT TEDDY BEARS (Figure 8.4)

The bears lived in the forest. They saw a house and the bear went in the house then went upstairs and went to sleep in the bed. I dressed up as a bear. I was a koala bear from the North Pole. I put lots of clothes on because it could be cold up there.

KIRSTY MADE A HOUSE AND A BOOK (Figure 8.5)

I made a teddy bear's house. I needed five squares for the outside and four triangles for the roof. The three bears live in the house. Next time I would make the house bigger so it is nicer for the bears.

I made some teddy bear books for my mum. I found the writing easy but the pictures were hard because they are a bit difficult.

KATE MADE A BEAR AND A BOOK (Figure 8.6)

I found it hard to put the fingers on. I made the head with bits of plastic. I made the legs with toilet rolls. When I made the body I had to use bits of circles. I stuck these things with glue. You must only use a little bit of glue because otherwise it won't stick. I like my bear. Next time I will paint my bear. I made a book about bears. I found it easy to draw the pictures. I found it hard to do the right words. I will give it to you to read.

These examples show what is possible for children to achieve when they are encouraged to plan and reflect on their learning and self-initiated activities. Lucy demonstrates emerging geographical knowledge, even though she located koala bears in the wrong hemisphere. Kirsty and Kate are competent technologists and designers. They use precise mathematical language and are using and applying mathematical knowledge. They also indicate their abilities to reflect on their learning, and reflect on how they

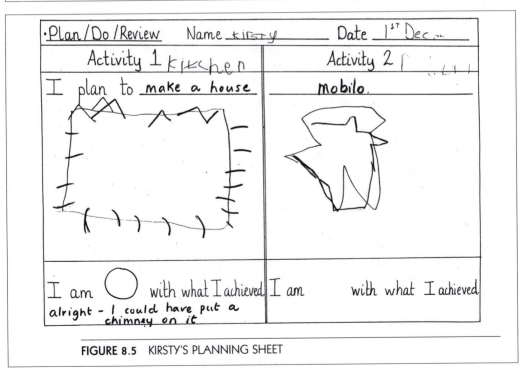

·Plan/Do/Review   Name LUCY   Date Mondays

Activity 1	Activity 2
I plan to **writing table.**	**Goldilocks and the3 bears** Me bears
teddy Book	
I am 😊 with what I achieved i Lik BoKs	I am 😊 with what I achieved I Lik Be Ba Bears

FIGURE 8.4   LUCY'S PLANNING SHEET

·Plan/Do/Review   Name kirsty   Date 1ˢᵗ Dec...

Activity 1 kitchen	Activity 2
I plan to **make a house**	**mobilo.**
I am ◯ with what I achieved alright - I could have put a chimney on it	I am with what I achieved

FIGURE 8.5   KIRSTY'S PLANNING SHEET

would do things differently in future. The plan–do–review approach creates time and opportunities for encouraging self-assessment and teaching children language about learning. The examples above show children's ability to sequence events, reflect on action using the past tense, link cause and effect, and plan further activities. The children also integrate discipline-based knowledge in technology, mathematics, geography and literacy.

DEVELOPING A SENSORY GARDEN

In developing a new Foundation Stage unit, the teachers had the opportunity to remodel the outdoor play area. In collaboration with the children they decided to make part of the area into a sensory garden. This involved much citizenship and democracy in action as the children recorded their suggestions and voted on 'plants that have a nice smell' and 'plants that you can eat'. Parents were involved in raising funds and donating plants from gardens, seeds and cuttings. The children visited a local plant nursery, and a member of staff directed them towards herbs and flowering shrubs that would be safe to touch and eat.

They set up the role-play area as a garden shop, and used many of the activities they had observed: ordering and cataloguing plants, writing orders and receipts, and displaying pictures of pests and diseases (which they found fascinating). When the plants in the garden grew, the children were able to describe and record their appearance, smell, and colour. They used many different forms of representation, including observational drawings, watercolour paintings, collage, tapestry and other mixed media. They dried leaves and flowers and made bags of pot pourri – the small net bags used with washing powder tablets were ideal for this purpose. There was much interest in this project from older children, and the young ones got more practice at citizenship and democracy in action as they negotiated access to the garden for other children, deciding on the times and rules (taking care of the garden, not walking on the plants). Subsequently a much larger project was undertaken, with funding from a charitable organization, to revamp the school grounds. All children were involved in the planning, and the younger ones were delighted when the planners came to see their garden as a model.

This play/work theme also became the focus of a school development and improvement project. The teachers in Key Stage 2 had little understanding

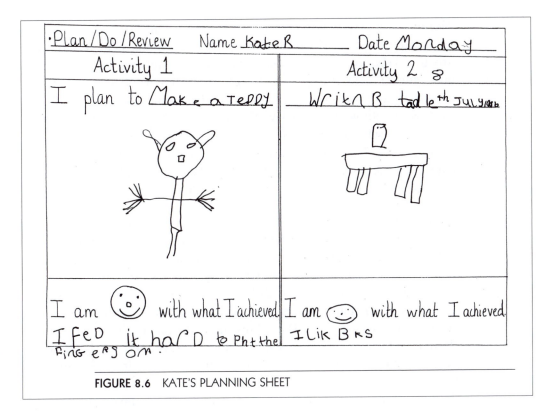

·Plan/Do/Review   Name Kate R   Date Monday

Activity 1	Activity 2. 8
I plan to Make a Telly	Writn B tadle th July
I am 😊 with what I achieved	I am 😊 with what I achieved
I feD it harD to Pht the Fingers on.	I Lik BKS

FIGURE 8.6 KATE'S PLANNING SHEET

of what happened in the Foundation Stage, and thought that it was all 'play and fun'. They did not see the principles underlying the practices, or the valuable skills, knowledge and concepts that the children were learning. They were also amazed at the competence of the youngest learners in their school, which contrasted with some of the older children who were already switching off from the routines of the Literacy and Numeracy Strategies (especially the boys). All the staff began a long but interesting process of developing more holistic approaches to teaching and learning, which integrated the PDR approach, and led to continuity and progression across stages.

CREATIVITY IN A NURSERY CLASS: CATHIE'S STORY

Cathie wanted to stimulate the children's creativity through a wide variety of media. Materials and resources were made accessible to the children, including different kinds of paints, pencils, chalks and crayons, sizes of brushes, types of paper, equipment for printing, glues, tools and a wide range of collage materials. The team planned some experiences where the children were taught how to use the materials and resources as well as specific techniques, which they then developed in their self-initiated activities. These included observational drawing, mixing paints, selecting tools, media and equipment to create different effects, combining techniques and learning specific skills such as sewing and weaving. The children also looked at other works of art and regular exhibitions were held in the school, which combined children's, teachers' and parents' contributions. The children's work was displayed well but it was not 'edited' by the adults. The children were also responsible for taking care of the tools and resources and tidying up after themselves.

Through these processes the children were encouraged to explore the materials, play with ideas, make novel combinations, represent their ideas and experiences, learn to use and apply techniques and skills, and value their own and each other's creativity. They had opportunities to work at easels, on flat surfaces and on the floor for larger projects. They worked individually, in pairs, in groups and occasionally produced pieces involving the whole class. The adults did not draw outlines for them to fill in: the children's work was valued and displayed sensitively and there were no adults' representations in the room. The children were inspired by the quality of the materials available, their freedom to choose, their ability to play with materials and ideas, and the support provided through sensitive interactions with the practitioners. They combined workfulness and playfulness in these experiences and learnt that creativity is not the preserve of the gifted few. The study by Anning and Ring (2004) provides further fascinating insights into children as artists and designers.

DEVELOPING A PLAYFUL SCHOOL

A primary school appointed a curriculum coordinator for play across both key stages. She gave advice and support for developing a whole-school approach and identified each teacher's requirements. She drew up a rolling programme of resource acquisitions over a three-year period and was allocated time to play alongside the children to model her role and support the children with some of the more demanding technical and constructive equipment. The older children were encouraged to play with the younger ones on a regular weekly basis to extend the concept of peer tutoring. A further spin-off from this whole-school approach was the redesign of the outdoor play environment, again with additional re-sources, delineated areas for ball games, chasing games and for sitting. The teachers, mealtime assistants and children learnt traditional games and, within a short space of time, these approaches eradicated behaviour problems. The daily lunchtime line-up outside the headteacher's office became a thing of the past.

In each of these examples, the practitioners involved conceptualized play as an integral part of the curriculum. They provided enabling conditions to improve the quality of play in the different settings. They were prepared to change or adapt the learning environment, provide appropriate resources and support, and make time available for different kinds of play tutoring. Their approaches indicated their values and beliefs about the role of play: they had the confidence and expertise to implement these and, to a certain extent, to take risks in their practice.

RIGHTS AND RESPONSIBILITIES

The United Nations Convention on Children's Rights enshrines children's rights to play (Nutbrown, 1996). However, adults are responsible for ensuring that those rights become a reality, rather than an abstract aspiration. We cannot assume that when children are playing they are automatically learning, or that their activities are pro-social. Play takes many forms and serves different purposes, which can include relaxation, fun and enjoyment as well as anarchy and subversion. Practitioners need to clarify what purposes play serves in their individual settings. If claims are made about the educational and developmental value of play, these should be substantiated with good evidence to parents and other professionals. Play can provide children with opportunities to act powerfully and competently through making choices, exercising will and self-determination. In an adult-dominated world, children need time, space and opportunities to play, regardless of their age. Becoming master players is an aspiration that can be achieved across a lifespan, and can contribute to lifelong learning.

While remaining enthusiastic about the potential of play, we perhaps need to be more critical about play in educational contexts. Improvements in the quality of learning through play can only come about by addressing the relationship between playing, learning and teaching as an integral part of the curriculum. So how can such improvements be made?

IMPROVING THE QUALITY OF PLAY

Education policies in England for the early years (birth to seven) have provided a framework of basic entitlements, which, in theory, should ensure a broad, balanced curriculum (DfEE, 1997; DfES, 2003). As many of the studies reviewed in this book have shown, this aspiration has not been achieved. The intensification of policy directives has not worked consistently towards improving the quality of children's educational experiences and outcomes. Many commentators remain concerned about the focus on literacy and numeracy, and the persistent use of formal, sedentary approaches to learning. Although practitioners have welcomed the Foundation Stage, there remain problems with transition to Key Stage 1, and many areas of discontinuity in children's learning and curriculum experiences (Wood and Bennett, 2001; Adams *et al*, 2004). In spite of much valuable and reliable evidence from research, both nationally and internationally, play remains vulnerable. Early childhood practitioners, particularly Reception teachers in primary schools, also remain vulnerable to downward pressures from colleagues, parents and the media.

This is not to imply a state of helplessness. Policy frameworks should not be a rigid straitjacket, but an enabling framework within which local developments can take place. Practitioners are in a powerful position to create detailed pedagogical knowledge through becoming more conscious of their educational practices and the theories that inform them. Practitioners, not policy-makers, are at the heart of improving the quality of teaching and learning in schools. Most of the practical examples given throughout this book have arisen from practice-based research, where early childhood specialists have worked collaboratively and individually on problems and challenges in their own settings. The wealth of knowledge that they have generated has been immediately useful, and has been disseminated to a wider audience through this book. They have provided positive role models of practitioners reclaiming their pedagogical expertise, as we recommended in the first edition. The professional development activities at the end of this chapter are based on those used successfully with practitioners on in-service courses, and Masters-level modules.

Implementing curriculum development and change can be a daunting process: however, if it is in the best interests of the children and the adults involved, then both the processes and outcomes can be challenging and energizing. Some practitioners may be able to build on existing good practice, while others may undertake a wholesale reconceptualization of their beliefs, provision and practice. It is not just the quality of play that needs to be improved: the quality of learning and teaching through play also needs to be addressed: practitioners should strive to maintain a balance between:

- child-initiated activities   *and* adult-directed activities
- play   *and* work
- children's intentions   *and* adults' intentions
- children's meanings   *and* adults' interpretations
- potential learning outcomes   *and* planned learning outcomes
- individual needs   *and* group/whole class needs
- familiarity and security   *and* challenge and risk
- flexibility and spontaneity   *and* structures and routines.

The following characteristics of high quality environments can help practitioners to create unity between playing, learning and teaching:

- a learning environment that offers high-quality, varied resources that allow for progression and extension

- rich provision of materials and resources to support creativity, inventiveness and originality

- experiences that promote self-reliance, cooperation, collaboration, responsibility and interdependence so that children are involved in their own learning

- practitioners who have the expertise and take the time to act as co-players

- practitioners who engage in sustained shared thinking and sustained shared playing, and can recognize teachable moments

- practitioners who help children make connections between areas of learning and experience, and support children's independence, interdependence, choices and decisions

- managerial and organizational strategies that empower children as learners and develop their confidence as master players and learners

- opportunities for children to play alone, in pairs, in small and large groups

- play activities that are content-rich, relevant and meaningful

- practitioners who value and extend children's ways of knowing, thinking, reasoning and understanding

- practitioners who help children to acquire the tools for thinking, learning and playing, and enable them to become master players and successful learners

- a curriculum that is diverse, inclusive and reflects the languages, customs, cultures and lifestyles of different ethnic groups

- a curriculum that is enabling and empowering for children and practitioners

- a curriculum that involves parents and other adults in playing, learning and teaching.

PROFESSIONAL DEVELOPMENT ACTIVITIES

1. SHARING VALUES, BELIEFS AND ATTITUDES ABOUT PLAY

This task can be carried out in a team, in collaboration with parents, or could be used as part of a whole-school or whole-setting focus on the quality of play.

Each member of staff should write a short account of an episode of good-quality play. The episode can be indoor or outdoor play; solitary, parallel, or cooperative; with or without an adult present.

Members of staff should work together in small groups to discuss what characterizes good-quality play. The following framework could be used for analysis:

- the type of play observed

- number of children

- resources available

- how the resources were used

- whether an adult was present, and what role the adult played

- time available, layout of the classroom/play area

- what learning processes, dispositions and outcomes were observed.

The outcomes of the analysis should be written on a large sheet of paper and shared/ contrasted with another group. If the task is used as part of a whole-school focus on play, the analysis could inform the development of a policy on play, taking into account continuity and progression across the Foundation Stage and Key Stages 1 and 2.

What implications does this analysis have for your practice? See Tasks 2 and 3.

▨ 2. ARTICULATING PERSONAL BELIEFS AND THEORIES ABOUT PLAY

Drawing on your knowledge and experience, and the analyses of play in practice from Task 1, brainstorm and discuss the following questions:

- How are playing and learning linked?

- How do different play contexts promote different areas of learning?

- What conditions are needed to support children's learning through play?

- Are these conditions always present in your classroom/ setting?

- Are there differences between your idealized vision of the value of play and what actually happens in your practice?

- Can you identify what constraints there are in your practice, and how these impact on the quality of your provision for play?

- What targets do you need to set in order to improve the quality of play in practice?

- How might some of the constraints you have identified be addressed?

Discuss and share your ideas within a group. You could use some of the examples and transcripts of play in this book, or carry out and analyse your own observations. A ten-minute episode can provide much valuable information for discussion and analysis. What targets would you prioritize for improving the quality of play? (See Task 3.)

■ 3. EVALUATING AND IMPROVING THE QUALITY OF PLAY

This task can be used to carry out an audit of existing provision and set targets for improvements across a period of time (short, medium and long term). The audit can be used flexibly to examine:

- ■ individual areas of provision, e.g. construction, tactile play, socio-dramatic play

- ■ features of provision, e.g. resourcing, curriculum planning, classroom management, teaching and learning styles, adult interaction, assessment and evaluation

- ■ current provision

What issues and concerns arose from Tasks 1 and 2 in relation to supporting good-quality play in pre-school and school settings? Organize these issues into the following areas.

PLANNING

How do you set aims and objectives for play activities – short, medium and long term?

Do you provide opportunities for intended learning outcomes, and possible learning outcomes?

Do you provide opportunities for teacher-directed and child-initiated activities? (accurate match, negotiated curriculum)

Are your aims and objectives related to the Foundation Stage Stepping Stones and Key Stage 1 programmes of study (breadth and balance)?

Are the activities appropriate for the children in the class? You should consider individual rates of development, learning styles, equal opportunities, differentiation.

Does your planning reflect equal-opportunities issues – ethnicity, gender, special educational needs, cultural and linguistic diversity, cultural sensitivity?

Does your planning identify opportunities/strategies for assessment?

What rules are set and how are these negotiated and communicated to children and staff?

What kinds of play activities and behaviours are encouraged, tolerated, ignored, or banned? And why?

ORGANISATION AND IMPLEMENTATION

Are you using the available space to good effect? (consider provision for indoor and outdoor play)

Are there any shared spaces outside classrooms that could be used effectively for play areas? How might this be negotiated with other members of staff?

What resources are available?

Are they of good quality and variety?

Do the resources support children's progression in learning through play?

Are the resources clearly labelled and accessible to the children?

How much time is made available for play?

What are children's agendas in different play contexts?

Can children's agendas be accommodated within the overall planning framework?

Do children have opportunities for extended periods of time to follow through their planning and investigations and develop themes and ideas?

What opportunities are provided for teaching through play, either through intended learning outcomes or spontaneous responses to activities?

What are the nature and quality of interactions between children/between adults and children in different play contexts?

Are the adults in your setting 'good players'? Are they responsive to children's agendas, and can they engage sensitively in play activities without taking over or directing the play?

ASSESSMENT AND EVALUATION

What opportunities exist for play-based observation and assessment?

What strategies for assessment do practitioners use?

Are these strategies used effectively to understand and discuss children's learning through play?

Do practitioners understand and use the six forms of assessment (Chapter 7)?

Do practitioners discuss children's play at home, with parents and caregivers?

Do practitioners share documentation with parents and caregivers to compare/contrast perceptions of children in different contexts, and chart their progress?

TARGET-SETTING

What areas have been identified for curriculum development? (short, medium and long term)

What strategies will be used to achieve the targets set?

Who will be involved (including parents and carers)?

What help is needed?

How will that help be provided?

4. DESIGNING A PARTICIPATORY CURRICULUM

What opportunities do you currently provide for children to participate in making choices and decisions?

What further opportunities might be provided?

You might like to consider:

- the design and organization of the learning environment
- the use of space
- the use of adults
- the location and labelling of resources
- gaining access to materials and resources
- opportunities for adult-directed and child-initiated activities
- opportunities for free play, negotiated play, directed play
- opportunities for children to express their ideas, opinions and concerns
- opportunities for children to represent their ideas, opinions and concerns through a variety of media
- your own beliefs, values and attitudes (see PDR in Chapter 5).

How might you work towards or extend a participatory curriculum?

FUTURE DIRECTIONS

Improving the quality of play in both pre-school and school settings is a continuing concern. The expansion of pre-school provision has brought an unprecedented focus on the curriculum for young children, and on their transition to school (Adams *et al*, 2004; Ofsted, 2004). This expansion has occurred in many other countries as well as in the UK. Creating unity between playing, learning and teaching is a significant challenge for all early childhood specialists. The extent of this responsibility should not be underestimated: there is substantial international research evidence to indicate that the quality of children's early experiences influences their success in later life. We hope that the second edition of this book provides opportunities for practitioners to think critically and creatively about their provision, and to articulate the theories that guide their practice. In order to improve the quality of play, early childhood specialists also need to articulate the nature of excellence in their practice to enable children to become master players and lifelong learners.

Bibliography

Abbott, L. and Nutbrown, C. (eds) (2001) *Experiencing Reggio Emilia: Implications for Pre-school Provision*, Buckingham, Open University Press.

Adams, S., Alexander, E., Drummond, M.J. and Moyles, J. (2004) *Inside the Foundation Stage. Recreating the Reception Year*, London, Association of Teachers and Lecturers.

Anning, A. (1995) A National Curriculum for Key Stage 1, in A. Anning (ed.) *A National Curriculum for the Early Years*, Buckingham, Open University Press.

Anning, A. (1997) *The First Years at School* (2nd edition), Buckingham, Open University Press.

Anning, A. and Edwards, A. (1999) *Promoting Children's Learning from Birth to Five*, Buckingham, Open University Press.

Anning, A. and Ring, K. (2004) *Making Sense of Children's Drawings*, London, Sage.

Anning, A., Cullen, J. and Fleer, M. (2004) (eds) *Early Childhood Education: Society and Culture*, London, Sage.

Athey, C. (1990) *Extending Thought in Young Children*, Paul Chapman, London.

Attfield, J. (1992) The Possibilities and Value of Assessing Children's Learning Through Play at Key Stage 1, Unpublished M.Ed. thesis, University of Exeter.

Beardsley, G. and Harnett, P. (1998) *Exploring Play in the Primary Classroom*, London, David Fulton.

Beetlestone, F. (1997) *Creative Children, Imaginative Teaching*, Buckingham, Open University Press.

Bennett, N. and Kell, J. (1989) *A Good Start? Four Year Olds in Infant Schools*, Oxford, Blackwell.

Bennett, N., Wood, E. and Rogers, S. (1997) *Teaching through Play: Teachers' Thinking and Classroom Practice*, Buckingham, Open University Press.

Bishop, J.C. and Curtis, M. (2001) *Play Today in the Primary School Playground*, Buckingham, Open University Press.

Blakemore, S.J. (2002) More Questions than Answers?, *Interplay*, Summer 2002, 24–30.

Blenkin, G. and Kelly, A.V. (1994) (eds) *The National Curriculum and Early Learning. An Evaluation*, London, Paul Chapman.

Booth, D. (1994) *Story Drama: Reading, Writing and Roleplaying Across the Curriculum*, London, Pembroke Publishers.

Boyce, E.R. (1946) *Play in the Infants' School* (2nd edition), London, Methuen.

Bradburn, E. (1976) *Margaret McMillan Framework and Expansion of Nursery Education*, Surrey, Denholm Press.

Bredekamp, S. and Copple, S. (eds) (1997) *Developmentally Appropriate Practice in Early Childhood Programs Serving Children from Birth Through 8* (revised edition), Washington, DC, National Association for the Education of Young Children.

Broadhead, P. (1997) Promoting Sociability and Co-operation in Nursery Settings, *British Educational Research Journal*, 23 (4), 513–531.

Broadhead, P. (2001) Investigating Sociability and Co-operation in Four and Five Year Olds in Reception Class Settings, *International Journal of Early Years Education*, 9 (1), 24–35.

Broadhead, P. (2004) *Early Years Play and Learning, Developing Social Skills and Co-operation*, London, RoutledgeFalmer.

Brooker, L. (2002) *Starting School – Young Children Learning Cultures*, Buckingham, Open University Press.

Broström, S. (1999) Drama Games with 6-year-old Children: Possibilities and Limitations, in Y. Engeström, R. Miettinen and R-L. Punamaki (eds) *Perspectives on Activity Theory*, Cambridge, Cambridge University Press, 250–263.

Bruner, J. (1966) *Toward a Theory of Instruction*, Cambridge, Mass., Harvard University Press.

Bruner, J. (1991) The Nature and Uses of Immaturity, in M. Woodhead, R. Carr, and P. Light (eds) *Becoming a Person*, London, Routledge/Open University Press.

Bruner, J. (1996) *The Culture of Education*, Cambridge, Mass., Harvard University Press.

Bruner, J.S., Jolly, A. and Sylva, K. (eds) (1976) *Play: Its Role in Development and Evolution*, London, Penguin.

Carr, M. (2000) Technological Affordance, Social Practice and Learning Narratives in an Early Childhood Setting, *International Journal of Technology and Design*, 10, 61–79.

Carr, M. (2001a) *Assessment in Early Childhood Settings: Learning Stories*, London, Paul Chapman.

Carr, M. (2001b) A Sociocultural Approach to Learning Orientation in an Early Childhood Setting, *Qualitative Studies in Education*, 14 (4), 525–542.

Chazan, S. (2002) *Profiles of Play*, London, Jessica Kingsley.

Chazan, M., Laing, A. and Harper, G. (1987) *Teaching Five to Eight Year Olds*, Oxford, Basil Blackwell.

Cohen, D. (1993) *The Development of Play* (2nd edition), London, Croom Helm.

Cohen, D. and MacKeith, S.A. (1991) *The Development of Imagination: The Private Worlds of Childhood*, London, Routledge.

Cook, J.S. (2003) Progression and Continuity in Role Play in the Foundation Stage, Unpublished M.Ed. thesis, University of Exeter.

Cowie, B. and Carr, M. (2004) The Consequences of Socio-cultural Assessment, in A. Anning, J. Cullen and M. Fleer (eds) *Early Childhood Education: Society and Culture*, London, Sage, 95–106.

Department for Education and Employment (1997) *Excellence in Schools*, London, DfEE.

Department for Education and Employment (1998) *The National Literacy Strategy*, London, DfEE.

Department for Education and Employment (1999) *The National Numeracy Strategy*, London, DfEE.

Department for Education and Employment (2001) *Code of Practice for the Identification and Assessment of Special Educational Needs* (revised), London, DfEE.

Department for Education and Science (1989) *Aspects of Primary Education: The Education of Children Under Five*, London, HMSO.

Department for Education and Science (1990) *Starting With Quality: Report of the Committee of Inquiry into the Quality of Educational Experiences Offered to 3- and 4-Year Olds* (Rumbold Report), London, HMSO.

Department for Education and Skills (2003) *Excellence and Enjoyment: A Strategy for Primary Schools*, London, DfES.

DeVries, R. and Kohlberg, L. (1987) *Programmes of Early Education – The Constructivist View*, New York, Longman.

Drake, J. (2001) *Planning Children's Play and Learning in the Foundation Stage*, London, David Fulton.

Drifte, C. (2002) *Early Learning Goals for Children With Special Educational Needs: Learning Through Play*, London, David Fulton.

Duffy, B. (1999) *Supporting Creativity and Imagination in the Early Years*, Buckingham, Open University Press.

Du Pré, H. and Du Pré, P. (1997) *A Genius in the Family: An Intimate Memoir of Jacqueline Du Pré*, London, Vintage.

Edwards, C., Gandini, L. and Forman, G. (eds) (1993) *The Hundred Languages of Children: The Reggio Emilia Approach to Early Childhood Education*, Norwood, N.J., Ablex.

Egan, K. (1991) *Primary Understanding: Education in Early Childhood*, London, Routledge.

Feinburg, S. and Mindess, M. (1994) *Eliciting Children's Full Potential*, California, Wadsworth.

Fisher, J. (2002) *Starting From the Child?* (2nd edition), Buckingham, Open University Press.

Fisher, R. (1995) *Teaching Children to Learn*, Cheltenham, Stanley Thornes.

Fleer, M. and Richardson, C. (2004) Mapping the Transformation of Understanding, in A. Anning, J. Cullen and M. Fleer (eds) *Early Childhood Education: Society and Culture*, London, Sage.

Fromberg, D. (1987) Play, in P. Monighan-Nourot, B. Scales, J. VanHoorn and M. Almy (eds) *Looking at Children's Play*, New York, Teachers College Press.

Garvey, C. (1991) *Play* (2nd edition), London, Fontana.

Gopnik, A., Meltzoff, A.N. and Kuhl, P.K. (1999) *The Scientist in the Crib: Minds, Brains and How Children Learn*, New York, William Morrow and Company.

Guha, M. (1988) Play in School, in G. Blenkin and A.V. Kelly (eds) *Early Childhood Education: A Developmental Curriculum*, London, Paul Chapman.

Gura, P. (ed.) (1992) *Exploring Learning: Young Children and Block Play*, London, Paul Chapman.

Hakkarainen, P. (1999) Play and Motivation, in Y. Engeström, R. Miettinen and R-L. Punamaki (eds) *Perspectives on Activity Theory*, Cambridge, Cambridge University Press, 231–249.

Hall, N. (1994) Play, Literacy and the Role of the Teacher, in J. Moyles (ed.) *The Excellence of Play*, Buckingham, Open University Press.

Hall, N. (2000) Literacy, Play, and Authentic Experience, in K. Roskos and J. Christie (eds) *Play and Literacy in Early Childhood: Research from Multiple Perspectives*, New Jersey, Lawrence Erlbaum, 189–204.

Hall, N. and Abbott, L. (1992) *Play in the Primary Curriculum*, London, Hodder and Stoughton.

Hall, N. and Robinson, A. (1995) *Exploring Writing and Play in the Early Years*, London, David Fulton.

Hendy, L. and Toon, L. (2001) *Supporting Drama and Imaginative Play in the Early Years*, Buckingham, Open University Press.

Hughes, F.P. (1991) *Children, Play and Development*, Massachusetts, Allyn and Bacon.

Hurst, V. (1994) The Implications of the National Curriculum for Nursery Education, in G. Blenkin and A.V. Kelly (eds) *The National Curriculum and Early Learning. An Evaluation*, London, Paul Chapman.

Hutt, S.J., Tyler, C., Hutt, C. and Christopherson, H. (1989) *Play, Exploration and Learning*, London, Routledge.

Jones, E. and Reynolds, G. (1992) *The Play's The Thing: Teachers' Roles in Children's Play*, New York, Teachers College Press.

Jordan, B. (2004) Scaffolding Learning and Co-constructing Understandings, in A. Anning, J. Cullen and M. Fleer (eds) *Early Childhood Education: Society and Culture*, London, Sage, 31–42.

Kelly-Byrne, D. (1989) *A Child's Play Life: An Ethnographic Study*, New York, Teachers College Press.

Lambert, E.B. and Clyde, M. (2003) Putting Vygotsky to the Test, in D.E. Lytle (ed.) *Play and Educational Theory and Practice, Play and Culture Studies*, Vol. 5, Westport, Conn., Praeger, 59–98.

Lytle, D.E. (ed.) (2003) *Play and Educational Theory and Practice*, Play and Culture Studies, Vol. 5, Westport, Conn., Praeger, 59–98.

Macintyre, C. (2001) *Enhancing Learning Through Play: A Developmental Perspective in Early Years Settings*, London, David Fulton.

MacNaughton, G. (2000) *Rethinking Gender in Early Childhood Education*, Buckingham, Open University Press.

MacNaughton, G. and Williams, G. (1998) *Techniques for Teaching Young Children: Choices in Theory and Practice*, Australia, Addison Wesley Longman.

Malaguzzi, L. (1993) For an Education Based on Relationships, *Young Children*, November, 9–13.

Marsh, J. and Hallett, E. (1999) *Desirable Literacies: Approaches to Language and Literacy in the Early Years*, London, Paul Chapman.

Marsh, J. and Millard, E. (2000) *Literacy and Popular Culture: Using Children's Culture in the Classroom*, London, Paul Chapman.

Meadows, S. (1993) *The Child As Thinker*, Routledge, London.

Meadows, S. and Cashdan, A. (1988) *Helping Children Learn: Contributions to a Cognitive Curriculum*, London, David Fulton.

Meckley, A. (1994a) Play, Communication and Cognition, *Communication and Cognition*, 27 (3).

Meckley, A. (1994b) Disappearing Pegs in the Road: Discovering Meaning in Young Children's Social Play. Paper presented to the American Educational Research Association Conference, 6 April.

Meckley, A. (1996) Studying Children's Play Through a Child Cultural Approach: Roles, Rules and Shared Knowledge, *Advances in Early Education and Day Care*, Vol. 7, *Social Development*, J.A.I. Press.

Meckley, A. (2002) Observing Children's Play: Mindful Methods. Paper presented to the International Toy Research Association, London, 12 August 2002.

Moyles, J. (1989) *Just Playing? The Role and Status of Play in Early Childhood Education*, Buckingham, Open University Press.

Moyles, J., Adams, S. and Musgrove, A. (2002) *Study of Pedagogical Effectiveness in Early Learning*, Research Report No 363, DfES, London, HMSO.

Newman, F. and Holzman, L. (1993) *Lev Vygotsky: Revolutionary Scientist*, London, Routledge.

New Zealand Ministry of Education (1996) *Te Whāriki Early Childhood Curriculum*, Wellington, Learning Media Ltd.

Nutbrown, C. (1996) *Respectful Educators – Capable Learners: Children's Rights and Early Education*, London, Paul Chapman.

Nutbrown, C. (1999) *Threads of Thinking: Young Children Learning and the Role of Early Education* (2nd edition), London, Paul Chapman.

Office for Standards in Education (2004) *Transition from the Reception Year to Year 1*, HMI Report number 2221, Ofsted. **www.ofsted.gov.uk**, accessed June 2004.

Ortega, R. (2003) Play, Activity and Thought: Reflections on Piaget's and Vygotsky's Theories, in D.E. Lytle (ed.) *Play and Educational Theory and Practice*, Westport, Conn., Praeger, 99–116.

Paley, V.G. (1981) *Wally's Stories*, London, Harvard University Press.

Parker, C. (2001) 'She's Back!' The Impact of my Visit to Reggio Emilia on a Group of 3- and 4-year olds, in L. Abbott and C. Nutbrown (eds) *Experiencing Reggio Emilia: Implications for Pre-school Provision*, Buckingham, Open University Press, 80–92.

Pellegrini, A.D. (1991) *Applied Child Study: A Developmental Approach*, New Jersey, Lawrence Erlbaum.

Pellegrini, A.D. and Blatchford, P. (2000) *The Child at School: Interactions With Peers and Teachers*, London, Arnold.

Pellegrini, A.D. and Boyd, B. (1993) The Role of Play in Early Childhood Development and Education: Issues in Definition and Function, in B. Spodek (ed.) *Handbook of Research on the Education of Young Children*, New York, Macmillan.

Peters, S. (1998) Playing Games and Learning Mathematics: The Results of two Intervention Studies, *International Journal of Early Years Education*, 6 (1), 49–58.

Piaget, J. (1962) *Play, Dreams and Imitation in Childhood*, New York, Norton.

Pound, L. (1999) *Supporting Mathematical Development in the Early Years*, Buckingham, Open University Press.

Qualifications and Curriculum Authority (QCA) (1999) *Early Years Curriculum for Under Five's Conference Report: The Review of the Desirable Learning Outcomes for Children's Learning*. **www.qca.org.uk/**.

Qualifications and Curriculum Authority/Department for Education and Employment (2000) *Curriculum Guidance for the Foundation Stage*, Sudbury, QCA Publications, QCA/00/587.

Reifel, S. (2001) *Theory in Context and Out, Play and Culture Studies*, Vol. 3, Connecticut, Ablex.

Roberts, R. (2002) *Self-esteem and Early Learning*, London, Paul Chapman.

Rodger, R. (1999) *Planning an Appropriate Curriculum for the Under Five's*, London, David Fulton.

Roffey, S. (2001) *Special Needs in the Early Years: Collaboration, Communication and Co-ordination* (2nd edition), London, David Fulton.

Rogoff, B. (1993) The Joint Socialisation of Development, in P. Light, S. Sheldon and M. Woodhead (eds) *Learning to Think*, London, Routledge/OUP.

Rogoff, B. (2003) *The Cultural Nature of Human Development*, Oxford, Oxford University Press.

Roopnarine, J.L. (2002) *Conceptual, Social-Cognitive, and Contextual Issues in the Fields of Play, Play and Culture Studies*, Vol. 4, Connecticut, Ablex.

Roskos, K. and Christie, J. (eds) (2000) *Play and Literacy in Early Childhood: Research from Multiple Perspectives*, New Jersey, Lawrence Erlbaum.

Rubin, K., Fein, G. and Vandenberg, B. (1983) Play, in E.M. Etherington (ed.) *Handbook of Child Psychology*. Vol. IV, *Social Development*, New York, Wiley.

Saracho, O. (1991) The Role of Play in the Early Childhood Curriculum, in B. Spodek and O. Saracho (eds) *Issues in Early Childhood Curriculum*, New York, Teachers College Press.

Saracho, O. and Spodek, B. (2002) *Contemporary Perspectives on Early Childhood Curriculum*, Connecticut, Information Age Publishing.

Sawyer, R.K. (2003) Levels of Analysis in Pretend Play Discourse: Metacommunication in Conversational Routines, in D.E. Lytle (ed.) (2003) *Play and Educational Theory and Practice*, Play and Culture Studies, Vol. 5, Westport, Conn., Praeger, 59–98.

Sayeed, Z. and Guerin, E. (2000) *Early Years Play: A Happy Medium for Assessment and Intervention*, London, David Fulton.

School Curriculum and Assessment Authority/Department for Education and Employment (1996) *Nursery Education Scheme: The Next Steps. Desirable Outcomes for Children's Learning*, London, SCAA/DfEE.

Shayer, M. (2003) Not Just Piaget; Not Just Vygotsky, and Certainly Not Vygotsky as Alternative to Piaget, *Learning and Instruction*, 13 (5), 465–485.

Siraj-Blatchford, I. and Siraj-Blatchford, J. (eds) (1995) *Educating the Whole Child: Cross-Curricular Skills, Themes and Dimensions*, Buckingham, Open University Press.

Siraj-Blatchford, I. and Sylva, K. (2004) Researching Pedagogy in English Pre-schools, *British Educational Research Journal*, 30 (4), 713–730.

Siraj-Blatchford, I., Sylva, K., Muttock, S., Gilden, R. and Bell, D. (2002) *Researching Effective Pedagogy in the Early Years*, Research report No 356, DfES, London, HMSO.

Slentz, K.L. and Krogh, S.L. (2001) *Teaching Young Children: Contexts For Learning*, New Jersey, Lawrence Erlbaum.

Smilansky, S. (1990) Sociodramatic Play: Its Relevance to Behaviour and Achievement in School, in Klugman, E. and Smilansky, S. (eds) *Children's Play and Learning: Perspectives and Policy Implications*, New York, Teachers College Press.

Steedman, C. (1990) *Childhood, Culture and Class in Britain: Margaret McMillan 1860–1931*, London, Virago.

Sutton-Smith, B. (1997) *The Ambiguity of Play*, Cambridge, Mass., Harvard University Press.

Vygotsky, L.S. (1978) *Mind in Society* (translated and edited by M. Cole, V. John-Steiner, S. Scribner and E. Souberman), Cambridge, Mass., Harvard University Press.

Wall, K. (2003) *Special Needs and the Early Years*, London, Paul Chapman.

Wasik, B.A., Bond, M.A. and Hindman, A. (2002) Effective Early Childhood Curriculum for Children at Risk, in O. Saracho and B. Spodek (eds)

Contemporary Perspectives on Early Childhood Curriculum, Connecticut, Information Age Publishing.

Weare, K. (2004) *Developing the Emotionally Literate School*, London, Paul Chapman.

Webster-Stratton, C. (1999) *How to Promote Children's Social and Emotional Competence*, London, Routledge.

Wenger, E. (1998) *Communities of Practice: Learning Meaning and Identity*, Cambridge, Cambridge University Press.

Wertsch, J.V. (1985) *Vygotsky and the Social Formation of Mind*, Cambridge, Mass., Harvard University Press.

Whitehead, M. (1999) *Supporting Language and Literacy Development in the Early Years*, Buckingham, Open University Press.

Winnicott, D.W. (1971) *Playing and Reality*, Harmondsworth, Penguin.

Wood, D. (1998) *How Children Think and Learn*, Oxford, Blackwell.

Wood, E. (2004) Developing a Pedagogy of Play for the 21st century, in A. Anning, J. Cullen and M. Fleer (eds) *Early Childhood Education: Society and Culture*, London, Sage, 17–30.

Wood, E. and Bennett, N. (2001) Early Childhood Teachers' Theories of Progression and Continuity, *International Journal of Early Years Education*, 9 (3), 229–243.

Wood, E. and Holden, C. (1995) *Teaching History at Key Stage 1*, Cambridge, Chris Kington.

Woodhead, M., Carr, R. and Light, P. (1991) *Becoming a Person*, London, Routledge/OUP.

Worthington, M. and Carruthers, E. (2003) *Children's Mathematics: Making Marks, Making Meaning*, London, Paul Chapman.

Wright, S. (2002) Teaching and Learning Through Play, Unpublished module assignment for the degree of M.Ed., Exeter University.

Author Index

Adams, S. 26
Anning, A. 9, 19, 21, 34, 58, 86
Athey, C. 80

Bennett, N. 9, 16, 17, 58, 101, 159
Blenkin, G. 19
Booth, D. 145
Boyce, E.R. 32, 35, 189–90
Broadhead, P. 45, 56, 58, 209
Brooker, L. 170
Broström, S. 154
Bruner, J. 94, 107, 173

Carr, M. 126, 141, 142, 187, 193
Chazan, M. 2, 15
Cohen, D. 12, 14, 30, 84
Cook, J.S. 109, 140, 170
Cudmore, D. 217

Drifte, C. 131, 142, 148, 215

Egan, K. 84

Fisher, J. 132
Fromberg, D. 6

Garvey, C. 3
Guha, M. 17
Gura, P. 47

Hall, N. 5, 166, 167
Hughes, F.P. 153
Hurst, V. 19
Hutt, S.J. 2, 85

Jones, E. 172
Jordan, B. 104

Kelley-Burne, D. 43, 52, 54
Kersey, A. 221

Macintyre, C. 119, 216
MacNaughton, G. 58
Malaguzzi, L. 127–8
Marsh, J. 12, 50, 148
Meadows, S. 9, 60, 67, 68
Meckley, A. 4, 5, 43, 55
Moyles, J. 160

Newman, F. 102, 111, 116

Ortega, R. 94

Paley, V.G. 52
Pellegrini, A.D. 6, 50
Piaget, J. 39–41, 78, 91, 104, 108–9, 111

Saracho, O. 6, 33
Sayeed, Z. 105, 214
Smilansky, S. 40, 48
Sutton-Smith, B. 14, 49

Vygotsky, L.S. 90–117 *passim*

Weare, K. 80
Winnicot, D.W. 103
Wood, E. 7, 22, 67, 152
Worthington, M. 5, 56, 78

Subject Index

access 169–72
accommodation 40
active learning 130–1
activities in play 52–7
adult's role 46–52
affordance 141–3
ambiguities 2–3
articulation of beliefs/theories 233
assessment 139 (Fig.)
   see also documentation
   and evaluation 186–7, 235–6
   forms 186–7
   process 188–90
   purposes 184–5
   socio-dramatic play 207–16
   techniques/strategies 191–3
assimilation 40
assisted performance 104–5
attitudes 1, 26–7, 121 (Fig.)
   sharing 232–3

balance 231
beliefs
   articulation 233
   sharing 232–3
Boyce, Miss 32–3, 35–6, 189–90
brain functions 60–3, 122
   educational implications 65–8
   and play 63–5
Brontë, Charlotte, Emily and Branwell 15

child-adulthood links 14–16
children, and play 4–5
children's rights 229
co-construction 104–5
   curriculum 139 (Fig.)
   and teachers 129 (Fig.)
cognitive processes/skills 121 (Fig.)
collaboration 129 (Fig.)
communication 129 (Fig.), 165–6

skills/processes 212–13
communities of practice 92
constraints 10–11
constructive play 46–9
creative skills/processes 214
creativity 84–7
   example 227
credit-based assessment 187
criteria 6
cultural experience 189–90
curriculum
   coordinator 228–9
   design 122–3, 138–52, 236
   models 120 *Fig/*, 123–4, 137–8
   see also National Curriculum
Curriculum Guidance for the Foundation
   Stage (CGFS) 22–7, 126

definitions 2–9
Desirable Outcomes for Children's Learning,
   The 21–2
development, and learning 90–3,
   116–17
Dewey, John 30
diagnostic assessment 186
dilemmas 188–90
discussion, and documentation 193–6
dispositions 6 (Fig.), 121 (Fig.)
documentation 129 (Fig.), 139 (Fig.)
   see also assessment
   and discussion 193–6
   and interpretation 196–207
dramatic *see* socio-dramatic play
Du Pré, Jaqueline and Hilary 14–15

Education Reform Act (1988) 18
Effective Provision for Pre-school Education
   (EPPE) 105–6
emotional literacy 80–3
enthusiasm 166–9

environment 129 (Fig.)
  high quality 231–2
epistemic play 85
equal opportunity 169–72
equilibrium 40
evaluation 6 (Fig.), 139 (Fig.)
  and assessment 186–7, 235–6
  and improvement 234–6
evidence, interpretation 196–207
exploration skills/processes 213

formative assessment 186
forms of play 5–6, 14, 38–9
foundation stage 22–4, 152, 225
  and Key Stage 1 26, 230
Froebel, Friedrich 29–30
future directions 237

High/Scope curriculum 130–1
history and play 152

ICT (information technology) and play
    151–2
ideology
  past and present 33–7
  pioneers 28–33
imagination 84–7
imaginative skills/processes 214
implementation 139 (Fig.), 230–2
improvement, and evaluation 234–6
independent performance 107
individual play/educational plans 190,
    214–16
information technology (ICT) and play
    151–2
informative assessment 186
inter/intrapsychological planes 93,
    114–15
internalisation 92–3
interpretation of evidence 196–207
intersubjectivity 94
investigation skills/processes 213
involvement 173–9
ipsative assessment 186
Isaacs, Susan 31–2

joint activity 96–7, 99–100
joint performance 105
joint problem solving 94

Key Stage 1, and foundation stage 26,
    230
knowledge and play skills 211–12

language 97–9
learning
  environment 129 (Fig.), 140–1
  example 217–20
  links with play 118–23
  outcomes 161
  spiral 107–8
lifelong learning and play 13–14
listening and play 165
literacy
  and play 143–9
  strategy 24–5
ludic play 85

MacMillan, Margaret 31
meta-communication 165
meta-memory 68–9
metacognition
  practice 70–6
  theory 69–70
metacommunication 76–8
Montessori, Maria 30–1
motivation 94
  and real-life plans 112–15
multi-modality 86

National Curriculum 10, 18–22
  see also curriculum models
  foundation stage 22–4
neuroscience see brain functions
new technologies 12–13
New Zealand 124–7
numeracy
  and play 149–51
  strategy 25

observation 162–4
organisation 139 (Fig.)

paradoxical nature 7–9
parents 129 (Fig.)
participation 92, 129 (Fig.)
PDR see plan-do-review
pedagogy
  dilemmas 188–90

framing/strategies 102, 103–4, 138–40, 158–60
of play 159
definition 182–3
skills/strategies 172 (Fig.)
performance
assisted 104–5
independent 107
joint 105
self-assisted 106–7
Piaget's theories 39–41, 78, 91, 104, 108–9, 111
plan-do-review (PDR) 131–7, 141
example 221–5
planning 139 (Fig.), 234
flexibility 160–1
for progression and continuity 152–7
play spiral 161 (Fig.)
play/non-play continuum 6–7
players' dispositions 6 (Fig.)
popular culture 11–12
problem-solving skills/processes 213
problematizing skills 94, 101–3
problems 12–13
professional development 232–6
progression
and continuity 152–7
through play 13
Progressive movement 34–5, 40
protagonists 129 (Fig.)
psychological tools 92
purposes of play 37–8

real-life plans 112
reception children 26
Reggio Emilia principles 127–30
research 129 (Fig.), 179–82
Researching Effective Pedagogy in the Early Years (REPEY) 105–6
responsibilities 229–30
revolutionary aspects 115–16
rhetoric-reality divide 10–11
rights and responsibilities 229–30
roles and identities 52–7
rough-and-tumble 49–52
rules 111–12
Rumbold Committee 20

safety 169–72
scaffolding 94–5, 104, 107

schema theory 78–80
self-assisted performance 106–7
self-speech 99
semiotic activity 108–9
sensory garden 225–7
sharing values/beliefs/attitudes 232–3
social cognition 80–3
Social Play Continuum (SPCP) 45–6
socio-affective skills/processes 212–13
socio-cultural theories *see* theories
socio-dramatic play 41–6
assessment 207–16
special educational needs 122, 155, 166
status of play 9–10
beyond childhood 13
Steiner, Rudolf 30
Stepping Stones 126, 137
subordination to rules 111–12
summative assessment 186
superhero play 49–52
sustained shared thinking/playing 105–6

target-setting 236
Te Whāriki curriculum 124–7
teachers
as co-constructors/researchers 129 (Fig.)
as co-players 172–3
teaching 103–4
teaching *see* pedagogy
themes in play 52–7
theories 37, 57–8, 59–60, 87–8
articulation 233
Vygotsky's 108–17
transformational processes 92–3

unifying mechanism 109
United Nation Convention on Children's Rights 229

values, sharing 232–3
Vygotksian theories 90–117 *passim*

work-play divide 16–17
Wright, Frank Lloyd 14

zone of proximal development (ZPD) 96–7
joint activity 96–7, 99–100
language 97–9
problematizing skills 101–3